EDITION
FROM EVERY
SIDE

Consultants:

ing. arch. Petr Chotěboř, CSc. and PhDr František Kadlec
(the part Prague Castle), ing. František Mysliveček, Bořek Neškudla

ISBN 80-901891-5-6

Prague Castle
Hradčany

Content

(I) On the way to Prague Castle and to the Hradčany Town

Introductory walk: . . . 10

(II) Prague Castle

First walk:
Throught Prague Castle acros the centuries . . . 26

Second walk:
Through three Castle courtyards . . . 44

Third walk:
The Cathedral of St Vitus . . . 60

Fourth walk:
The Old Royal Palace . . . 94

Fifth walk:
Through Vikáfiská Street to the Convent of St George . . . 112

Sixth walk:
Through Jifiská Street to Golden Lane and the Old Castle Stairs . . . 124

Seventh walk:
From the Garden At the Bastion to the Stag Moat
and via the Powder Bridge to the north forefield of Prague Castle . . . 134

Eighth walk:
Through the Royal Garden . . . 144

Ninth walk:
Through the southern garden of Prague Castle . . . 152

(III) The Hradčany Town

First walk:
Through the history of the town . . . 164

Second walk:
Around Hradãany Square . . . 170

Third walk:
From Hradãany Square to the Loretto and back . . . 178

Fourth walk:
From Pohofielec to the Strahov Monastery . . . 196

(IV) Where one can sit, eat and drink

Final walk: . . . 214

Key figures of the Czech history . . . 221

Significant artists in Bohemia . . . 229

Vocabulary of special terms . . . 237

Prague is undoubtedly a city which has many visitors and admirers. By which does it attract people and why did it fascinate nearly everyone who walked its streets? There are many answers to this question, however, nearly all of them have one in common: The atmosphere and beauty of Prague is not given only by the unique combination of sights and pieces of art dated from various periods, but also by the life which is present here and which bears the heritage of the old times. The French historian Ernest Denis once wrote about it: „Each of its stones reminds us of a heroic drama. At no place life was more tossed about, upheavals more frequent, passions more mad, fights more fierce and violent... Prague is one of the places which dictate history."

A person who regards this city as a large museum can admire it, however, s/he will not experience anything, s/he will not understand anything. You have to roam about, to wander about, to walk through Prague. As one of its admirers said, you have „to acquire the art of poetical walking through the city". When you walk and perceive, the time barrier is removed. You walk and suddenly you have the feeling that the boundaries between the past and the present are being removed.

Unfortunately, only few people can wander about through the city for hours and weeks. Guidebooks facilitate orientation, but they put certain restrictions upon you. Therefore it is good for you not to take them quite seriously and, as wanderers say,to deviate from the course occasionally into a lane, a passage or a pub which is not mentioned in them. The following walks would like to bring besides information a little bit entertainment and relaxation. Nothing more. Everybody has to find the soul of the city in his/her own way, as did such „wanderers" as Jaroslav Seifert, Vítězslav Nezval, Franz Kafka, Gustav Meyrink, Jaroslav Hašek, Guillaume Apollinaire, Angelo Maria Ripellino, Maria Cvetajeva, and many others.

(I)
On the way to Prague Castle and Hradčany

Introductory walk

The Czech lion in a bend of Chotkova Street is guarding the lower entrance to the Stag Moat

At present you can enter Hradčany and Prague Castle from more directions than you could in the past. The original access road to the Castle led to the eastern gate through the steep Street *Na Opyši*, to the southern gate through a steep path (called Lezka) crossing the present *Zámecké schody* (Castle Stairs), and to the western gate through *Hradčanské náměstí* (Hradčany Square) and a ravine. The entrance to the Hradčany Town was guarded by three gates: by the Strahov Gate west of the main entrance to the Strahov Monastery, the Špitálská Gate (Hospital Gate) in *Kanovnická Street* and St Benedict's Gate on the site of the present *Radniční schody* (Townhall Stairs). Obviously, one could enter Hradčany directly from Prague Castle, since the fortifications of both the units were connected. As Prague developed, the number of access routes increased; now we will mention the most picturesque of them.

Naturally, you can arrive at Hradčany and Prague Castle simply by car (the *Na Pohořelci* car park), by a tourist coach (the car park in *Jelení* street) or by metro (Underground; the *Hradčanská* or the *Malostranská* station) and by tram (the *Pražský Hrad*

/Prague Castle/ stop, or the *Královský letohrádek* /Royal Summerhouse/ or the *Památník písemnictví* /Museum of the National Literature/ stop of the number 22 line). The way by tram has its own charm, since its track ascends from the *Malostranská* metro station through the winding road of *Chotkova* street, from which you can have a surprisingly impressive view of Prague.

In the past people mainly used to walk, only nobility and wealthy burghers had their own coaches or they even saddled a horse. From 1712 a visitor could order, besides coaches and carriages, a sedan chair carried by two showily liveried men. It was not a cheap way of transport, since each hundred steps cost one kreutzer. At the end of the 18th century stagecoaches called fiacres appeared (they were named after the Paris Saint Fiacre Hotel, where their first stand was established). From 1829 omnibuses for more passengers drawn by horses were introduced. In 1908 one could arrive in Hradčany through *Nerudova* Street by a motor bus of the Fiat make. A drive from *Malostranské náměstí* (Small Quarter Square)

In the background of the Old Castle Stairs
stands the Black Tower of Prague Castle

The Old Castle Stairs

took 15 minutes, however, it was not safe because of the steepness of the road (one bus crashed). The traffic was soon closed, and even now you cannot go onto the Hradčany hill by a city transport bus. It may be a good reason why to choose a pleasant and aesthetically richer coming on foot.

The following access footpaths are numbered in accordance with the numbers of the street map.

1. Up the Old Castle Stairs (Staré zámecké schody).

You can come to the rear (easter) gate of Prague Castle *up the Old Castle Stairs*, which ascend from the Small Quarter Street *Pod Bruskou*, about one hundred metres distant from the *Malostranská* metro station. At one time a footpath led in their place, the stairs were built here only before 1683. At present they have 101 steps and they are surrounded by a wall from each side. The wall on the left side

built in 1848, unfortunately, deprives you of the view of the *Fürstenberk Garden* (in the middle of the stairs you pass the Baroque garden house number 113/3 belonging to the garden). Behind the wall on the right side is hidden the garden of the Classicist **Richter Summerhouse** (No. 251) surrounded by Street *Na Opyši* on the other side, the street is probably the oldest carriage access route to the Castle, it was used even in the 10th century.

The garden is called St Wenceslas' Vineyard, since - as says a legend - Prince St Wenceslas made wine for the communion there. However, it is more probable that the vineyard was not founded here before 1358, when Emperor Charles IV issued the decree about founding vineyards and orchards around the Prague towns. St Wenceslas' Vineyard belongs to Prague Castle and its opening for the public as well as the conversion of the Richter Summerhouse into a restaurant are being taken into consideration.

On the site of the small park at the foot of the

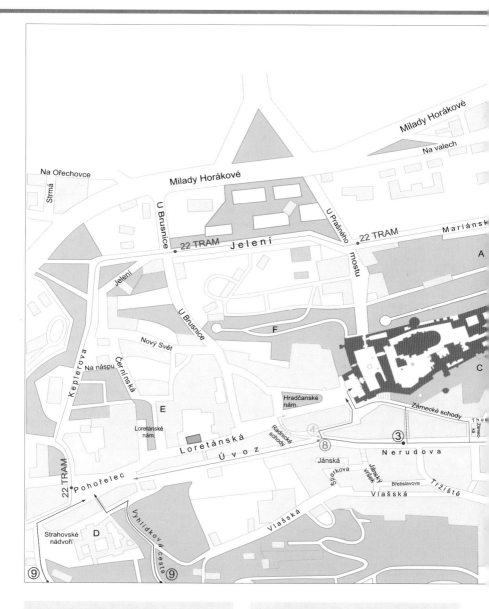

THE ROUTE:

1. Throught the Old Castle Stairs
2. Through the Castle Stairs
3. From Nerudova Street through Ke Hradu Street
4. Via the Townhall Stairs to Hradčany Square
5. Through Pod Bruskou Street and the Chotek Park to the Royal Summerhouse
6. From the Hradčanská metro station to the Royal Summerhouse
7. Through the palace gardens of the Small Quarter into the southern gardens of Prague Castle
8. Through Úvoz Street to Hradčany
9. From Petřín to Hradčany

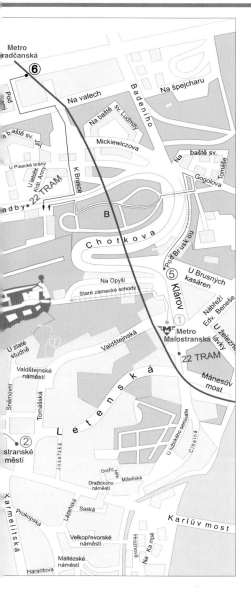

stairs used to stand an army warehouse till the beginning of the 20th century, and even before (in the 14th century) here used to be **a royal limehouse** where lime used at the constructions at Prague Castle was slaked. The Classicist building on the right side is the **dům U Verdugů** (House At the Verdugs, also called Richter's House, No 150/2); the outstanding Czech actor Eduard Vojan lived and died there in 1920. There also lived the married couple writers Růžena Svobodová and František Xaver Svoboda and also for a short time before his death Václav Vojtěch Štech, the art historian and significant specialist in Prague.

The stairs and Street *Na Opyši* lead into the small open space outside the **eastern gate** of the Castle. The open space came into being in 1797 after demolishing the late Gothic barbican. The space is partly surrounded by a toothed wall build in 1848. There you can have a magnificent view of Prague with the Small Quarter gardens and the roofs of the palaces in the foreground.

At the corner of the house No 192/8, at the end of *Na Opyši* Street, there is a copy of **a statue of St Barbora** (the 17th century), the patroness of the dying; in the past it used to stand higher at the open space and reminded people that there used to be an execution place. The nobles kept in prison and sentenced at Prague Castle were executed there. On the left of the Castle gate you can enter the *southern gardens of Prague Castle* (see the ninth walk through the Castle), on the right side is the *Na Opyši Garden* in the west adjacent to the late Gothic fortifications of the Castle.

2. Up the Castle Stairs (Zámecké schody)

The Castle Stairs lead to *Hradčany* Square and to the main (western) entrance to the Castle. The stairs were called New in the past so that they could be distinguished from *the Old Castle Stairs*. There used to lead a path even in the 13th century, at that time between gardens and vineyards. Real

A - the Royal Garden
B - the Chotek Park
C - the Garden Na Valech
D - the Strahov Monastery
E - the Loretto
F - the Stag Moat

The Castle Stairs

The look-out place in front of the eastern gate of Prague Castle

stairs were built in the 15th century, they were rebuild into the approximately contemporary form in 1674. They are more than 183 metres long and have 209 steps. You can approach them through two picturesque paths leading from *Malostranské* (Small Quarter) *Square*, either through *Thunovská Street* (in fact the stairs are its extention), or from *Nerudova Street* via a narrow passage up the stairs between the Baroque Thun-Hohenstein Palace (now the Italian Embassy) and the Churches of the Virgin Mary and of St Kayetan.

The Castle Stairs were originally considerably narrower and alongside of them led a steep waggon road, which was used till 1663, when a more comfortable road called Nová cesta (the New Route), today's Street Ke hradu, was widened. At the bottom of the stairs a gate was built, which, however, was pulled down after six years, as it was unsuitable. Since the 15th century on the right side of the lower half of the stairs new houses began to be built. Since the end of the 16th century the upper half of the stairs has been bordered by a high wall on the right side (the wall supports the hill below the Rajská zahrada /Garden of Eden/ of Prague Castle) with niches into which thirteen sculptural groups of the Stations of the Cross should have been placed at the beginning of the 17th century, which did not happen.

On the left side we can see in the parallel *Thunovská* Street the Renaissance facade of the large **Palace of the Lords of Hradec**, to which a small Baroque covered bridge leads from the stairs. The commemorative plaque reminds us that in 1911-24 the famous Czech painter Alfons Mucha lived there. Further, next to the steps stands a small Baroque house (No 191/3) connected with the Kayetan monastery, to which the following objects also belonged. The houses on the right side of the stairs are mostly Renaissance, adapted in the Baroque and Classicism. In the 16th and 17th centuries craftsmen and artists had their shops in them, and sold there mainly luxurious goods. The row of windows (the former shop windows) with an exposed wide stone plate reminds us of the shops; some

Above the Castle Stairs towers the Mathias Pavilion in the Garden of Eden of Prague Castle

The entrance to the Garden of Eden from the top of the Castle Stairs

of them are used as shops up to now. In the house **U pelikána** (At the Pelicane) lived the outstanding Czech modern painter Jan Zrzavý. Some of the houses have terraced gardens towards the Castle.

It is worth noticing that the houses were supplied by water from the Castle water system, since it was impossible to push water there from the Small Quarter water house tower. The water from the Castle was high-quality spring water, however, this water supply system had also one disadvantage; when someone from the Emperor's family arrived at the Castle, the water supply into the Small Quarter houses was always closed, so that the Emperor (or his family) did not suffer from shortage of water. However, another time there was a surplus of water; after the big rainstorm in 1647 one of the houses was so damaged by the flood from the royal gardens that it had to be demolished.

At the top of the stairs on the left side stands the Baroque **statue of St Philip of Nerea** by Ferdinand Maxmilian Brokof. Behind it begins the terrace of *Hradčany Square* with a beatiful view of Prague; the

main Castle entrance is not far from there. (If you turn to the right immediately at the end of the stairs, you can enter the south gardens of Prague Castle.)

The view from the terrace above the *Castle Stairs* is a real reward for climbing 209 steps. It was also the opinion of the famous composer Hector Berlioz in the 19th century, who wrote: „It is perhaps for the first time I did not regret an exhausting climb, of course with the exception of an ascent of Vesuv; ... Seriously, the gradient is really steep, but how charming the continual row of churches, palaces, battlements, belfries and turrets is ... How charming the view from the top of the hill bordered by the stone beauty is!"

3. From Neruda Street via Ke Hradu Street

To *Hradčany Square* and to the main entrance to Prague Castle also *Ke Hradu* Street leads; coronation processions of Czech kings used to march this way. The street was hewn out in the rock as late as in

A platform in place of the Chapel of the Virgin Mary of Einsiedeln

The Townhall Stairs

1639-43 and mainly after its improvement and widening in 1663 and in 1683 it took over most of the traffic from the older roads leading to Hradčany and Prague Castle.

The street begins from *Nerudova Street* in an oblique direction having as its opposite the picturesque *Radniční schody* (Townhall Stairs), leading to the farther end of *Hradčanské Square*. On the left side above the street towers a large block of the **Swarzenberk Palace** with a rich Renaissance sgrafitto facade, on the right side you can see over a stone wall the panorama of *Neruda Street* and further on of a large part of the Small Quarter. The street leads into the same look out terrace as the *Castle Stairs*. At its beginning remained a fenced platform on the site of the ground floor of the upper part of the **Chapel of the Virgin Mary of Einsiedel** built in 1672 and closed in 1783 at the time of the Enlightenment reforms of Emperor Josef II.

Soon afterwards (in 1791) the upper part of the chapel was demolished, since the Castle authorities were afraid that the deteriorating architecture could cause harm to the delicacy of the nobility preparing for the approaching coronation of Emperor Leopold II. Since then the Prague officials have solved the problem of deteriorating architecture spoiling public ceremonies several times in a similar way; let us hope it was last time in 1985, when the historically and artisticaly highly precious (though deteriorating) neo-Renaissance Denis train station in the New Town was demolished.

On one side of the entrance to the former chapel **a sculptural group of the Pieta** was placed at the end of the 17th century, on the other side is placed the **statue of St Wenceslas** by Čeněk Vosmík dated from the beginning of the 20th century. It stands on a Baroque pedestal, the remnant of the damaged statue of St Wenceslas by Otavio Most (at present placed in a lapidary) moved into this place from the Charles Bridge in 1791.

The look-out pavilion
of the Barnabite Monastery

The passage in place of the former gate
of St Benedict

4. Via the Radnické schody (Townhall Stairs) to Hradčany Square

Townhall Stairs *begin at the end of* Nerudova Street *nearly at the same place as Street* Ke Hradu, *however, they lead in the opposite direction, and therefore lead to the other end of* Hradčany Square. *They are one of the most beatiful quiet places of Hradčany, they lead throught its oldest fortifications. At the beginning they are embellished by two statues, on the left by the statue of St John of Nepomuk by Michal Josef Brokoff, on the right by a statue of St Joseph by an unknown sculptor. On the right side they are bordered by the buildings of the former Monastery of the Barnabites (No 184/2 and 183/4), today's Carmelitan Convent. You can notice a glazed look out arbour with sgraffito, which was adapted on the top of the former castle tower at the beginning of the second half of the 20th century. On the left side you pass a rear line of three houses whose fronts lead to Street* Úvoz. *The next*

house (No 172/7) is called **U černého ježka** (At the Black Hedgehog). Next is a side wall of the **Hradčanská radnice** /Hradčany Townhall/ with an original literary coffee bar U zavěšenýho kafe /At the Hung Coffee/. In three quarters of lenght the stairs are spanned by a covered passage connecting the Monastery of the Barnabites with the townhall. In the past on this site stood the **St Benedict Gate** guarding the entrance to the Hradčany Town from the Small Quarter. Above the passage you can notice the shop Karmel, where you can buy handmade products from the Carmelitan Convent. The stairs lead to the boundary of *Hradčany Square* and *Loretánská Street* (between the townhall and the convent), directly opposite the corner of the Toscan Palace embellished by a Baroque statue of St Michael. These places, however, will be the topic of our walks through Hradčany.

The Bílek Villa

The sculptural group Komenský bids farewell to his homeland

5. Via Street Pod Bruskou and the Chotkovy sady (Chotek Park) to the Královský letohrádek (Royal Summerhouse/ Belvedere)

It is also interesting to walk from the *Malostranská* metro station upwards for a short time along the tram rails through *Klárov* Street and then through *Pod Bruskou* Street which soon turns to the right and becomes nearer. The narrow street leads at first between a picturesque row of several Baroque and Classicist houses typical of the border part of the historic built-up area. In the first of them called **U černého (červeného) jelínka** (At the Black (Red) Stag; No 135/4) used to be a tavern, the next house **U Krásných** (At the Krásný's; No 136/6) is embellished by a picture of St John of Nepomuk, the house **V balónu** (In the Balloon; No 137/8) was renovated in early 1970s by the writer and painter Adolf Hoffmeister. Behind the last houses the street becomes even narrower changing into a path called *Myší díra* (The Mouse Hole) hewn out in the

rock at the beginning of the 17th century by the soldiers of Albrecht of Valdštejn.

At the beginning of the narrow part of Street *Pod Bruskou*, between the Hoffmeister Hotel (No 144/5; a postmodern building in harmony with the other buildings) and the **house U Krásných** (No 136/6) used to stand the **Písecká brána** (Písek Gate; also called Bruska). It was a part of the late Gothic fortifications of the Small Quarter and after building the Baroque fortifications it lost its importance. You can approach the remnants of the Baroque fortifications at the end of *Pod Bruskou* Street; a large part of the neighbouring streets is built in place of its demolished bastions, of which one is reminded by the names of the streets (the streets *Na Baště sv. Ludmily, Na Baště sv. Tomáše* /At the Bastion of St Ludmila, At the Bastion of St Thomas/ etc.).

At the top the path *Mouse Hole* changes into the pavement along *Chotkova silnice* (Chotkova Road), along which you can approach a large crossroads, on whose opposite side you can see the unique **villa**

*The Kramář Villa. In the foreground
the building of the Govenment
of the Czech Republic*

*The monument of the writer Julius Zeyer
in Chotek Parks*

and studio of the sculptor František Bílek, a representative of the spiritually tuned Art Nouveau. In the garden at the entrance towers his monumental sculptural group Komenský bids farewell to his homeland, in the interior (also open for the public) his further works are exhibited. However, the way to the Castle runs to the right several metres via *Gogolova Street* and then once more to the right on the route to the former *Kramářova vila* (Kramář villa; No 212/1). In 1908-11 Dr. Karel Kramář, the later first Prime Minister of the Czechoslovak Government had it built according to the plans of Bedřich Ohmann. Nowadays it serves to the Government of the Czech Republic.

The villa stands on the site of the former **bastion No XIX** - the bastion of St Mary Magdalena. In fact, it was a small stronghold built at a strategic place opposite Prague Castle. It had both defensive and guarding function; even at the time of telegraph and telephone a torch used to be fastened there prepared to flare up, whenever an enemy would approach the walls.

Cannonades in honour of a childbirth in the ruler's family were fired here. If a daughter was born, only 21 gunshots were fired, when a boy, the successor to the throne was born, 121 gunshot were fired. The last ceremonial cannonade was fired probably in March 1868, when daughter Valerie was born to Empress Elizabeth. Between 1891 - 1918 a gunfire from the bastion No XIX also announced noon. The officer observed a signal given by a pennon at the astronomical tower of Klementinum in the Old Town and then immediately he ordered to fire.

We will turn off the path leading to the Kramář Villa via a small bridge across *Chotkova Road* to the *Chotek Park*.

Emperor Rudolf II bought the lot of the future park in 1589 with the intention to extend the *Royal Garden*. However, a garden was not founded there. The lot was used as a building site for the near Royal Belvedere, later as an open riding school (arena), and then as a carpenters' yard and a timber store for the needs of Prague Castle. In 1833-41 a park was founded in place of the yard from the iniciative of the

The mask on the front of the Písek Gate

*The House At the Golden Star
at the beginning of Úvoz Street*

Prague Burgrave Count Karel Chotek - the second modern public Prague park.

In the park stands the romantic large monument of the writer Julius Zeyer having the shape of a cave in which are some characters of his works sculptured by Josef Mauder. From the romanticaly quiet park you can get easily to the **Royal Belvedere**, whose high side wall encloses the park. The summerhouse stands at the eastern end of the *Royal Garden*, whose visit is the theme of the last but one walk through Prague Castle.

6. From the Hradčanská metro station to the Royal Belvedere

Another path to the **Royal Belvedere** is the walk from the *Hradčanská* metro station via *K Brusce* Street, through which you can get to **Písecká Gate**, a remnant of the massive Baroque fortifications of Prague. The gate was built by Emperor Charles VI in 1721 according to the plans of

Kryštof Dientzenhofer. From it leads a direct path to the **Royal Belvedere**.

7. Through the palace gardens of the Small Quarter into the southern gardens of Prague Castle

Since 1997 a new access to Prague Castle is opened through the palace gardens *Ledebourská* and *Malá* (small) *Pálffyovská* (after reconstruction also the gardens *Velká* /large/ *Pálffyovská, Kolowratská* and *Malá* /small/ *Fürstenberská* will be opened). The entrance to the Small Quarter gardens leads at present from the Small Quarter *Valdštějnské Square* through the passage in the Baroque **Ledebourský Palace** (No 162/3). The gardens ascend from the palaces at their foot along the south slope to the Castle, where they are connected with the castle garden *Na Valech*. However, we recommend all visitors to connect the viewing tour of the Small Quarter gardens rather with the tour of the

The palace gardens below the eastern part of Prague Castle

Small Quarter, where these gardens belong from the historical and aesthetical point of view. Walks through the Prague gardens will be the theme of the next volume of our edition „From every side".

8. Through Úvoz Street to Hradčany

An ancient access route to Hradčany, namely to *Pohořelec* Square, leads through *Úvoz* street starting at the upper end of *Nerudova Street*. The houses in the lower part of the street were being built after the middle of the 14th century and created a certain suburb of Hradčany. They adjoined by their rear part the Hradčany fortifications, which at that time ceaced to fulfil their function, since after sprawling the Small Quarter and building its walls it remained inside the connected towns.

The southern (left) side of the street is made up at the beginning of five houses, of which the first is the most important - the Baroque House **U bílého jablka** (At the

White Apple; No 230/1). Next is the wall of the *Strahov Garden*, discontinued in the middle by the House **V presu** (In the Press; No 157/11), originally a wine press of the Strahov Monastery converted into a monastery bakehouse in the second half of the 16th century and into a residential building in the 20th century. It has an interesting modern sign by Josef Klimeš - crossed ropes spliced into a knob chiseled in stone. Behind the house you will certainly be delighted by the view of the vast *Strahov Garden* with the silhouette of the monastery on the hill and the slopes of the *Petřín* hill in the background.

The northern (right) side of the street begins by the corner House **U zlaté hvězdy** (At the Golden Star; also called At Three Kings; No. 171/2), originally medieval, rebuilt in the Renaissance and Baroque styles. The main front faces *Nerudova Street*, the north side faces *the Townhall Stairs*. The rich Baroque facade is embellished on the gable by the symbol of God's eye. Above the gate is fastened a beaten lattice

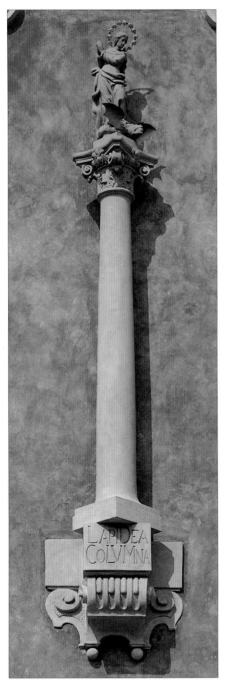

*The housesign of the House
At the Stone Column*

with a small crown. Next is the House **U tří červených růží** (At Three Red Roses; No 170/4), today the Hotel U krále Karla (At King Charles). Above its stucco house sign of three roses is a picture of the Virgin Mary in a rich stucco frame. It is worth noticing the Baroque House **U tří sekyrek** (At Three Hatchets; No 169/6) with three crossed hatchets in the housesign in a cartouche above the gate. The House **U bílé čelisti** (At the White Jaw; No 164/16) comes from the second half of the 16th century and was rebuilt in the classicist way. On the first floor are preserved painted wooden Renaissance ceilings. The House **U zracadla** (At the Mirror; No 161/22) has a Rococco facade with a relief of Madonna with little Jesus in a rich stucco frame.

Perhaps the house **U kamenného sloupu** (At the Stone Column; also called U Slunce a Luny - At the Sun and the Moon; No 160/24) is the most interesting in the whole street. It has a Renaissance core, it was rebuilt in the Baroque by the painter Kristián Luna, who placed stucco busts of the Sun and the Moon on the sides of the front. An interesting motiv is the stone column with a statue of the Virgin Mary placed on the sockle above the windows of the first floor.

Three following houses belong to *Úvoz* street, the main fronts of all the others face the parallel but much higher lying *Loretánská Street* and *Loretánské Square*. Because these houses are built on a steep slope, on the *Úvoz* side they have up to five storeys, whereas on the front side only one.

The street leads to *Pohořelec* Square between the **Trauttmannsdof House** (No 110) on the right side and the **Strahov Hospital of St Elizabeth** (No 155/15) on the left side. We will mentions both buildings in the last walk through Hradčany.

The Gothic wall on the Petřín slope

The Baroque fortifications near the former Strahov Gate

9. From Petřín to Hradčany

You can get to *Pohořelec* Square directly to the main gate of the Strahov Monastery also from the top of *Petřín* via the *Strahov path*. It is interesting, as it leads partly between a **Gothic wall** on one side and a massive brick **Baroque wall** on the other side. From the Petřín Look-out Tower you can walk up the stairs and then via the *Vyhlídková cesta* (Look out path) on the slope of *Petřín* to the *Strahov Garden* and *Úvoz* Street. On the way an impressive panoramatic view of the Small Quarter and the whole Prague valley basin is opened. The walk through the Petřín parks will be the theme of the next volume of our edition „From every side".

(II)
Prague Castle

Almost from the beginning of the Czech history people's
attention turned to the elongated hill above the Vltava
whose shape was compared by the chronicler Kosmas to
„*the back of a dolfin or sea pig*".
On this hill there grew over the centuries the unique group
of buildings of Prague Castle, whose significance
was heightened because it became not only the secular
but also the religious centre of the country.

First walk:

THROUGH PRAGUE CASTLE ACROSS THE CENTURIES

The survey of the styles: from the Gothic and the Baroque to the classicist modern style. The view from the Garden Na Valech

Founding Prague Castle

Founding Prague Castle is immediately connected with the history of the first Czech princely (later royal) Přemyslide dynasty ruling at the beginning only central Bohemia. The first centre of Přemyslide Bohemia was not Prague but the fortified settlement Levý Hradec lying near the north border of today's Prague (above the town Roztoky) on a high hill above the left bank of the Vltava. In Levý Hradec in the seventh decade of the 9th centrury, Prince Bořivoj (the first historicaly documented Přemyslide ruler) built the oldest Christian church in Bohemia, dedicated to St Kliment, the Roman Pope, considered the apostle of the Slavs. After his return from the Great Moravian Empire where he was christened (probably in 882), Bořivoj I moved to a parched hill above a bend of the Vltava called Praha (Prague). (According to the latest arecheological excavations the hill was inhabited before 850, its significance increased, however, with the coming of the ruler). Between 882-84 Prince Bořivoj founded here the second Christian church in Bohemia dedicated to the Virgin Mary and next to it a new princely residence, the foundation of the future castle and town.

We can only guess the causes of moving from Levý Hradec to Prague; perhaps it was motivated by both strategic and economic reasons. The Prague basin, above which the new castle towered, was relatively densely populated and made up a natural crossroads of trade routes of which the one leading from Regensburg via Prague to Krakow and further to Kiev and to the region along the Volga river was the most important. The existence of an easily accessible ford across the Vltava was surely also important, near Levý Hradec there was no ford. The castle itself was easily accessible from the Prague basin, however, it was well protected by the natural fortification; in the south and the east the narrow rocky ridge steeply declined to the Vltava valley (later here the Small Quarter was built), in the north it declined into a deep ravine (later called the *Jelení příkop* /Stag Moat/). The western part of the castle was separated from the ridge by a natural moat called the Hradčany furrow.

At first the castle had the appearance typical of an early medieval fortified settlement whose fundamental ground plan layout (distinctly different from typical medieval castles) has preserved up to now despite all later changes of the inner division and of the character of the buildings. The core of the fortified settlement with probably a timber house of the prince was approximately on the site of today's *third courtyard* and *Jiřské Square* with the Convent of St Jiří (George). After 900 the settlement was fortified by about 5 metre wide mound of earth and stones reinforced by a grating of logs and branches. Roughly on the site of today's *first* and *second courtyards* used to be the western castle area fortified by the above mentioned natural moat and later also by an artificial mound. The existence of the often mentioned eastern castle area between the contemporary Convent of St George and the Black Tower is not documented for that time. The inhabitants used to live in small timber houses and underground shelters of timber and earth scattered all over the area.

While for modern historians the beginning of Prague Castle remains a mystery in many aspects, Czech legends and the old chroniclers describe the oldest history of the Castle in a great detail, however, in contradiction with the found reality. The author of the oldest Czech chronicle, dean of St Vitus Chapter Kosmas (died in 1125) ascribed founding the Castle to the legendary Princess Libuše, wife of Přemysl the Tiller, the legendary founder of the Přemyslide dynasty. She foretold (probably on the Petřín slopes) the fame of Prague which „will touch the stars". Allegedly it happened in 723; the top of chroniclers' accuracy is, however, the data of Daniel Adam of Veleslavín (died in 1599), who determined the date of founding the Castle to 2 November of the mentioned year. The Nuremburg chronicle expresses quite a different opinion, according to it Prague was founded at the times of the biblical forefather Abraham. Only much later, in the period of Emperor Charles IV, the opinion that the oldest Prague Přemyslide castle was not Prague Castle but Vyšehrad began to spread. This belief prevailed for a long time thanks to the chronicler Václav Hájek of Libočany (died in 1553) and it was refuted only by the modern archeological excavations.

Prague Castle in the pre-Romanesque period

As early as at the end of the 9th century Prague Castle became the natural centre of the consolidating Přemyslide state and soon it became a permanent symbol of the Czech statehood. It was also manifested in the care which was given to it by many Czech rulers during history. (The exceptional position of the Castle had also its negative side. The Castle was considered the key to ruling the Czech state, and also to gaining the princely crown, and therefore during the first two centuries of its existence it was endangered more by the struggle for power between the members of the Přemyslide dynasty themselves than by an external enemy.)

The first stone building in the Castle was the above mentioned Church of the Virgin Mary, whose traces were found in today's west section between the *second* and the *fourth* courtyards (the Garden *Na Baště*), that is in the western part of the castle area. Its foundations can be seen through the transparent glass on the northern side of the passageway. Inside the walls after 920 Prince Vratislav I built another Prague church dedicated to St Jiří. His son, Prince Wenceslas, founded before 929 the third church, the Rotunda of St Vitus. This church soon became the religious centre of the whole country, since its founder himself was buried there, who soon after his assasination (about 935) was worshiped as saint and became the patron saint of Bohemia. In 973, un-

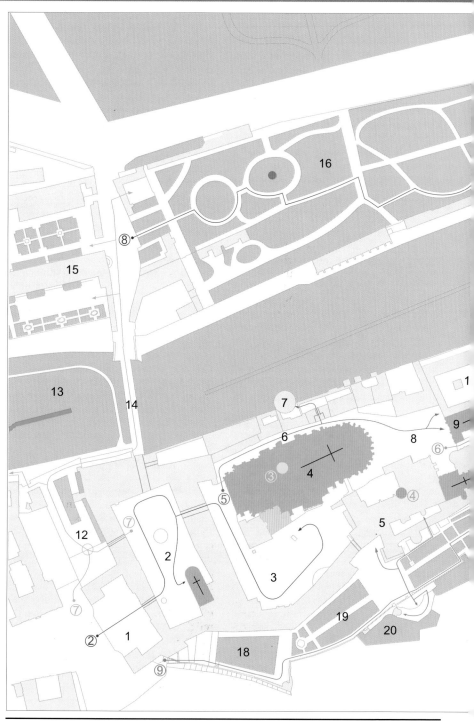

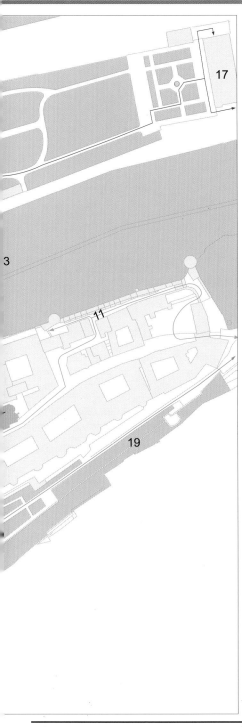

1 - first courtyard
2 - second courtyard
3 - third courtyard
4 - the Cathedral of St Vitus
5 - the Old Royal Palace
6 - Vikářská Street
7 - the Powder Tower
8 - Square U sv. Jiří
9 - the Basilica of St Jiří (George)
10 - the Convent of St George
11 - Golden Lane
12 - the fourth courtyard and the Garden
     At the Bastion
13 - the Stag Moat
14 - the Powder Bridge
15 - the Riding School
16 - the Royal Garden
17 - the Royal Summerhouse
18 - the Garden of Eden
19 - the Garden na Valech
20 - the Hartig Garden

THE WALK:

① Through Prague Castle across centuries
② Through three Castle courtyards
③ The Cathedral of St Vitus
④ The Old Royal Palace
⑤ Through Vikářská Street to
   the Convent of St George
⑥ Through Jiřská Street to Golden Lane
   and the Old Castle Stairs
⑦ From the Garden At the Bastion to the
   Stag Moat and via the Powder Bridge
   to the north forefield of Prague Castle
⑧ Through the Royal Garden
⑨ Through the Southern Gardens
   of Prague Castle

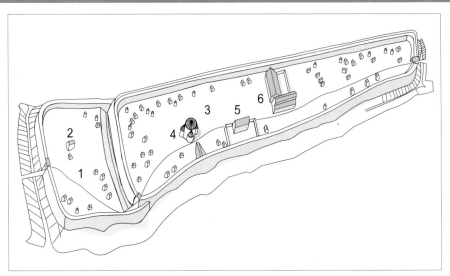

Prague Castle at the end of the 10th century

der Prince Boleslav II, the Prague bishopric was established and the Church of St Vitus became a cathedral. (The significance of the church even increased, when the relics of the second Prague bishop St Vojtěch were buried there.) In 973, next to the Church of St Jiří (George), the first convent in Bohemia was founded, run by Benedictine nuns; their first abbess was Mlada, the sister of Boleslav II. The connection between the secular and the religious centre was established at that time.

The relation between the secular and the church power was not always harmonious. The chronicler Kosmas for examples tells a story how at building the wall near the Convent of St George the future Prince Spytihněv pulled down the furnace belonging to the abbess with the words „today the abbeyss will not taste warm cakes". After this the relations between the abbess and the ruler were strained, and there were many mutual wilful acts. Finally after years the Prince expelled the abbess from the country admitting at that time that „there was no merit in pulling down

the furnace, now, however, he has a reason to be satisfied". More serious controversies arose between the ruler and the bishop (who was often the ruler's younger brother), which sometimes grew into an open clash and in the 11th century they even caused a temporal departure of the ruler from the Castle.

The years 1002-04 at Prague Castle were characterized by bloody fights for power in the country between the sons of Boleslav II - Jaromír, Boleslav III the Redhaired and Oldřich. The Castle was occupied several times (usually by treason and a ruse). The conflict incited by the domestic barrons even crossed the borders of the country; in 1003 the Polish King Boleslav the Brave occupied the Castle. The next year Emperor Henry II intervened militarily in Prince Jaromír's favour.

It is characteristic that this time of turmoils and violence borne the ruler who was perhaps afflicted with bad luck most of all European rulers. It was the above mentioned Prince Jaromír. In 999 he was castrated by his brother

1 - the western area outside the walls
2 - the Church of the Virgin Mary
3 - the central part of the fortified
   settlement
4 - the Rotunda of St Wenceslas
5 - the Princely Palace
6 - the Church of St George with
   the Convent

*The Romanesque style: stone masonry
of the fortifications of Prince Soběslav II*

Boleslav III the Redhaired and soon he escaped into the Empire. In 1003 seated on the princely throne by the German Emperor Henry II, soon he was expelled perhaps by Vladivoj (about whom nearly nothing is known, except the fact that in one year of the reign he drank himself to death) and certainly by the Polish King Boleslav the Brave, he was entroned again by the Emperor in 1004. Then he ruled till 1012, when he was overthrown by his younger brother Oldřich, he escaped to the Emperor again, who, however, handed him over back to Oldřich. After 21 years in jail he was entroned by Emperor Konrad II in 1033, after a year he was overthrown by Oldřich, blinded and again imprisoned. When the same year (1034) Oldřich died, Jaromír ascended to the princely throne again, however, nearly immediately he handed over the reign to Břetislav I. After a year he was killed.

In 1041 the German Emperor Henry III besieged Prince Břetislav at Prague Castle. He managed to set fire to the wooden parts of the fortification and the Prince was forced (again also by treason)

to surrender. Drawing a lesson from these events, he built soon afterwards new fortifications, which consisted at least partly of a stone wall (dry-rubble stonework).

Prague Castle
in the Romanesque period

After 1070 some princes, Vratislav II being the first of them (who acquired the royal title and crown for his person) preferred to have their seat at Vyšehrad, which became the second Prague castle; the reason was Vratislav's continuous controversies with his brother, bishop Jaromír. (However, there was no doubt about the importance of Prague Castle as the permanent centre and the main castle of the country.) Parallel with building the Vyšehrad Church of St Peter and Paul a new basilica founded by Vratislav's brother Prince Spytihněv II (consecrated in 1096) was completed on the site of the Rotunda of St Vitus. Completing the construction of the basilica is often considered the first evidence of the new Romanesque style, which manifested fully at the beginning of the 12th century.

In 1135 Prince Soběslav I decided to perform an extensive reconstruction of Prague Castle „according to the style of Latin towns". He built new stone fortifications (using mortar) which surrounded the central part of the Castle with the eastern part of the Castle area. The wall was very high (at some places up to 14 m), the external and internal faces of the wall were of carefully shaped limestone ashlars, the inside was of poured stonework. The southern side of the fortifications was reinforced by numerous towers, which were a unique fortification element at that time. The entrance to the Castle was guarded by three towers: by the White Tower in the southwest (the gate stood along its southern side), the southern tower with a passage through it next to the princely palace and the Black Tower with a passage through it on the eastern side. The middle of the western wall was reinforced by the Bishop tower, and also the eastern part of the northern wall was reinforced by a tower (next to the later Residence of the Prague Burgrave). Next to the southern wall of the Castle a stone princely palace was built. It became a part of the fortifications, and therefore it was reinforced by the above mentioned towers.

Soběslav's son Prince Vladislav II (from 1158 King) moved from Vyšehrad to Prague Castle for good in 1140. The new fortifications soon went through a test. In 1142 the Castle was besieged for five weeks by the Přemyslide apanage Prince Konrád of Znojmo. It was not conquered, however, it was severely damaged by fire, after which extensive reconstructions and renovations of the Castle area followed.

In the last quarter of the 12th century a long dynastic crisis began; at fights for power the Castle was besieged twice in 1178, then in 1182, 1184, 1192, and 1193.

1 - the western area outside the walls
2 - the White Tower
3 - the Bishop's Tower
4 - the Basilica of St Vitus
6 - the Monastery of the Prague Church
7 - the Princely (Royal) Palace
8 - the Basilica of St George
   with the Convent
9 - the tower of the Burgrave's Residence
10 - the Black Tower
11 - the Church of the Virgin Mary

It was not conquered, but three times (1178, 1192 and 1193) the desperate military and political situation forced the defenders to surrender. Only in 1197 when Prince Vladislav Jindřich handed over the rule after an agreement to his brother Přemysl I Otakar, a long period of peace began and a time of flourishing the Czech Kingdom set in.

Prague Castle in the period of the last Přemyslide rulers

In the first half of the 13th century Prague castle remained in the shape which was determined by Prince Soběslav. The Early Gothic, which was applied in Bohemia after the 1340s, was not manifested in the Castle.

In 1248 the barons rose up in rebellion against King Wenceslas I. The leader of the rebellion was his son, later King Přemysl II Otakar, who fortified his position at the Castle, however, he was forced to

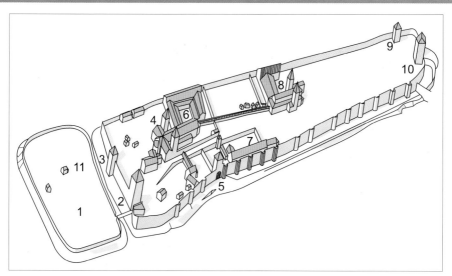

Prague Castle at the beginning of the 13th century

surrender because of lack of water. The conflict ended in reconciliation, and in 1253 Přemysl II Otakar (as Václav's co-ruler) could start rebuilding the royal palace. One year later, now as the only ruler, he concentrated on the renovation and extending of the castle fortifications (especially the moats), whose southern part was connected with the walls of the newly founded Small Quarter (1257). Next to the south section of the northern wall the Burgrave Palace was built.

At first, instead of Přemysl's successor Václav II his guardian, the Margrave Ota of Brandenburg ruled (1278-83); in fact, it was no rule but looting the country. In 1280 the Castle was damaged by a storm and a heavy downpour; the roof timbers of the towers were swept away, and the northern fortifications, the Convent of St George and the Chapter House of St Vitus Cathedral were seriously damaged. Under the long and lucky rule of Wenceslas II the Castle was repaired and experienced one of its cultural climaxes (troubadour poetry). However, at the end of Wenceslas' rule in 1303 fire damaged seriously the royal palace. It was an omen of the unfortunate years which followed. In 1305 the King died and one year later his son and successor Wenceslas III was assassinated in Olomouc. The Přemyslide dynasty died out on the spear side.

Prague Castle in the period of the Luxembourg dynasty rule

At the time of turmoils after the assassination of the last Přemyslide ruler Prague Castle deteriorated and was in serious danger several times. In 1306 Henry of Kärten gained the throne, but in the same year Rudolf of Hapsburg (called Kaše - the Weak) seized the rule, and after his death in 1307 Henry of Kärten ascended the throned again. In 1310 John of Luxembourg, the son of Emperor Henry VII, gained the throne.

The decline continued also under the rule

1 - the western palace
2 - the Old White Tower
3 - the Chapter Deanery
4 - Cathedral of St Vitus
5 - the foundations of the northern tower
of the Cathedral
6 - the Powder Tower
7 - the Royal Palace
8 - the Church of All Saints
9 - the Basilica of St George with the
Convent
10 - the New White Tower
11 - the Burgrave's Residence
12 - the Black Tower
13 - the Daliborka Tower
14 - the barbican in front of the eastern gate
15 - the artillery bastions of the southern
moat wall

The high Gothic: the Cathedral of St Vitus

of John of Luxembourg, a chivalric king and a skillful diplomat, who made Bohemia famous in numerous war expeditions abroad, however, he came home mostly only to collect money for his further adventurous enterprises. The Castle deteriorated, the only significant change in the first three decades of the 14th century was founding the tributary town Hradčany in 1321 on the western forefield of the Castle; its fortifications were connected with the defence system of Prague Castle and the Small Quarter.

When in October 1333 Prince Charles, later King and Emperor Charles IV (the son of John of Luxembourg and the last Přemyslide Eliška), arrived in Prague, he found the Castle so desolate that at first he had to stay in the Old Town. However, he soon moved into the Castle building of the Burgrave's residence, and began an extensive repair and reconstruction of the royal seat. He rebuilt and enlarged the royal palace having built new residential and official rooms (mainly the throne

hall). In 1344 in the presence of his father John of Luxembourg he laid the foundation stone of the Cathedral of St Vitus, which gradually replaced the old Romanesque basilica. The Cathedral built by Master Mathias of Arras and Master Petr Parléř became the permanent dominant feature of the Castle and the whole city. In 1470s the Church of All Saints was completed on the site of the Romanesque palace chapel considered a wonder of Gothic architecture. By these and other adaptations (gilding the roofs of the White and the Black Towers) Charles IV made a respectable emperor's seat out of Prague Castle. He paid less attention to the fortifications, he founded only a new moat and a moat wall outside the south wall opposite the Small Quarter.

The construction continued at a lower pace also during the rule of Wenceslas IV; the building of the Cathedral continued, and also the Royal Palace was adapted (especially its residential rooms). After the King died in 1419, and after the out-

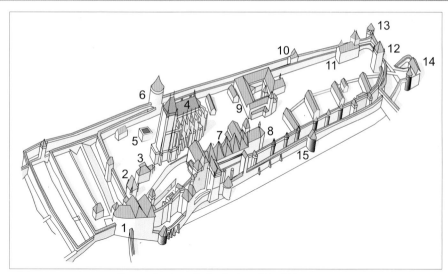

Prague Castle at the beginning of the 16th century

break of the Hussite Wars in 1420, the building activity was interrupted. The Castle was occupied and plundered by the Prague Hussites, and then by the treason of the Prague Burgrave it was opened to the troops of Wenceslas' brother Emperor Zikmund of Luxembourg, who had himself crowned on 28 July 1420 (after the lost Battle of Vítkov) and soon he left Prague. From 1421 the Castle remained in the power of the Prague Hussites till the end of the Hussite wars (1434), with the exception of the years 1425-27, when the castle garrison consisted of the soldiers of Zikmund Korybutovitch, the unsuccessful Polish pretender to the rule over Hussite Bohemia.

Prague Castle in the late Gothic period

After the end of the Hussite Wars the Czech rulers Emperor Zikmund of Luxembourg, King Albrecht II of Hapsburg, Ladislav the Posthumous, Jiří of Poděbra-

dy and at first also Vladislav Jagellon resided mostly in the Králův dvůr (King's Court; on the site of today's Obecní dům - the Public House) in the Old Town and the Castle continued deteriorating. After the town upheavals in 1483 King Vladislav Jagellon decided to move back to Prague Castle because of his safety. He had it rebuilt in the late Gothic style, which emphasised not only the official purposes of the building but also the personal comfort of the ruler. He chose luckily as the builder the outstanding architech Benedikt Ried, whose first task was to rebuild the fortifications.

The old Romanesque fortifications were not only deteriorated, but it became very dated when considered the development of warfare, mainly because of the spreading and the fast development of fire weaponry. The Castle was endangered most on the north side, one time reliably protected by a deep ravine of the *Stag Moat*; however, it was so narrow, that now the quality cannons of invaders could easily shoot behind it. Therefore Benedikt Ried built a

The late Gothic: the Vladislav Hall

moat wall outside the Romanesque wall, founded on the slope of the moat, and reinforced it by three artilery bastions. Their task was to cover by the fire of their weapons both the opposite side of the Stag Moat, the proper space of the moat, and the space at the foot of the moat wall, which otherwise could not be reached. The most massive tower was the Prašná (Powder) Tower (later called incorrectly Mihulka) standing opposite the Cathedral of St Vitus, the slenderest was the middle Bílá věž (White Tower, called the New, to be distinguished from the old White Tower next to the western gate), on the east side of the northern fortification stood the Daliborka Tower, lying in the moat.

The most significant work by Ried was rebuilding the Royal Palace, where among others, he built in place of the throne hall of Charles IV the large Vladislav Hall, at that time the largest secular vaulted space in Middle Europe. A noteworthy example of the late Gothic architecture was also the Jezdecké schody (Riders Staircase) leading to the hall. On the windows of the Vladislav Hall and at building the transversal palace wing (called Ludvík's) elements of the Renaissance style manifested in Ried's work; it was the first evidence of the new style in Bohemia.

The general appearance of Prague Caste of that time was completed by a number of smaller buildings around the whole castle area. They mostly belonged to noblemen, the Church and the court officials. The extensive palaces along the eastern part of the southern fortifications were built by the lords of Švamberk, the Lords of Rožmitál, and the Lords of Rožmberk. At the western gate next to the White Tower the house of the castle captain was built.

Prague Castle in the period of Renaissance and Mannerism

The rule of the Polish Jagellon dynasty ended by the tragic death of King Ludvík

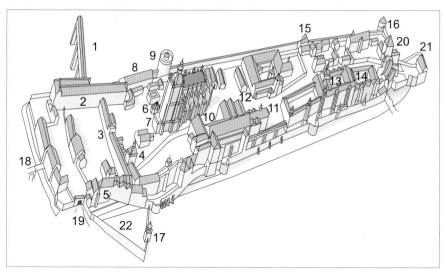

Prague Castle at the beginning of the 17th century

Jagellon after the lost battle with the Turks at Mohács (1526). After complicated diplomatic negotiations in the same year young Ferdinand I Hapsburg was elected Czech King, which started the nearly four centuries long rule of the Hapsburg family in the Czech lands.

The fortified Gothic residence did not suit the developing new Renaissance lifestyle, which made headway fully with the arrival of King Ferdinand I Hapsburg. Also the existing space of the Castle turned out insufficient for the ruler's grand plans, and therefore it was extended by the northern forefield on the other side of the ravine (the later *Stag Moat*). In 1534 the Renaissance *Královská zahrada* (Royal Garden) was founded, built at the cooperation with Italian masters. Even now it is dominated by the Renaissance building of the Velká míčovna (Great Ball-game House) and mainly by the Royal Summerhouse (built from 1538), a top work of the Renaissance architecture north of the Alps. The garden was

1 - the Powder Bridge
2 - the northern wing
3 - the Bishop's (Astronomical, Mathematical) Tower
4 - the Old White Tower
5 - Rudolf's Palace (the Summer Building)
6 - the Chapel of St Vojtěch
7 - the Cathedral of St Vitus
8 - the foundry
9 - the Powder Tower
10 - the Royal Palace
11 - the Church of All Saints
12 - the Basilica of St George with the Convent
13 - the Rožmberk Palace
14 - the Pernštejn Palace
15 - the New White Tower
16 - the Daliborka Tower
17 - the Tower of the Trumpeters
18 - the western gate
19 - the gate to the Castle Stairs
20 - the Black Tower
21 - the barbican in front of the eastern gate
22 - the Garden of Eden

accessible from the Castle across a hight wooden bridge with five stone pillars.

After the disasterous fire of the Castle, the Small Quarter and the Hradčany Town in 1541 the King began an extensive reconstruction of the residential premises and had new palace buildings built along the southern fortification west of the old palace. When the king was not present the building work was run by his wife Anna Jagellon and after her death by King's son, Archduke Ferdinand of Tyrol. His delicate taste and art talent manifested favourably at building the Castle; among others he established a building office headed by the significant architects Paolo della Stella and from 1556 by Bonifác Wolmut. The Archduke had a private garden, later called *Rajská* (the Garden of Eden) built on the southern slope of the Castle. The building activity continued even during the rule of Ferdinand's successor Emperor Maxmilian II (the central Chapel of St Vojtěch in front of the western front of the Cathedral).

In the 16th century the rulers considered all objects which were their property and an occasional residence a part of their private household. Therefore they issued instructions even about the smallest details of the adaptation of the castle space. For example the building office did not even dare to decide which colour to use for painting the fence of the garden around the Royal Summerhouse, and solved the issue lengthily by correspondence with Emperor Maxmilian II, who stayed in Austria at that time.

On the plots cleared by the fire palaces of noblemen were built, of which the Rožmberk Palace (belonging to a significant noble family from Southern Bohemia) was the largest (along the southern fortifications east of the Royal Palace) and also the Pernštejn Palace standing next to it. The castle residence of the Burgrave was rebuilt in the Renaissance style. In front of the west front of the St Vitus Cathedral the central Chapel of St Vojtěch was built (demolished during the neo-Gothic completion of the Cathedral).

The Castle went through an extraordinary development in the last third of the 16th century in the period of Rudolf II's rule, when Prague became the Emperor's residence and the centre of the empire for the second time in its history. Significant artists and scientists of that time used to arrive in Prague (for example the painters Hans von Aachen, Bartolomeus Spranger, Giuseppe Arcimboldo, the scultor Adrian de Vries, the astronomers Tycho Brahe and Johannes Kepler; even Giordano Bruno visited Prague). The Emperor acquired a famous and immensely extensive collection of works of art and various curiosities, of which only a negligible torso remained in the Castle up to now.

The Emperor had the southern palace wing next to the old White Tower extended by the so called Summer Building, where were his private rooms. The largest Rudolf construction was a new palace on the northern side of the Castle (the construction began in 1589) with two halls, nowadays called the Spanish Hall and Rudolf's Gallery. The new palace was connected with the palace complex next to the old White Tower by a narrow wing with a passage, the foundation of today's central wing between the *second* and the *third courtyard*. Simultaneously the adaptation of the *Royal Garden* continued, where among others the Lion Court, the Pheasant Farm, the aviary, and the open summer riding school were built. Behind the Pheasant Farm a fish pond was founded. The ravine between the Castle and the Royal Garden was converted into a deer park; probably from that time it is called *Jelení příkop* (the Stag Moat). In the northeast part of the fortifications between the old Romanesque wall and the late Gothic moat wall the castle riflemen settled, whose dwellings became the

The Renaissance: the giardinetto and the Royal Summerhouse in the Royal Garden

The Baroque: the presidential banner above the late Baroque first courtyard

foundations of the famous *Zlatá ulička* (Golden Lane).

The building development ceased after dethroning Rudolf in 1611. During the short reign of his brother Mathias (1611-19) the south wing was completed, and the late Renaissance garden summerhouse was built in the *Garden of Eden*. The grand western Mathias Gate was completed (1614), considered the first building implementation of the early Baroque style in Prague.

In May 1618 the uprising of the Czech Estates against the Hapsburg dynasty broke out, which started the Thirty Years War. In the next year the leader of the Protestant Union Fridrich of Fal, a son-in-law of the English King James I, was elected Czech King, and Prague became a busy residence again for fourteen months. The short episode ended by the defeat of the Czech Estates in the Battle of the White Mountain on 8 Nov 1620 and by the King's flight from the country; the power of the Hapsburgs and the Catholic Church

was not only renewed but gradually also significantly enlarged. The importance of Prague, however, dedined.

Prague Castle in the Baroque period

During the Thirty Years War the Castle was occupied twice, in 1631 by the Saxon army, and in 1648 by the Swedish troops. The Swedish army plundered a large part of the valuable collections of Rudolf II and caused an explosion in the Powder Tower, which damaged it severely. The building activity (except for the necessary fortification work) nearly ceased at that time. Only in the 1640s in the middle part of the south wing the New House of the Empress was built and the connecting wing of Rudolf II was extended by a number of houses, partly intended as the dwellings of the Empress' retinue. The attempt at the Baroque completion and rebuilding of the Gothic Cathedral of St Vitus remained fortunately unsuccessful.

The significance of the Castle declined after the end of the Thirty Years War. Therefore at Prague Castle there are only few early Baroque buildings and nearly no buildings from the period of the high Baroque (unlike the Prague Towns). At the end of the 17th century the Castle was included into the general Baroque fortifications of Prague, in its northern forefield several bastions were built and in 1721 the new Písecká Gate was also built.

The Hapsburg rulers resided mostly in Vienna and Prague Castle revived only during their temporal stays and mostly at holding coronation ceremonies (1679 the coronation of Emperor Leopold I, 1723 of Charles VI, 1743 of Maria Theresa, 1791 of Leopold II, 1792 of Franz II, 1836 of Ferdinand V). The Castle experienced a ceremonial reviving also in 1680, when Emperor Leopold and his court came from Vienna afflicted by plague to Prague. Unusual ceremonies took place in the honour of the memory of St John of Nepomuk (in 1721 his beatification, in 1729 sanctification), but otherwise the Castle remained in the backgroung of events.

Only in the second half of the 18th century, under the rule of Empress Maria Theresa, a time for a large adaptation of the Castle came. A joint French, Bavarian and Saxon occupation of Prague in 1741 (the Bavarian Emperor Elector Charles Albrecht was proclaimed Czech King for a short time) and a Prussin occupation in 1744 preceded to it . In 1757 the Castle was seriously damaged by the Prussian artillery at another, this time unsuccessful, siege.

The rebuilding was run by the imperial architect Nicolo Pacassi. First he rebuilt the former Rožmberk Palace into the Ústav šlechtičen (Home for Noble Women), then he rebuilt the south wing of the Royal Palace, the central wing between the *second* and the *third courtyard* and the buildings around the *second courtyard*, where he built the new Chapel of the Holy Cross. After demolishing several buildings in the western part of the Castle and filling the moat the west wing with two short projecting parts was built, which together with a decorative grill created the *first courtyard* (the court of honour). The newly built and rebuilt buildings were later united by a late Baroque facade, the interiors were rather in the Roccoco style. Pacassi's rebuilding joined the Castle space together and gave to the formely picturesque Castle a balanced and grand palace appearance of the prestigous architecture.

However, the costly rebuilt Castle did not find a respectable use. Maria Theresa's son, Emperor Josef II, sold in auction the remnants of the one time valuable collections, and since the last offices (the country government and the court of appeal) moved from the Castle into the town in 1784, the deserted Castle was offered to the army. They Royal Belvedere became an artillery laboratory, in the closed Convent of St George artillery barracks were established.

Prague Castle in the 19th and 20th centuries

At the beginning of the 19th century the significance of Prague Castle even declined.

The emperor's residential rooms were so much deserted, that if by chance an important guest were to be accommodated in them, the Castle administration had to borrow the interior equipment including carpets and cuttlery from the private residences of nobility.

Reviving came in 1832-36, when the Castle served as an exile residence of the French King Charles X, expelled from Paris by the revolution in 1830. Although the seventyfive years old King liked Prague (he left it only for numerous game

The modern styles: the wedge-shaped corridor modified by Otto Rothmayer belongs to the youngest parts of Prague Castle

hunts and to the Teplice Baths), this living was not much comfortable, for at occasional visits of the Emperor's family from Vienna, he had to leave his rooms. The last reminder of the past fame was the coronation of Emperor Ferdinand V the Czech King (1836), the last coronation Prague experienced.

Ill and unable Ferdinand V was forced to resign in favour of Franz Josef I in the revolutionary year 1848, he chose Prague as his residence. Only in 1866, during the Prussian-Austrian war, he left Bohemia for a longer time. Then, after the lost Battle of Sadová, the Castle was occupied for two and half months by the Prussian army. The ex-emperor became a popular Prague figure because of his eccentricity (and also generosity). It was possible nearly every day to see him walking to check the tenement house which belonged to him, and taking off his hat to every passer-by. Prague dwellers were indulgent to Ferdinand, since he was the last crowned Czech King, and they called him Ferdinand the Kind.

In the second half of the 19th century the reconstruction and modern Gothic completion of the Cathedral of St Vitus started. The building of the new part of the Cathedral became an extraordinary chance for the contemporaneous Czech artists at the end of the 19th and the beginning of the 20th century; besides the prevailing historicism mainly in the interior equipment and decoration also the elements of the Art Nouveau appear. At that time also the neo-Gothic Chapter Deanery and two residences for the canons were built in Square *U sv. Jiří* (At St George). The Basilica of St George was restored into a Romanesque appearance (not very fortunately).

After the disintegration of Austria-Hungary and the formation of the Czechoslovak Republic in 1918 it was decided to renew the residential traditions of the Castle and to transform it into a prestigous presidential residence.

The neo-Gothic style: a window rosette of the western front of the St Vitus Cathedral

The first president of the republic, Tomáš Garrigue Masaryk, gave the task of the Castle adaptation to the Slovenian architect Josip Plečnik. At first Plečnik modified the southern gardens of Prague Castle - *the Garden of Eden* and *the Garden Na Valech*, later he also modified the Garden *Na Baště* (at the Bastion). He also modified the open castle space, mainly he unified to the same level both parts of the *third courtyard*, which had different height. In the west wing (between the *1st* and the *2nd courtyard*) he created the monumental Sloupová sín (Pillar Hall), modified and equipped newly a number of official rooms including the flat of the president. Plečnik's buildings and modifications are complemented by a number of perfectly handicraft done and artisticaly designed details, giving the Castle rooms unusuality and a new aesthetic dimension. (Plečnik did not hesitate, for example, to use in an original way motives from Ancient Egypt, Crete and the Antiquity, which complete suprisingly the character of the place.)

The modern styles: the decoration of the Bull Staircase from the Garden Na Valech

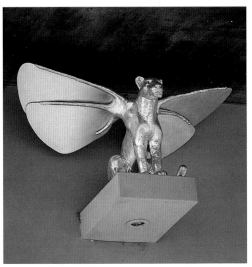

The presence: a post-modern sculpture by Bořek Šípek in the 2nd courtyard

His pupil Otto Rothmayer continued in Plečnik's spirit at the adaptations of the Castle. The architect of Prague Castle became Pavel Janák, who after the WW II among others reconstructed the Riding School, the Great Ball-game House and the Royal Summerhouse. Fortunately, the war year 1939-45 did not mark Prague Castle significantly. The occupation administration rejected clearly Plečnik's modifications because of ideological reasons, however, their removal was prevented (often only thanks to great personal courage). Only on the last days of the war the Great Ball-game House in the *Royal Garden* was seriously damaged.

Modifications and reconstructions were performed at Prague Castle even later, in the period of the Communist rule, however, a number of Castle spaces remained closed. Prague Castle was declared the national cultural treasure number one by a law passed in 1958. Since 1990 new parts of the Castle area have gradually been being opened for the public, the Castle expositions have been being enlarged, extraordinary exhibitions have been held. Since 1925 a detailed archeological survey has been going on nearly without interruption, still bringing new findings. Thus the history of Prague Castle can surprise us by many new facts.

Second walk:

THROUGH THREE CASTLE COURTYARDS

*The entrance gate to the Castle is guarded
by the stone giants and the Castle guard*

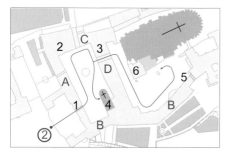

A - the western wing
B - the southern wing
C - the northern wing
D - the central wing

1 - the Mathias Gate
2 - the Picture Gallery
 and the Spanish Hall
3 - the Rudolf Gallery
4 - the Chapel of the Holy Cross
5 - the Bull Staircase
6 - the Old Deanery

At present the *first courtyard* of Prague Castle is connected directly with *Hradčany Square*. In the past the access to the Castle was not so easy. Between the courtyard and the square (approximately on the site of today's pavement in front of the decorative grill, was a ravine called the Hradčany furrow dividing the Hradčany ridge into two rises.

This natural fortification of the Castle was changed into the first **castle moat**, equipped by a drawbridge in the period of King Přemysl II Otakar. In the second half of the 15th century approximately at the eastern edge of the *first* and the *second courtyard* two artificial moats were dug, according to archeological surveys 20 metres wide and 10 metres deep. The bridges across the moats led to the fortified gates, which for tactical reasons were not built in one line, but in a way that the access road was bent as much as possible; the first gate stood approximately on the site of the north wing of the *first courtyard*, the second and the third gates were moved to the south. Both artificial moats we-

The first courtyard

re filled in the 16th century, but the moat on the site of the Hradčany furrow remained preserved till the large rebuilding of the Castle under Maria Theresa in the second half of the 18th century. Next to the furrow stood the house of the royal administrator of the collections from 1556 and an old arsenal from 1570. Both buildings were demolished under Maria Theresa. It is said that in the moat itself even before the Theresian rebuilding stood a small bakery; the smoke of its furnace displeased the nobility crossing the moat on the nearby bridge.

First courtyard

You can enter the *first courtyard* through the **entrance gate** with a Rococo grill with the initials of Empress Maria Theresa and her son Josef II. The large statues of the **fighting giants** on the entrance pillars were created by the Baroque sculptor Ignác František Platzer in 1770-71 (in 1921 they were replaced with the copies by Čeněk Vosmík). I. F. Platzner

also created the statues on the other pillars next to the gate, mainly the symbols of the Czech Kingdom (a lion) and of the Hapsburg monarchy (an eagle). At the gate stand the castle guard in festive uniforms designed by Theodor Pištěk (who is also the author of the decor and costumes of Forman's films Valmont and Amadeus).

The guard company did not always have it easy. The soldiers carried out their guard duty only in return for accommodation and firewood. Because of this they were obliged to take up other skilled crafts and from their earnings they not only supported themselves but also paid the cost of their uniforms and weapons. Their life was spent in endless disagreements with the members of the Prague craft guilds, who saw in the Castle guard unfair competition. In the 18th century the company was reduced to the minimum complement of 24 men and with its allocation of three cartridges would have been of little value in the defence of the Castle. The company was saved thanks only to the tradi-

The war trophies in the first courtyard

tion that it served as escort for the religious procession of Corpus Christi. The complaints against the guards were endless and so it is not surprising that one of the Castle Captains, the Lord of Svárov, tired by vain supplications for improving the conditions of the company, ended up insane in 1739 and eventually had a stroke.

The *first courtyard* was formed in 1763-71 under the rule of Empress Maria Theresa. The court architect Nicolo Pacassi gave it the character of a noble court (having the shape of the letter U) invitingly open from *Hradčany Square,* thereby denying the stronghold character of the Castle in agreement with the contemporary trend. A large part of all three wings of the noble court is made up of new buildings in the style of the austere imperial Baroque, decorated on attic gables by imperial **sculptures of allegories of war and peace** by the sculptor Ignác František Platzer (today there are copies). The monumental decoration and austere facade express the imperial majesty of the residence and therefore it differs from the playfulness of the palaces and houses of the Prague Baroque.

Even the great philosopher G. W. F. Hegel liked Pacassi's design, who in 1824 saw the reflection of his absolute idea in the clear design of architecture: „imperial castle - imagine a modern palace, no such an angular, zigzag, shapeless ... five-pointed, undefinable objects as the castle in Nuremburg."

At present the north and the south transversal wings are used for accommodating state guests and the middle wing is used for offical puposes. The paving, the illuminations and the 25 m high flag poles (originally of fir trunks, since 1962 sticked of parts) were made according to the designs of Josip Plečnik from 1920-22.

Incorporated into the front of the building is the festive sandstone **Mayášova brána** (Mathias Gate), originally standing separately, which was inspired by the Roman triumphal archs. It is consi-

The Mathias Gate

The Pillar Hall

dered one of the first early Baroque buildings in Prague; it was completed in 1614 under the rule of Emperor Mathias, however, it was being built under Rudolf II, probably according to a design of the significant architect Giovanni Maria Filippi. Below the ledge of the gate are placed the coats of arms of the countries ruled by the Hapsburgs, on the gable under the gold commemorative inscription is a sculpture of Mathias' imperial emblem. On the right of the passage through the gateway leads a grand staircase to the state rooms on the first floor of the New Palace. (The staircase stands in place of a smaller staircase from the period of Rudolf II, which led to the private rooms of the Emperor.) On the left of the passage is the entrance to the monumental **Sloupová síň** (Pillar Hall) built by Josip Plečnik in 1927-31. In 1975 a staircase was placed in Plečnik's Hall because of the modifications to the entrance to the Spanish Hall.

Second courtyard

In place of the *second courtyard* was originally the western part of the Castle area and half of it was made up by the moat outside the Romanesque wall up to 1576 (when it was filled). The wall remained preserved in the central wing between the *second* and the *third courtyards*. The courtyard was gradually surrounded by Renaissance and Baroque buildings. Their facades were united by Nicolo Pacassi into the form of his own buildings on the *first courtyard*. By this unification the Castle lost the variety of volumes and proportions in favour of cold dignity.

At present most rooms on the first floor of all wings of the New Palace around the *second courtyard* serves for official purposes and the rooms of the second and the third floor serve for administrative purposes (the Administration of Prague Castle, the Offices of the President). The state rooms are open for the public twice a year.

The Pillar Hall, a detail

The Baroque fountain in the second courtyard

The paving of the courtyard comes from 1965-67, it was designed by Jaroslav Fragner. The courtyard is decorated by a **Baroque fountain**, the work of the stone mason Francesco de Torre and the sculptor Jeroným Kohl from 1686. On the ledge of the central fountain stand the statues of Hercules wearing a lion's skin, Neptun with a dolphin, Volcano with a hammer and an anvil and Mercury with small wings at the ankles and on the helmet. On the bowl they support stand three sea gods Tritons bearing the upper bowl on which are three lions spouting water out of their mouths. The nearby **well** is 14 m deep and comes probably from the 16th century. It is covered by an ornamental grill from 1719.

The oldest source of drinking water was the spring sunk in the rock in the *third courtyard* nearby the Chapel of St Wenceslas of the Cathedral of St Vitus. When the water supply from it was not sufficient, in the southwest part of the *third courtyard* a well was sunk above 60 m deep, probably the deepest one

in the historic Prague. Under Charles IV a pipeline was installed in the Castle running from Kajetánka in Břevnov, where it ended in the fountain outside the Royal Palace decorated by a statue of St George. In the Renaissance after founding *the Royal Garden* water run through tunnels from wells in Střešovice. Under Rudolf II a new pipeline was built, reportedly according to the plans of the astronomer Tycho Brahe. Drinking water came through the pipeline from the game preserve around the Hvězda Summerhouse to the royal kitchen, to the fountain in *Jiřské Square*, to the Old Residence of the Burgrave, to the Lobkovic Palace, and to several houses in the Small Quarter. Water for general use was brought here from the lake below the Hvězda Summerhouse into the Stag Moat, where it was cleaned and then pumped to the Castle fountains and to several houses in the Small Quarter. According to a legend the water sprite Paklt takes care of Castle water; he is exceptional in this that unlike the other Prague water sprites he does not live in running water but in wells.

A well with a Baroque grill   *The Rothmayer Hall*

West wing

The long west wing separates the *second courtyard* from the *first courtyard* and from the *fourth courtyard* (the Garden *At the Bastion*). In the northern part of the wing (behind the passage to the *fourth courtyard*) on the first floor is the high **Rothmayer Hall**, which makes a vestibule of the Spanish Hall in the north wing.

In the passage to the *fourth courtyard* you can see the stonework of **the foundations of the first Prague Church of the Virgin Mary** coming from the last quarter of the 9th century, which was uncovered in 1950. In the church skeleton remains were found, belonging probably to Prince Spytihněv I and his wife.

In the past south of the church stood two houses from the Gothic period, originally owned by the St Vitus Chapter, from the 16th century extended for the High Chamberlain and from 1758 adapted into the kitchen of Maria Theresa (in its place is the Pillar Hall today).

There were also stables, the flat of the butler and a shed for fire engines.

South wing

In the short south wing (which, however, continues to the *third courtyard* up to the Royal Palace) there are several important state rooms. In the corner section by the *first courtyard* is a cloakroom connected to Pacassi's staircase (leading from the Mathias Gate) decorated by a precious Gobelin from the 17th century, behind the cloakroom is the **Entrance Salon** (also decorated by a precious Gobelin). Considerable part of the length of the south wing is made by the **Throne Hall**, where most official audiences take place. Next is the **Brožík Salon**, called after Václav Brožík, the author of the paintings placed here, of which the largest is the picture from 1878 called The message of King Ladislav to the French court in 1457. The following **Hapsburg Salon** preserved as the only one the original form from the end of the 18th century. Its

The Hapsburg Salon

walls are covered by wood lining, into which portraits of Maria Theresa's family members are put. Further on, at the place where the central wing is connected, there is the **Glass Salon** with a valuable Indian carpet from the middle of the 19th century.

In the past in place of the south wing used to stand a Romanesque wall. On its foundations in the southeast corner of today's courtyard a separate palace was built at the end of the 15th century (under King Vladislav Jagellon). It was designed by Benedict Ried. Later the wife of Ferdinand I Anna Jagellon lived in the palace, and after the Castle fire in 1541 it was rebuilt into the New House of Archduke Ferdinand of Tyrol by the architect Hans Tirol. Westwards of this place, aproximately on the site where the western wing is connected, there stood another palace building given to the Count of Thurn by Ferdinand I; next to it to the west another building was built. Emperor Maxmilian gained both buildings back, and he had them connected (by a building of Bonifác Wohlmut) with the New House of Archduke Ferdinand. Emperor Rudolf II had the whole palace rebuilt and new floors built, where he established his private rooms (called the Summer House).

North wing

Through the middle of the north wing a passage leads to the Prašný most (Powder Bridge) via the Stag Moat. Inside the passage is preserved a **Renaissance gate**, from the outside is a pillar portal built in 1722 according to the design of N. Pacassi (called **Pacassi's Gate**). On both sides of the passage are long vaulted **Renaissance stables** built for Spanish horses at the end of the 16th century by Emperor Rudolf II (stables used to be at this place as early as under Ferdinand I). Two parallel hall spaces of the stables on the west side of passage were converted into the Castle **Picture Gallery**, one hall space in the east serves as a separate exhibition hall called **Emperor's stable**. The court accessible from the right of the passage

The Spanish Hall

belonged originally to the stables, behind it there is the building of the former foundry from 1569, nowadays adapted for the Vikárka Restaurant.

The core of the **Picture Gallery** is the famous painting collection of Emperor Rudolf II, the major part of which, however, was not preserved; a part of it was transported to Vienna before the beginning and during the Thirty Years War, a part was robbed by the Swedish in 1648. After the end of the Thirty Years War Emperor Ferdinand III and mainly his brother Archduke Leopold William restored the picture gallery. From the 1720s the collection was reduced, some pictures were carried to Vienna, some works were sold to Saxony, some pictures were sold at auctions under Josef II. A new picture gallery was opened in 1965. Among the most precious works connected with the old Picture Gallery are Tizian's „Toilet of a Young Woman", Rubens' „The Gathering of the Olympian Gods", and Tintorett's „The Whipping of Christ". There are also paintings by Hans von Aachen, Domenic Fetti, Bartolomeo

Spranger, Paolo Veronese and others. In the first half of the of the 20th century the collection was enriched thanks to President T. G. Masaryk and his daughter Alice by the representatives of the Czech art of the 18th, 19th and 20th centuries. The castle collections have some of the paintings by Petr Brandl, Jan Kupecký, Norbert Grund, Josef Mánes, Adolf Kosárek, Jan Preisler, Antonín Slavíček and others.

The most important hall of the Castle is besides the Vladislav Hall in the Old Royal Palace mainly the **Spanish Hall** (originally called the New Hall) going through two floors of the north wing of the New Palace. It is 12 m high, 21 m wide and 43 m long. It was built at the beginning of the 17th century, originally had two naves and a line of wooden pillars in the middle, in the first half of the 18th century it was made higher and the new construction of the roof timbers enabled removing the pillars. It was modified at Pacassi's rebuilding of the Castle, again in 1836 and last time in 1865-68 in

The sunblind above the entrance to the offices
(the second courtyard, the central wing)

connection with the prepared but not carried out coronation of Emperor Franz Josef I as Czech King.

The hall was designed for safekeeping the Emperor's collections but also for other official purposes. On several occasions it was the venue for eccentric behaviour by the crowned heads. For instance in 1680 Emperor Leopold had a wild tomcat released into the hall. Together with his children and dogs he organised a hunt and the animal was speared to death. (Leopold withdrew to Prague then to escape the plague in Vienna, to pass the time he held a fancy dress ball on Shrove Monday 1680). No less deadly were the intentions displayed later by Emperor Charles VI, who from the window of the hall shot at deer driven out from the Stag Moat.

Rudolf's Gallery next door was established by Emperor Rudolf II for his collection of paintings. The rich relief wall decoration comes from the second half of the 19th century.

Rudolf's Gallery was originally called the Spanish Hall. The name was derived probably not only from taking the attribute of the stables on the ground floor, where Spanish horses were bred, but it was also a frequent name of galleries in the Hapsburg countries. The galleries came into being as a building type in France, and therefore they were generally called French halls, which, however, was unacceptable for the Habsburgs (being France's enemies). Because the immediate inspiration for building Rudolf's Gallery were Spanish Galleries, it was called the Spanish Hall. Today's Spanish Hall was originally called the New Hall, from the 17th century the New Spanish Hall, later the present name. The original Spanish Hall changed its name into the Gallery, the German Hall, and finally Rudolf's Gallery.

In Rudolf's Gallery on 14 November 1944 The Committee for the Liberation of the Russian Nations was proclaimed and the Vlasov army was established, which fought on the side of Germany against the Soviet Union but in May 1945 it helped to liberate Prague.

The Chapel of the Holy Cross

The interior of the Chapel of the Holy Cross

Central wing

The long central wing (between the second and the thrird courtyards) was rebuilt into the present form by N. Pacassi in 1759-75. Its rooms serve mainly as administrative and official spaces of Prague Castle. In the east on the floor above the former western gate is the **Old Hall** between the original Romanesque wall and the stonework of the White Tower. North of the gate is preserved the 18 metres high Romanesque limestone **White Tower**.

The tower was over 30 m high and together with the bastion from the first half of the 12th century guarded the main entrance to the Castle. It also served as a dungeon, for instance the Přemyslide Prince Soběslav II was imprisoned in it (1147 and 1162), as well as Záviš of Falkenštejn (1288), the husband of Kunhuta, Queen Dowager after the Přemysl II Otakar, King Wenceslas IV (imprisoned in 1394 by the rebelious nobility and in 1402 by his brother Zikmund of Luxembourg) and the Polish pretender to the throne of the Hussite Bohemia - Zikmund Korybutovič. In the Baroque period fireworks were let off its flat root, the upper floor was demolished during Pacassi's rebuilding.

Further to the west are placed the **New Salons**, adapted in the 1960s and named after the painters who performed their decorations. These are Mánes', Chitussi's, Purkyně's, Navrátil's and Čermák's salons. There is a room of the New Gallery, not much fortunate examples of the so called Brussels style of the 1950s which made the Czechoslovak architecture famous at the world exhibition Expo '58 in Brussels.

In the past in place of today's central wing originally stood the stone Romanesque wall of Prince Soběslav I with the Bishop Tower (approximately in the middle of the wing) and with the White Tower (at the souther end). Houses were built next to the wall, at first on the side from the *third courtyard*. In the second half of the 16th century a narrow wing was built to the wall from the side

The Plečnik Staircase with the lift to the former flat of the president

The Lion Fountain at the exit from the flat of the president into The southern gardens of the Castle

of the *second courtyard*, which connected the palace buildings in the north with the south buildings. The medieval **Bishop Tower** was integrated into this wing (into which Emperor Rudolf II deposited his collections). In the tower a staircase was built which connected the floors and led into a lookout terrace. The tower served as Rudolf's observatory, therefore in that period it was called Astronomical or Mathematical. In the 1640s in place of Rudolf's wing a continuous wing was built by order of Emperor Ferdinand III. It served to accommodate the Empress' female retinue.

Approximately in the middle of the wing there is a **sun blind** above the new entrance to the offices of the President and the Prague Castle Administration. The entrance is embellisted by a sculpture of a leopard with wings by the Castle architect Bořek Šípek. Alongside the central wing the **Chapel of the Holy Cross** juts out from the south into the courtyard, it was built as a replacement for the closed Chapel of St Wenceslas

in the southwest corner of the *third courtyard*. It was built in 1758-63 according to N. Paccassi's plans on the site of the court building office from the 16th century and the kitchen established for the coronation feast of Emperor Charles VI in 1723, later used as the main guardroom. From the original equipment was preserved mainly the marble main altar with sculptures of angels by František Platzer and with a picture of the Crucifixion by František Xaver Balk. The other decoration comes from 1852-56, when the chapel was adapted into a private chapel for the ex-emperor Ferdinand the Good. The ceiling paintings depicting the scenes from the Old Testament and the wall paintings depicting the scenes from the New Testament are ascribed to Vilém Kandler. In 1961-90 part of the St Vitus treasure was exposed in the chapel and the adjacent rooms.

South of the chapel in the closed passage to the *second courtyard* is hidden a late Gothic

The third courtyard from the tower of the St Vitus Cathedral

tower gate from the period of Vladislav Jagellon. It protected the main (west) entrance to the Castle which from the beginning led alongside the White Tower, nowadays hidden deeper in the buildings. The passage was adapted by Josip Plečnik into the private entrance to the flat, respectively to the office of the President. Some details of Plečnik's modifications can be seen through the glazed door of the passage.

Third courtyard

You can come to the *third courtyard* outside the front of the Cathedral of St Vitus through the passage nearby the Baroque fountain. You will pass the Romanesque ashlar stones of Soběslav's fortifications. If you turn to the right behind the nowadays post office, you will find yourself at a closed passage, the entrance to the former flat of the president. Above the entrance is placed a gilt sculpture of a girl's head by Damian Pešan, Plečnik's fellow worker. From this place neglected by visitors, you can have a general view of the courtyard, whose monumental paved surface is in impressive contrast with the verticality of the Cathedral, stressed by Plečnik's monolith made of Mrákotín granite 16.38 m high. Under the mosaic of the granite paving are hidden among others the foundations of the Church of St Bartholomew from the 12th century, which used to be connected by a covered passage with the Basilica of St Vitus.

The *third courtyard* represents the central area of the Castle. According to not substantiated reports, here used to be a raised area called „Žiži", used for cult purposes. The latest archeological excavations showed that the southern part of the courtyard was originally outside the fortifications and served as a burial ground. Not even in later times did the courtyard form a unified whole. It was divided into two areas of different heights eventually levelled by Plečnik's paving of large granite slabs. By that the area gained in monumentality, but on the other hand a part

The pillar portico of the New Palace

of the Old Palace found itself below the level of the courtyard.

South wing

The buildings of the south wing of the New Palace were unified by the facade according to the design of N. Pacassi in 1755-61. The facade in the middle of the wing is enlivened by a massive portico bearing the so called presidential balcony, from where, according to the tradition, the President speaks at festive occasions to the audience gathered in the courtyard. Near the Old Royal Palace the baldachin of the **Bulls' Staircase** juts out from the building of the south wing. The staircase connects the *third courtyard* with the southern gardens of Prague Castle in an original way. When building it, Josip Plečnik was inspired by the antique, Egean and Egyptian mythology and architecture.

The official rooms on the first floor of the south wing are connected directly with

The granite monolith in the third couryard

The Bull Staircase

A detail of the decoration
of the Bull Staircase

the official rooms of the south wing a-bove the *second courtyard*. In the southwest corner there is **Janák's Hall** (named after the castle architect who adapted it in 1937) and the so called **Oktogon**, an octagonal official salon established in place of the court Chapel of St Wenceslas from 1644, closed at Pacassi's rebuilding. Behind the Octagon is placed the **Small Salon.** Eastwards are the **Mirror Salon** serving as a dining room, the **Salon With a Fireplace**, the **Musical Salon** with a Roccoco stove and Brussels Gobelins from the 17th century, the **Social Salon** and a cloakroom.

In the past in place of the south wing origi-nally stood the Romanesque wall. In the southwest corner of today's courtyard, next to the White Tower stood the above mentio-ned palace built under Vladislav Jagellon II. and adapted into summer rooms for Rudolf II. East of it stood the building of the New House of the Empress, which Emperor Ferdi-nand III had built for his wife Maria Anna of Spain in 1638-42. In 1832-36 there lived the exile French King Charles X. Further to the east used to stand the kitchen of Empe-ror Maxmilian II.

Next to the main entrance to the Ca-thedral of St Vitus is the Baroque Chapter Deanery, decorated with a statue of St Wenceslas from 1662 by Jan Jiří Bendl. Originally a Romanesque episcopal pala-ce was there, whose wall with its tiny windows is visible on the east side of the building. Adjoining the house was the **Chapel of St Mořic** (Maurice), demo-lished in 1880 during work on the completion of the Cathedral. The cha-pel's foundations are preserved under Plečnik's covered area next to the Cathedral. There are also the foundations of the Caroline rotunda and of the Roma-nesque basilica of St Vitus.

Near to the monolith made of Mrákotín granite stands a copy of a renowned Gothic **statue of Sv. Jiří** (St George), whose original is in the National Galle-ry. We will end the walk through the

The statue of St Wenceslas at the corner of the Chapter Deanery

The statue of St George

three courtyards beside this precious monument.

The statue was cast in 1373 by the iron founders Jiří and Martin from Kluž. It is considered probably the oldest surviving, free-standing statue in Bohemia. (Gothic statues are normally connected to walls of churches and monasteries, forming only an addition to the decoration and frequently not even finished at the back. The statue of St George, however, was regarded as a work of art in its own right.) Originally it stood on the southern side of the later *third courtyard*, from 1761 in the middle of the courtyard, it has been standing on its current site since the time of the Plečnik alternations to the Castle.

Third walk:

ST VITUS CATHEDRAL

*The Cathedral of St Vitus,
the pre-Romanesque rotunda*

The Gothic Cathedral is an exceptional achievement. For centuries it has been considered not only the main church of the Castle but also the spiritual centre of the whole country.

Pre-Romanesque rotunda

About 925 Prince Wenceslas founded the Rotunda of St Vitus in order to house a gift from Emperor Henry the Fowler, the shoulder of St Vitus, the defender of the Holy Roman Empire and henceforth also a patron saint of Bohemia. This third Prague church stood on the highest place of the Hradčany ridge, and by doing so he determined once and for all the layout of the secular and religious buildings in the *third courtyard*. It was a four-apse central building with an inner gallery and platforms upstairs, the rotunda was probably vaulted. Its nave had the inner diameter 13 m. The main church of the country gained even more significance, when in its southern apse

A - the Golden Gate
B - the southern Cathedral tower
C - the covered passage to
      the Royal Palace
D - the western modern front

I - the former tomb of St Vojtěch
      in the demolished central Chapel
      of St Vojtěch
II - the Royal Mausoleum
III - the main altar
IV - the northern arm of the transept
V - the southern arm of the transept

1 - the Chapel of St
   Agnes of Bohemia
2 - the Schwarzenberk
   Chapel
3 - the New Archbishops
   Chapel
4 - the New Sacristy
5 - the Choir Chapel
6 - the Chapel
   of St Zikmund
7 - the Old Sacristy
8 - the Chapel
   of St Anne
9 - the Pernštejn Chapel
10 - the Chapel of St John
    the Baptist
11 - the Chapel of the
    Virgin Mary
12 - the Chapel
    of the Holy Relics
13 - the Chapel of St
    John of Nepomuk
14 - the Chapel of St
    Mary Magdalene
15 - the Cathedral
    vestibule with the
    Royal Oratory
16 - the Chapel of the
    Holy Cross with the
    entrance to the
    Royal Crypt
17 - the Chapel
    of St Andrew
18 - the Chapel
    of St Wenceslas
19 - the Hasenburg
    Chapel (on the
    ground floor of the
    southern tower)
20 - the Chapter library
21 - the Thun Chapel
22 - the Chapel
    of Christ's tomb
23 - the Chapel
    of St Ludmila

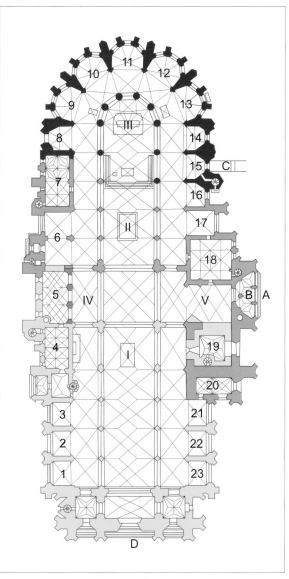

The Cathedral of St Vitus, the ground plan

red - the building of Master Mathias of Arras
blue - the building of Master Petr Parléř
green - the Renaissance masonry
yellow - the masonry from the 19th century

metre long basilica, in the building of which his brother and successor Vratislav II continued from 1061.

The three naved basilica had two choirs, the easter, main, was dedicated to the country's patron saints - St Vitus, St Wenceslas and St Vojtěch, the western choir to the Virgin Mary. At the western end the main nave was crossed by a transept 26.6 metres long, with two adjoined towers. At the eastern choir the southern apse of the demolished rotunda with the tomb of St Wenceslas was incorporated into the southern transept. Under the western choir used to be a five naved crypt of St Martin, under the eastern choir the three naved crypt of St Kosmas and Damian, connected with the crypt of St Radim (Gaudentius) under the main nave. The basilica was completed in 1090, however, it was soon destroyed by fire, and it was consecrated again in 1096.

The Cathedral of St Vitus,
the Romanesque basilica

its founder himself was buried, Prince St Wenceslas, who became a patron saint of the Czech lands. In 973 the Prague bishopric was established and the rotunda became the catedral church. Next to it the residence of the Prague bishop was built; the bishop's house at St Vitus became later, after moving the bishops into the court in the Small Quarter, the seat of the dean of the St Vitus Chapter (today's Deanery next to the southwest side of the Cathedral). In 1039 the relics of the second Prague bishop, St Vojtěch, who died as a martyr in 997, were carried from Polish Hvězdno to the Cathedral.

Romanesque basilica

The rotunda was soon unable to accommodate all the believers coming to pay tribute to the holy relics of Prince Wenceslas and Bishop Vojtěch. Therefore Prince Spytihněv had it demolished in 1060, and on its site started to build a 70

The grandeur of the new church was probably connected with the effort of the princes to gain the elevation of the bishopric to the status of an archbishopric, unsuccessful to that time. Also the chapter house (nearby the north facade of the basilica) was rebuilt, which gained the form of a quadrature with a cloister around the paradise court (the so called **Monastery at the Prague Church**). Even before its completion in the basilica Vratislav II was crowned the first Czech King in 1085, and after him other rulers were crowned here, last time John of Luxembourg with his wife Eliška Přemyslovna. In the church also their son Wenceslas was christened, who at his confirmation accepted the name Karel (Charles). It is Charles as king and emperor, who deserves recognition for the building of the Gothic cathedral.

Gothic Cathedral

In 1344 from the initiative of the future King Charles IV the Prague bishopric

A view of the Cathedral from the third courtyard

was elevated to the status of an archbishopric. The significant change was to be symbolised by the building of the new Cathedral of St Vitus.

The term cathedral has two distinct meanings: ecclesiastical and architectural. From the ecclesiastical point of view a cathedral church is every church under the jurisdiction of a bishop's or archbishop's chair or cathedra; therefore there are in the country as many cathedral churches as

The western front of the St Vitus Cathedral

there are bishoprics. From the architectural point of view the Gothic cathedral is a type of church construction whose essential difference is the gallery with the garland of chapels enclosing the main nave in such a way that the main altar stands in the centre and can be walked around at to back to gain access to the chapels. In the Czech Republic only four churches of cathedral type exist: in addition to St Vitus there is the Cathedral of St Bartholomew in Kolín, the Cathedral of the Virgin Mary in Sedlec near Kutná Hora and the Cathedral of St Barbora in Kutná Hora.

The foundation stone for the new building was laid on 21 November 1344 by King John of Luxembourg in the presence of the heir to the throne Charles, Archbishop Arnošt of Pardubice and other religious and secular dignitaries. From the beginning the old basilica was still in use, however as the work progressed, the old building was gradually taken down, to make room for the new.

The first architect of the Cathedral was Matyáš of Arras during the years 1344-52, who, in the classical linear style of the French cathedrals, built eight polygonal chapels at the end of the Cathedral and the gallery. Four years after his death Charles IV chose as the architect, 23 years old Petr Parléř from Swabian Gmund. Parléř was and architect and sculptor of genius of the final phase of the late Gothic. He co-operated closely with the King, who is probably the author of the original concept of the Cathedral. Thanks to the mutual agreement of the architect and the King a work was built which ranks by right among the most important buildings of this type.

Among the characteristic features of Parléř's work are the network of ribbed vaulting, the flamboyant curvilinear style, the sculptured supporting pillars and bold, protruding ceiling bosses. The young architect also changed the groundplan of the chapels from a triangular to a rectangular shape. This change is clearly visible in the layout of the

The Gothic commemmorative plaque with the data about the building of the Cathedral

A detail from the southern front

The slate roof of the Cathedral

chapels where Parléř linked up with the unfinished work of Master Matyáš of Arras. For the sake of interest, in the bills of the construction from the years 1372-73, an item for 10,260. eggs is preserved. They were added into mortar to achieve better hardening of the mixture.

Until his death in 1399 Parléř managed to build the rest of the choir chapels, to roof the Chapel of St Wenceslas (consecrated in 1367), create the triforium and roof the choir (1371-76, it was consecrated in 1385), build the complicated supporting system (1371-85). He started to build the transept (from 1392) and the tower (from 1396). Just before his death he closed up the choir by constructing a temporary wall, so that the completed part could even during the construction of the nave serve to its purpose. This „temporary solution" was to last nearly 500 years (in the Baroque the temporary wall was embellished from the outside by a wall painting of All the Saints). Thus the Cathedral was not

then completely finished and remained approximately half of today's length. Admittedly the Parléř iron foundry continued with the building until 1419, but it concentrated on finishing the decoration of the parts already completed. At the beginning of the Hussite Wars the Cathedral was plundered in 1421, it was consecrated again in 1437.

The incomplete state of the St Vitus Cathedral was nothing unusual. Gothic cathedrals were always very costly and therefore subject to lengthy building schedules. During the construction the craftsmen who participated in it, were based in iron foundries - a type of building workshop set up on large construction sites. The foundry gathered together masters of different crafts and frequently even had a family character. Within this family framework building techniques, pattern books and „trade secrets" were passed from generation to generation. The members of the foundry stood apart from the craft guilds and were personally autonomous. The best of them travelled

The covered passage from the Old Royal Palace

The Baroque helmet of the southern tower of the Cathedral

from town to town and hired local stonemasons, bricklayers and carpenters. The most respected craftsmen were stonemasons and wood carvers who, on the ground, carved and sculpted individual pieces of the structure and decoration. In addition there were bricklaying, carpentry and other crafts. A Gothic cathedral was usually started at the east end, where the main altar was to stand. At the same time the foundations of the church tower were laid so that the weight of masonry could settle slowly. When the walls reached the height at which the vaulting could be started, the nave was roofed and only then the Gothic vaulting would be built underneath it. The load bearing ribbing of the late Gothic created a sort of skeleton construction bearing the vaulting.

Period of the late Gothic, the Renaissance and the Baroque

The Hussite Wars meant a long interruption of the building activity. Only at the end of the Gothic period the royal orato-ry was built in the Cathedral (architects Hans Spiess and Benedikt Ried), in the Renaissance period the architect Bonifác Wolmut covered the top of the tower by a copper roof and closed the main nave by an organ loft. Outside the western side of the Cathedral (on the place of the future main nave) the central **Chapel of St Vojtěch** was built, an outstanding example of the late Renaissance and mannerism. In 1589 in the main nave the Renaissance royal mausoleum was completed, an outstanding work of Alexandr Collin. In the period of the reign of the Winter King Friedrich of Falc in 1619 the Calvinists plundered the Cathedral, after they left the major part of the damage caused by them in the interior was remedied. In the Baroque the inner equipment was newly modified and a large silver tombstone of St John of Nepomuk was installed. During the Prussian siege of Prague in 1757 the Cathedral was seriously damaged.

*The pinnacle above
the crossing of the main
nave and the transept
of the Cathedral*

*The deanery with the remnants
of the demolished Chapel
of St Maurice*

*A detail of the decorative
grill of the southern
Cathedral vestibule*

Completion of the Cathedral

During centuries two unsuccessful attempts to complete the Cathedral were made, in the years 1509-11 under King Vladislav Jagellon, who had the foundations of the northern tower laid, and in 1673, when Emperor Leopold I built the pillars of the Baroque three naved space.

The second attempt was motivated by the then spread prophesy that the one who completes the Cathedral, will drive the Turks from Europe. Paradoxically, it was the consequence of the Turkish danger, that the construction was interrupted at the very beginning, which was lucky in a way, since a Baroque completion would probably violate the unique Gothic building.

Only the third attempt at the completion was successful. It began in the era of Romanticism, when the idea of completing important buildings from the Middle Ages spread through Europe. (For instance the well known Cologne Cathedral was completed among others.) In Prague, in 1859, the Union for the Completion of the St Vitus Cathedral was established. In 1861, under the leadership of the architect Josef Kranner, work commenced on the renovation of the Cathedral and from 1873 under the direction of Kranner's successor Josef Mocker, the construction of the new western end of the Cathedral with towers began.

The craftsmen who participated in the completion of the Cathedral faced many problems. They had to acquire the long forgotten art of the Gothic vaulting and many other technological and artistic procedures. In this sense the activity of the modern St Vitus iron foundry meant an important contribution to the renovation and support of the crafts. The Cathedral builders were not afraid to use also new elements at the completion, and so the modern part of the roof timbers is not made of wooden beams but of iron girders.

Because of the completion, unfortunatelly, the Chapel of St Vojtěch had to be

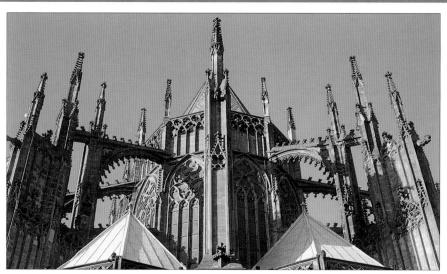

The end of the Cathedral viewed from Jiřské Square

demolished, and the Chapel of St Maurice at the St Vitus Deanery was demolished unnecessarily. Its foundations together with a part of the foundations of the St Vitus Rotunda and Basilica are hidden under the roofed place built by Josip Plečnik in the *third courtyard* in the 20th century. Not even Josef Mocker lived to see the completion of the Cathedral, he died exactly 500 years after Parléř in 1899. Only the later architect, Kamil Hilbert, whose construction work was more sensitive to the older architecture, led the construction to the celebrated consecration in 1929 at the occasion of the millennium of the martyrdom of the main Czech patron saint - St Wenceslas.

The completion of the Cathedral met with much excitement but also much criticism, because it altered the centuries old silhouette of the Castle. Nowadays the completion is no longer condemned; time wipes away the differences between the old and the new and we can even admire the artistic decoration of the styles of the 19th and 20th centuries.

Although Emperor Charles IV called masters from Venice to realize the mosaic, the glass pieces were made by one of the Czech glassworks. Unfortunately, they had an unquality chemical composition, which did not have sufficient resistance to the weather influences, which are much more cruel here that the climate in sunny Italy. In the 19th century the mosaic was already seriously damaged, and a decision was made to replace it by a faithful copy. In 1890 the mosaic was taken down and deposited. A very precise documentation for making the copy was carried out at the scale 1:1 where each piece of glass was marked. However, the copy was not made, and that is why in 1910 the original was placed back on its place. The missing pieces of glass were taken from the ornamental frame which surrounded the mosaic and that is why the frame is now missing. During the 20th century the mo-

The Gothic gargoyles

The Gothic ribs of the southern Cathedral vestibule

saic was restored several times, however, it became more and more dilapidated. At present the Getty Institute in the USA studies the possibility of its restauration.

The Union for the Completion of the St Vitus Cathedral chose at the beginning of their activity the biblical motto: „The Lord told David: That you decided in your heart to build the house for my Name, you have done good, having had it on mind." By the long term work of many people the motto met its purpose.

Exterior of the Cathedral

The external appearance of the Cathedral captivates us mainly by the richness of the Gothic **buttressing.** Externally the Cathedral was to be reminiscent of „the City of God", so that everywhere we can see various „little towers" (pinnacles), suggestions of house gables, „passageways", galleries, staircases and balustra-

des. From Jiřské Square a veritable stone forest of flying buttresses, pillars and pinnacles can be seen, making the structure of the Cathedral most visible. Below the roof our attention is captured by the Gothic gargoyles, which drained away the water. They have the likeness of monsters, fiends and evil creatures. The Cathedral was protected by them against dark powers, because according to an old belief, a demon is frightened of its own image on a facade and flies away. The portrayl of monsters on the outside of a church also has another, more spiritual purpose. It reminds the believers that all the badness they possess should be stripped away outside so that they can come to the Cathedral freed from the impure temptations of life.

The main nave is encirled at the height of 14 metres by a gallery called the **external triforium**. It was used originally, but in the 19th century the passages through the pillars were walled up because of the statics. Above the walled passages of the old part

The mosaic of the Last Judgement on the front of the Golden Gate

The spiral staircase on the southern front of the Cathedral

The tombstone of St John of Nepomuk

of the Cathedral there are sculptures of fantastic beasts and faces and at the end of the choir (on the eastern side) busts of Christ, the Virgin Mary and the main country's patrons saint: St Vitus, Wenceslas, Vojtěch, Prokop, Ludmila, Cyril and Metoděj and Zikmund. At the height of 36 metres there is the second gallery running around the decorated slate roof.

Southern facade

A monumental view of the southern face of the old and new parts of the Cathedral is unveiled for us from the *third courtyard*. At first we will stop outside the festive entrance to the Cathedral, the **Zlatá brána** (Golden Gate). Its facade above three archs is decorated by the **mosaic picture of the Last Judgement**, an outstanding work of the Czech Gothic, created in 1370-71 of splitted quartz and glass in 33 hues according to a design of Venetian masters. In the centre sits Christ in a halo, judging the living and the dead, under him are kneeling as supplicants the earthly patrons, and even lower, on the edges of the centre arcade kneel Charles IV and his wife Eliška of Pomerania. In the picture on the left and the right, the Apostles are pleading on behalf of the sinners and below them are represented scenes from the Ressurection and the Day of Judgement. The small Gothic windows lead to the crown chamber, where the Czech coronation jewels are kept. Above the mosaic is the tracery of the largest Cathedral window, which ends the southern arm of the transept. Three pointed archs of the gate are opened into the southern vaulted **Cathedral vestibule**. The vestibule belongs to the part of the Cathedral with the most highly decorated masonry. Petr Parléř here relieved the Gothic ribs and even let them float freely in space! The walls of the vestibule are covered in mosaics called „Adam and Eve" and „Crucified Christ" by Karel Svolinský. The vestibule is separated from the courtyard by a grill decorated by bronze reliefs of the calendar and the zodiac signs by Jaroslav

Horejc from 1955. The inner door comes from 1964.

On the eastern side of the large window is a remarkable **spindle-shaped staircase**, probably designed by Petr Parléř. It is surrounded by a stone cover with the emblems of the Czech lands. A person who goes through the staircase makes three turns before s/he reaches the level of the external triforium. On the left external buttress of the Golden Gate is a stone plate in a frame. It comes from 1396 and contains a detailed commemorative record of the construction of the Cathedral.

East of the Golden Gate a covered passage from the Old Royal Palace is connected to the Cathedral. It leads to the late Gothic Royal Oratory of Vladislav Jagellon. A similar bridge used to stand here even during the reign of Emperor Charles IV, from whose time probably a pillar and an arch of the present bridge come. On the southeastern side of the choir, between the buttresses of the St John of Nepomuk Chapel is placed a sandstone symbolic tomb of St John of Nepomuk by Ignác František Platzer from 1763.

Souther Cathedral tower

The 96.5 metre high southern **Cathedral tower** is (probably intentionally) placed asymetrically on the south side of the Cathedral close to the grave of St Wenceslas, the defender of the Czech lands. It was here a symbolic substitute for the traditional defensive tower of Gothic castles, which in Prague is absent. The Gothic tower remained unfinished because of the outbreak of the Hussite Wars in 1419. Only in 1560-62 the Emperor's architects Bonifác Wolmut and Hans Tirol built a Renaissance gallery at the height of 56 metres and then topped the tower with an onion-shaped roof, newly modified in 1770 by Nicolas Pacassi. On the top of the tower is fastened a 3.5 metre high gilded Bohemian lion.

The gilded grill from the period of Emperor Rudolf II

73

The lower part of the western front of the Cathedral

On the first floor of the tower there is a remarkable gilded grill from the time of Rudolf II, whose monogram is displayed a little higher up. **The clock** which has two faces also comes from the same period. The higher face with the diameter of 4.5 metres shows only hours and the lower one with the diameter of 3.85 metres minutes. The clock machine, which turns them comes from the end of the 16th century. This solution used to be frequently adopted, because it

*Emperor Charles IV, Parléř's bust
in the triforium*

*Blanche of Valois, the first wife of Charles IV,
the bust in the triforium*

was very difficult to set the axes of both hands into the centre of one face. In the tower are four bells (there used to be seven bells). The bell called Zikmund, cast in 1549 by Tomáš Jaroš, is the largest in Bohemia, weighing between 15,000 and 16,000 kg and measuring 256 cm in diameter. The other bells are called Wenceslas (cast in 1542), John the Baptist (1546) and Josef (1602).

Until the introduction of the telephone the bells were used not only for liturgical purposes but also for emergency fire warnings. If there were fire in the Small Quarter, the bells rang three times, fire in Hradčany was announced by six bells sounds. The dwelling of the St Vitus bell-ringer was directly in the tower. The bell-ringers threw waste and dirt out of the window; at the beginning of the 18th century the gold faces of the clock were completely damaged by dirt, also the roofs and stone decorations of the Cathedral were polluted considerably. One of the legends about the St Vitus tower says that King Wenceslas IV ordered it demo-

lished, since it had been prophesied to him that he would die „před" (Czech, meaning either locally „in front of", or as a time preposition „before") the St Vitus tower. However, before the demolition started, the King had a stroke and died. The preposition „před" did not have the local but the time meaning.

Western facade

A visitor is forced to perceive the high new western facade of the Cathedral without a sufficient distance. The gable wall of the main nave is surrounded by two 82 metres high **towers**, one on each side, in the horizontal level the face is divided into three distinct parts. In the lower part are three richly decorated **entrance portals**. The reliefs of the bronze doors were created by Otakar Španiel in 1927-29; the middle door is decorated by scenes from the history of building the Cathedral, on the northern door is depicted a cycle from the life of St Vojtěch and on the southern door a cycle from

Petr Parléř, the bust in the triforium

The internal triforium

the life of St Wenceslas. On the sandstone tympana of the portals are reliefs with the themes of the Birth, Crucifixion, and Ascension of Christ coming from the 1950s and 1960s. The middle part of the facade is dominated by a large **window rosette** with the diameter of 10.40 metre, fixed in a raised pointed arch. Under the lower edge of the rosette are double portraits of the modern builders of the Cathedral by Vojtěch Sucharda both on the left and the right side; on the right are the architects Josef Mocker and Kamil Hilbert, on the left the art historian Zdeněk Wirth and the painter František Kysela, the author of the stained glass in the rosette. Under the baldachins on the buttresses of the towers stand statues of Emperor Charles IV and his counsellor Archbishop Arnošt of Pardubice, above them in niches and consoles are placed 14 statues of saints, a part of the originally intented but not carried out 46 sculptures. The third floor has a gable in the middle, which is richly decorated with blind traceries and on the

sides with the stone pyramids of the towers.

Interior of the Cathedral

The maximally complicated external buttressing contrasts with the nobility and peace of the interior of the Cathedral. The three naved Cathedral is 124 m long by 60 m wide measured at its widest point across the transepts and the height of the main vaulting is 33.24 m. Along the sides of the main nave are the narrower and lower side naves, encircled by a row of chapels opened into the Cathedral. Under the southwest tower are plates with the plastic groundplans of the excavations of the Rotunda and the Basilica of St Vitus. The window is decorated according to a design by Cyril Bouda.

The windows of the Cathedral transmit a subtle and frequently coloured light. It used to have not only aesthetical but symbolic significance.

The view of the main altar

The net vaulting in the St Vitus Choir

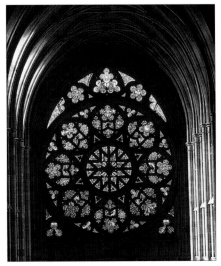

The circular window rosette of the western Cathedral front

The interior of the Cathedral was considered a holy place ripped out of this world, a „heavenly Jerusalem", which is not illuminated by natural light (by the sun and the moon) but by unearthly and mystical light of God's glory. According to another explanation the windows were regarded as the dividing line between this and God's world, into which we can glance or even uplift ourselves.

The edges of the high windows of the main nave are slanted on the sides inwards, and therefore they partly cover the pillars between the windows. This intensifies the impression of a nearly immaterial wall seemingly made up only of a stone grating filled with glass.

Above the archs of the arcades between the main nave and the side naves runs a gallery at the height of 14.3 m, called the **internal triforium.** In the old part of the Cathedral it used to be a functional gallery, since it was possible to go through the passages in the buttresses. However, they were walled up because of

the statics in the 19th century, and not even in the new part of the Cathedral were passages built. Above the former passages are sculpted portrait busts; in the old part of the Cathedral is a unique Parléř **sculptural portrait gallery** consisting of eleven portraits of the members of the Emperor's family (Charles IV, his parents, brothers and sisters, four wives, children), portraits of three Prague archbishops, five master builders of the Cathedral and two architechts - Matyáš of Arras and Petr Parléř. On the remaining pillars are sculpted three sculptures, one gryphon, a dog and a cat. The placing of the portrait busts of the builders among the important secular and ecclesiastic dignitaries testifies to the increasing status of artists, considered in the Middle Ages more as craftsmen and servants. The sculpture gallery thus in its way anticipates the Renaissance, displaying genuine respect for the genius of artists. In the modern part of the Cathedral the gallery has busts of artists and important persons meriting recognition for their

The Renaissance organ loft in the northern arm of the transept

A pelican feeding the young by its own blood; a neo-Gothic sculpture in the gallery of the southern arm of the transept

work towards its completion. The Parléř sculpture gallery continues even in the chapels which contain very important stone tombs with reclining figures of the Přemyslide rulers.

Main nave

We are impressed by the **net vaulting** of the main nave and the choir connected to it. The net vaulting was used for the first time in the Continental Europe (that means in Europe without Great Britain and Ireland) by Petr Parléř when he built the choir. The vaulting is not divided into separate rectangular vault sections with crossed Gothic ribs but it makes a continuous net so that the eye can easily slip along from the entrance towards the altar and back. The „softness" of the Cathedral space is created optically besides the vanlting also by the slanted edges of the large windows in the main nave.

The western side of the main nave is dominated by the large **pointed window with a circular rosette**. It consists of 261 stone parts nad 27,000 pieces of coloured glass. In the stained glass window there are depicted the scenes of the individual days of the creation of the world according to the design of František Kysela. In the centre of the new part of the main nave a site is marked on the floor where used to be the tomb of St Vojtěch in the central Renaissance Chaple.

Transept

We will advance further through the main nave up to the crossing with the transept. The transept is equally high as the main nave and makes a border between the old and the new part of the Cathedral. On the pillars of the crossing of the nave and the transept are fixed eight wooden **statues of the Czech patron saints**, which stood originally on the pillars of the choir. They were carved in 1696 according to the design of František Preiss and portray these saints: Vitus, John of Nepomuk, Zikmund, Vojtěch,

The stained glass window depicting the Last Judgement in the southern arm of the transept

The Royal Mausoleum

Ludmila, Wenceslas, Prokop and Norbert. The **northern arm of the transept** is enclosed by the Renaissance organ loft, a work by Bonifác Wolmut from between 1557-61. It originally enclosed the choir, onto its present site it was transferred in 1924 during the completion of the Cathedral. The Roccoco embellished **organ** from 1763 was created by Antonín Gärtner from Tachov. We will treat the Chaple of the Choir in connection with the other chapels of the Cathedral.

In the **southern arm of the transept** are the marble tombstones and the relief monument to the killed soldiers in the World War I by Karel Pokorný from 1921. Next to it stands a font of black marble and green striped serpentine embellished by a bronze statue of young St Wenceslas by Karel Dvořák from 1929. Above the arcade of the side nave you can see a large mosaic emblem of the Czechoslovak Republic (used between the world wars) consisting of the historical countries including the part of Ukraine west of the Carpathians. Nearby the corner of the St Wenceslas Chapel stands a statue of Jesus Christ of carara marble, a work of Čeněk Vosmík from 1897. Under the baldachin at the corner of the St Wenceslas Chaple is sited a late Gothic statue of the Madonna with little Jesus from the 16th century. The upper part of the southern front of the transept is filled by a **neo Geothic window**, the largest one in the Cathedral. On its top is placed a stone St Wenceslas crown. The stained glass created according to the design of Max Švabinský from 1939 depicts the theme of the Last Judgement. Above the glazed grill exit to the *third courtyard* is hung a relief emblem of the capital city Prague by Karel Štipl from 1946, on the left from the entrance is the picture „Taking off the Cross" from the 17th century.

Choir

In the choir of the Cathedral in front of

The early Baroque pulpit

The main altar of the Cathedral

the main altar is sited **the royal mausoleum**, the part of the tomb of the Czech Kings which is above the ground. This outstanding Renaissance work was built of white marble by the Dutch sculptor Alexander Collin from between 1571-89. On the upper surface of the tomb are carved the figures of standing ressurected Christ and lying Ferdinand I, his wife Anna Jagellon and son Maxmilian II. The sides of the tomb are embellished by eight medaillons with reliefs of the rulers whose remains were transfered at the end of the 16th century to the Royal Crypt under the mausoleum: Charles IV, his four wives, Wenceslas IV, Ladislav the Posthumous and Jiří (George) of Poděbrady. The tomb is enclosed by a fine Renaissance grill. Near the mausoleum by the pillar is a **pulpit** from 1631, richly decorated by carving, painting and gilding. The Baroque pews are also decorated by carving. **The main altar** is neo Gothic, created according to the design of Josef Kranner, modified by Josef Mocker.

Three neo-gothic stained glass **windows** at the end of the choir were created according to the designs of Max Švabinský in 1946-48. In the middle window is depicted the Holiest Trinity, in the north window the Virgin Mary with the St Wenceslas crown, beatified Mlada Přemyslide and St Ludmila. Below them kneels Prince Spytihněv II with a model of the St Vitus Basilica which he founded. In the right window are depicted St Wenceslas and St Vitus and below them Charles IV with a model of the Cathedral.

On the arcade walls of the choir under the balustrade of the internal triforium gallery are painted the **emblems of the countries** which belonged to the Hapsburgs in the 16th and the 17th centuries, and the emblems of the countries of the Czechoslovak Republic between the World Wars. Latin and Czech commemorative inscriptions are added to the emblems.

A wooden altar with crucified Christ

The early Baroque door to the Choir Chapel

Side chapels

We will start the visit of the chapels from the main (western) entrance from the left side along the north side of the Cathedral. The chapels are numbered in accordance with the plan of the Cathedral to ease your orientation.

1. Chapel of St Agnes of Bohemia (of the Bartoň family from Dobenín) is decorated with a mosaic of the Acts of Mercy by František Kysela and by the stained glass window with depicting the Eight Beatitudes by the same artist. On the altar of St Agnes is regularly displayed an outstanding sun reliquary by Alena Nováková, created in 1989 on the occasion of the sanctification of the patroness of Bohemia. The bronze sculptural group of St Agnes was created by Karel Stádník in 1989.

2. In the **Swarzenberk Chapel** is a captivating window with scenes from the life of Adam František Schwarzenberk and from the history of the relics of St John of Nepomuk. The design was by Karel Svolinský. In the Chapel is sited the late Gothic Čimelická arch depicting the Adoration of the Magi, an interesting example of Gothic panel painting. The panel painting the Ressurection of Christ from the last quarter of the 16th century is ascribed to Bartolomeo Spranger.

3. The New Archbishops Chapel (Horova) has been used since 1909 as the burial chapel of the Prague archbishops. The window was decorated by Alfons Mucha in the late Art Nouveau style and illustrates the lives of the Slavonic saints Cyril and Methodius. The last one buried in the Chapel is the Prague Archbishop and Cardinal František Tomášek (died 4 August 1992), one of the most important persons of the spiritual revival at the end of the Communist regime and in the first years after its fall.

We will notice a neo Gothic spiral staircase. It leads to **the New Treasure Chamber** (Cathedral treasury), modified in 1925 on the first floor. A substantial part of the St Vitus Treasure is kept there. The stained glass window behind the staircase is decorated with scenes from the life of St Stephen according to the design by Cyril Bouda.

4. Next is the **New Sacristy**, where by the inner wall stands a **large wooden altar with Crucified Christ**, an outstanding work of the sculptor František Bílek, a significant representative of the spiritually focused trend of the Czech Art Nouveau and symbolism. He created the relief of the Crucifixion in 1899, the other parts of the altar in 1927, using a combination of lime, oak and spruce wood.

5. We are entering the transept. **The Chapel of the Choir** is on the ground floor of the Wolmut organ loft previously mentioned and is enclosed by three carved doors, the middle of which is modern and the side doors come from 1639. Inside are sited an early Baroque archbishop's throne from the second half of the 17th century and a late Renaissance altar from 1579.

6. The Chapel of St Zikmund (Černínská) was built by Petr Parléř. Here were kept the remains of the Burgundian Kind Zikmund, whose body Charles IV himself had sent to Bohemia. Scenes from the life of the saint are depicted in the Renaissance fresco on the east wall of the Chapel by Daniel Alexei from Květná from the end of the 16th century. On the opposite wall we can see a wall painting „The Assumption of the Virgin Mary" from the same time. The Baroque altar was made according to a design by Ferdinand Maxmilián Kaňka. Further in the chapel are sited a number of Baroque and Classicist tombstones, the most important of which belongs to Humprecht Černín from Chudenice. Among others, the Transylvanian Prince Zikmund Báthory and Sylvia, Margravine of Baden are buried here.

The Archangel Michael by the wall of the Old Sacristy

7. Next is the **Old Sacristy** (previously the Chapel of St Michael), which is hidden behind a wall. The rectangular space of the Chapel was vaulted by Petr Parléř before 1362, two ceiling bosses of the vaulting belong to the most original contributions of Parléř's art. The eastern wall of the Chapel, however, comes from Parléř's predecessor, Master Matyáš of Arras. In the northeast corner of the sacristy is a spiral staircase, through which one can enter the treasury in which the St Vitus treasure was originally kept. Today it is used for keeping liturgical objects. On the exterior wall of the Chapel hang the pictures „The Baptism of Christ" by Petr Brandl from 1722, „St Maurice" by Jan Kryštof Liška and „The Visitation of the Virgin Mary" by Jan Jiří Hering probably from 1630. Above the confessional is hung a copy of the Tizian picture „The Entry of Christ into Jerusalem". On the console next to the entrance to the sacristy is placed a wooden statue of St Michael,

From the Chapel you can see well the cathedral character of the Church - the choir gallery with a ring of chapels encircling the presbytery (the high choir) with the main altar. Most of the following choir chapels are enclosed by a Baroque gilded forged grill.

Opposite the Chapel, in the gallery between the arcades of the choir, we can see a large wooden relief **picture** of **The Flight of Fridrich of Falc** (the Winter King) from Prague after the lost Battle of the White Mountain in 1620 by Kašpar Bechteler. The masterpiece was created before 1635 and one can see in it the panorama of the early Baroque Prague. The second part of the relief picture can be seen between the following arcades.

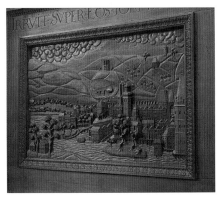

The second part of the relief picture
„The Flight of Friedrich of Falc"

a German work from the beginning of the 17th century.

8. The Chapel of St Anne (Nostická) belongs among the chapels created by Matyáš of Arras. The ceiling boss of the vaulting is decorated by a relief coat of arms of the Lords of Dražice (Jan IV of Dražice was the last Prague bishop), the vaulting boss in the gallery in front of the Chapel is decorated by the coat of arms of the Lords of Pardubice (Arnošt of Pardubice was the first Prague archbishop). In the neo Gothic altar is placed a silver Romanesque reliquary (called the Triers reliquary) from 1266, coming from the Church of St Martin in Triers. This important goldsmith's work embellished with enamelled pictures, filigree work, and precious stones contains 43 relics of saints. The original is now a part of the St Vitus treasure and in the Chapel it will be replaced by a copy. Under the paving of the Chapel are the tombs of the family of the Lords of Žďár and of the Nostic family.

9. In the **Pernštej Chapel** (the Old Archbishops' Chapel) Prague archbishops were buried between 1793-1899. On the left is the Pernštejn family tomb with a Renaissance sarcophagus of the highest chancellor of the kingdom, Vratislav of Pernštejn.

Opossite the Chapel is placed the large **statue of the kneeling Cardinal Bedřich Schwarzenberk**, one of the best works of the sculptor Josef Václav Myslbek (created in 1895).

10. Next is the **Chapel of St John the Baptist** (of Arnošt of Pardubice, of St Anthony the Hermit). It was founded by Archbishop Arnošt of Pardubice. Its stonework is not original, since it stood on shallow foundations, and therefore it had to be rebuild in 1863-64. Under the Parléř Gothic tombstones are buried Prince Bořivoj II (on the left) and Břetislav II (on the right). Into the wall are fixed the marble tombstones of the archbishops Antonín Brus from Mohelnice (died 1580) and Martin Medek (died 1590). The walls are decorated with a picture of St Philip of Nerea by Jan Jakub Quirin Jahn from 1772 and the picture „The

Death of St Joseph" by Francesco Trevisan from 1656. In a glazed frame is placed a Baroque wooden relief of „The Crucifixion", here is also placed the so called Jerusalem Candelabrum, an outstanding example of Romanesque metal casting (the arms of the candelabrum are, however, late Renaissance).

Allegedly, the Jerusalem Candelabrum was seized by the Czech warriors headed by King Vladislav I, who conquered Milan in 1158 as the allies of Emperor Friedrich I Barbarossa. (The Czechs excelled not only in bravery, but also in the ability of psychological pressure. They began to bake bread in the form of small figures and it seemed to the defenders of the city, that they were eating small children. The terror of „the raiders from the North" demoralised the defence of the town which was soon occupied.

The tomb or Přemysl II Otakar

Between the gallery pillars opposite the Chapel is hung the **picture of St John of Nepomuk** from the end of the 17th century, depicting scenes from his life.

11. The Chapel of the Virgin Mary (of the Holiest Trinity, the Emperor's, of the Cross, of St Ludmila, of the Berka family of Dubá) stands in the axix of the choir and the whole building. It was founded by Charles IV probably on the site where the building of the Cathedral began. Here are sited the Parléř Gothic tombstones of Prince Spytihněv II (on the left) and of Břetislav I (on the right, under the tombstone also the remains of his wife Jitka are buried). Zdeněk Lev of Rožmitál (died 1535) is also buried here, a significant leader of the Czech nobility, who pushed through the election of Ferdinand I to the Czech throne. Above the grill enclosing the Chapel is a beam with a sculptural group of the Calvary (of Crucified Crist) from 1621.

In the gallery in front of the Chapel stands the **tombstone of St Vitus** from 1840 with a sandstone statue by Emanuel

Max. In front of the tombstone, in the paving are fixed 14 tombstones of the Prague bishops.

12. The Chapel of the Holy Relics (Saxon, of the Šternberk family) was founded by the Saxon Duke Rudolf, a son-in-law of Charles IV. Along the sides are the stone tombs of Přemysl II Otakar (on the left) and Přemysl I Otakar (on the right). They are decorated by the reclining figures of the kings, an outstanding sculptural work by Petr Parléř. By the remains of Přemysl II Otakar his burial crown, sceptre and orb were found, wrought of gilded silver. The sceptre belongs among the oldest preserved ones in Central Europe. On the pillar is hung one of the cannon balls which hit the Cathedral during the siege of Prague by the Prussian King Friedrich II the Great in 1757. Under the paving is sited the tomb of the Šternberk family.

The Prussian siege caused much damage, between 31 May and 8 June several thou-

The tombstone of St John of Nepomuk

The Royal Oratory

sand balls were fired at the Cathedral, which destroyed the roof and caused damage to the stonework on 215 spots. In the Cathedral itself 770 balls were found. The town was afflicted as well.

13. In the **Chapel of St John of Nepomuk** (Vlašimská) is sited an altar decorated by silver busts of St Wenceslas, Vojtěch, Cyril and Vitus from the end of the 17th century. A casket with the remains of St Vojtěch is kept in the middle part of the altar. The picture of the Virgin Mary of Pasov above the altar comes from 1602. By the western side wall is the tomb of the second Prague Archbishop Jan Očko of Vlašim, a work of the Parléř foundry from 1370. The tombstone is made of red marble, it portrays the reclining figure of the Archbishop with a dog at his feet of white marble. In the Chapel one can be captivated by a bronze relief epitaf of Ludmila of Thurn (on the left on the eastern wall) from after 1558. The wall paintings from the 14th century are partly preserved.

In the ambulatory opposite the Chapel stands the Baroque **silver sarcophagus of St John of Nepomuk**, the largest work of a precious metal in Bohemia. It was designed by Josef Emanuel Fischer from Erlach and created between 1733-36. On the marble plinth are fixed two angels carrying the coffin, on which the saint's figure kneels. A baldachin donated by Maria Theresa hangs above the sarcophagus. The marble ballustrade is decorated with allegorical figureds of Silence, Wisdom, Strenth and Justice, made in 1746 according to a model by Jan Antonín Quittainer

14. Next is the **Chapel of St Mary Magdalene** (of the Holiest Heart of the Lord, of the Valdštejn family). The most significant monuments here are the two tombstones of both builders of the Cathedral, Matyáš of Arras (on the left) and Petr Parléř (on the right) with their carved portraits. They were transferred here from the original site in the paving in front of the old sacristy. The remnants of Gothic paintings depict the Virgin Mary with little Jesus, saints and kneeling donators. Under the Chapel is the tomb of the Valdštejn family, their family coat of arms is placed on the grill.

In the ambulatory among the arcades of the choir, opposite the Chapel, is placed a wooden **relief picture** depicting the **destruction of the Cathedral by the Calvinists in 1619.** This masterpiece of Baroque carving was created in the 1630s by Kašpar Bechteler. The second part of the picture can be seen among the other arcades.

15. Next to the Chapel of St Mary Magdalene stands the **Cathedral vestibule,** accessible from the outside via the Gothic portal from 1350. In the area of the vestibule (originally a Gothic chapel) hangs a fine Gothic carved crucifix from around 1410. **The Royal Oratory** is built into the upper part of the vestibule. It was built in 1493 on the command of king Vladislav Jagellon probably by Hans Spiess and Benedict Ried. It is decorated with naturalistically entwined branches and the monogram of King Vladislav Jagellon on the protruding corbel. On the ballustrade of the Oratory are placed the emblems of the lands over which this ruler reigned: the Czech and Hungarian emblems are in the middle, on the right side are the emblems of Moravia, Luxembourg, Silesia and Lower Lusatia, on the left the emblems of Dalmatia, Upper Lusatia, Bosnia and Poland. The Oratory is accessible via a covered bridge directly from the Royal Palace. On the pillars of the Oratory and on the opposite pillar of the choir arcade there are placed Baroque statues of miners with long skirts on which they slid down the mineshafts. They were created by the workshop of Matyáš Bernard Braun. The miners should remind us of the source of the riches (the silver mines in Kutná Hora) of which the Oratory and other buildings at the Jagellon time were financed.

16. Next to the Oratory is the **Chapel of the Holy Cross** (of St Simon and Judas). Its left (eastern) side is a work of Matyáš of Arras, the other walls and the vaulting were created by his successor Petr Parléř, who was the builder of further chapels of the old Cathedral. In this Chapel can be seen the difference between the ground plan conception of both masters. Whereas Matyáš of Arras began to build the Chapel as polygonal, Petr Parléř completed it as rectangular. On the wall we can see the remnants of Gothic paintings from the end of the 14th century, above the altar from the 18th century hangs a crucifix of cedar wood (the so called Milan cross), Italian craftmanship from the 15th century. The marble slab in the floor below the south (front) wall reminds us of the tomb of the Czech King Rudolf I, called Kaše (the Weak, it was originally a discrediting nickname because of his stinginess at royal feasts). In 1870 the burial insignia of gilded silver were found in the tomb. At present Rudolf I is buried in the underground Roayl Crypt, which one can enter from this Chapel.

The Royal Crypt was built at the end of the 16th century into the remnants of the former so called Monastery of the Prague Church (the seat of the St Vitus Chapter). It was modified last time by the architect Kamil Roškot between 1928-35. In the middle rests Emperor Charles IV, on our right King Ladislav the Posthumous, on the left King George of Poděbrady, in the second row on the right King Wenceslas IV and his wife Jane of Bavaria, on the left the wives of Charles IV, in the third row in the middle the original tin coffin of Emperor Rudolf II is artisticly the best (its copy can be seen in the Prašná věž /Powder Tower/), on its right the casket is embedded into the ground which contains the remains of Eleanora (daughter of Emperor Maxmilián II), the Austrian Duke Rudolf and the Czech King Rudolf I Kaše (the Weak). On the left from Ru-

The Royal Tomb   *The tombstone of Leopold Šlik*

dolf's coffin the casket with the remains of Wenceslas, a minor son of Charles IV. On the extreme right stands the neoclassical coffin of Maria Amalia, the Duchess of Parma (the daughter of Maria Theresa), on the extreme left is buried Jan Zhořelecký (the brother of Wenceslas IV) and other unknown persons. Under the ground the remnants of the pre-Romanesque Rotunda and Basilica can be seen.

17. The Chapel of St Andrew (of the Martinic family, originally of St Anthony and St Silvester) it the last choir chapel on the southern side of the Cathedral. It was built by Petr Parléř on a rectangular ground plan. There is sited the burial place of the Martinic and Lobkovic families. A Renaissance epitaf with a relief of Jan Popel of Lobkovice is set on the left (western) wall. In the crypt of the Martinic family Jaroslav Bořita of Martinice is buried, one of the governors who were thrown out of a window of the Royal Palace during the second Prague defenestration in 1618. The epitafs of the Lords of Martinice are sited on the wall below the window. Barbora Celská (died 1451), the second wife of Emperor Zikmund, rests also here. She was famous for her interest in magic and alchemy.

By the pillar opposite the Chapel stands the marble **tombstone of the Field Marshal Count Leopold Šlik** from 1723. It was designed by the Viennese architect Josef Emanuel Fischer from Erlach and built by František Maxmilián Kaňka. The bust of the Count is a work of Matyáš Bernard Braun, the other sculptural decoration comes from his workshop. On the console of the next pillar is sited a Renaissance wooden polychrome statue of the Virgin Mary the Painful.

18. Next is the **Chapel of St Wenceslas**, the most valuable and the most sacred place in the Cathedral. It is roofed by the perfect Parléř star-vaulting above the square ground plan, which by its size goes beyond the row of the preceeding

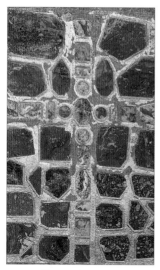

The precious stones and the gilded cross on the wall of the Chapel of St Wenceslas

The altar with the scene of the Crucifixion in the Chapel of St Wenceslas

chapels. In the Chapel the remains of St Wenceslas, Prince and Patron Saint of the Czech lands are kept. The Prince was originally buried in the rotunda he himself built, and his tomb has remained until now on the same site even after all following rebuildings. The contemporary freely standing tombstone of the saint is combined with an altar and is a modern reconstruction created according to the partly preserved tombstone from the period of Charles IV.

The decoration of the Chapel bears witness to the high level of the Czech art in the 14th century. The lower part of the walls below the large profiled ledge is studded with 1345 precious stones - violet amethysts, red jaspers and green chrysoprases.

The stone plates were cut by means of a thin rope and grinding powder, which was poured under the rope. They were fastened to the wall by a binding agent made of egg whites. The gaps between the stones are filled with plastic gilded patterns. The coloured shine of precious stones was to symbolise the Heavenly Jerusalem.

Among the precious stones is a **cycle of scenes depicting the suffering of Christ** by an unknown painter from the years 1372-72. This Passion cycle has its climax above the altar by the scene of the Crucifixion. On the sides of the Crucified Christ stand the Virgin Mary and St John, behind them is kneeling Emperor Charles IV and his fourth wife Eliška of Pomerania. At the feet of the cross kneel the small figures of Wenceslas IV and his wife Jane of Bavaria. Below the figure of Charles IV in the wall is placed the sanctuary (a casket for the holy sacraments), closed by a gilded Gothic grill by Master Wenceslas from 1375.

Above the Passion cycle runs the second series, illustrating on all walls **31 scenes from the life of St Wenceslas.** It is ascribed to the workshop of the Master

St Wenceslas among angels

The tower reliquary in the Chapel of St Wenceslas

of the Litoměřice altar, which was painted probably between 1506-09, and painted over in 1612 by Daniel Alexei from Květná in 1612. Above the altar and inserted into the cycle are the figures of King Vladislav Jagellon and his wife Anne de Foix-Candale. Directly above the altar on a pedestal is an outstanding **limestone statue of St Wenceslas** from 1373, made probably by Jindřich Parléř, a nephew of Petr Parléř. On the sides of the statue are portraied two angels that, according to a legend, accompanied the Prince at his audience with Emperor Henry the Fowler. Behind the angels are painted four Czech patron saints.

In the corner under the window of the chapel stands a **tower like reliquary**, an exquisite example of smith's work by Master Wenceslas from 1375. By the north entrance to the chapel is sited a **Renaissance bronze candelabrum** with a statue of St Wenceslas, made by the Nuremburg sculptor and metal caster Hans Vischer in 1532 ordered by the guild of Prague maltsters. Next to the candelabrum is hung a Renaissance panel painting „The Assassination of St Wenceslas" from 1543, a work of a Master signed by the initials I.W. The gilded chandelier comes from the beginning of the 20th century.

Under the window we can see a small door leading to the staircase to the **Coronation Chamber**, placed above the St Wenceslas Chapel. The doors, just like the armour plated cabinet for the jewels, have seven locks and their keys are in the keeping of distinguished representatives of the state, the church and the city of Prague. The preserved collection of the Coronation Jewels comprises the golden St Wenceslas crown from the time of Charles IV, the sceptre and orb from the time of Ferdinand I, the reliquary cross which was made out of an older cross in the 14th century and became a permanent part of the Coronation Jewels only in 1645, the coronation

The coronation jewels

robe, belt and stole from the 18th century. In the Middle Ages the collection also contained a ring, golden bangles and a crystal annointing vessel.

Prince Spytihněv II tried to gain the right to wear a royal crown. He did not manage it, but he acquired the right to wear a bishop's mitre. However his brother, Prince Vratislav II obtained for his person the title of king and a crown (in 1085). After his death (1092) the crown, which also had as its part Spytihněv's mitra of a hemisperical shape, was dedicated to the main patron saint St Wenceslas, who was pronounced the permanent ruler and heir of the Czech lands. Here the tradition begins, which was codified by Charles IV, to accept the crown from „the body of St Wenceslas", whose property it is.

The northern portal of the chapel is decorated from the outside with Gothic statues of Judas, whose tongue is being torn out by the devil, and St Petr denying Christ. In the portal are set iron doors, made in the second half of the 14th century using a Romanesque bronze ring inserted into a lion's mouth. According to tradition it is the ring from the Church of St Kosmas and St Damian in Stará Boleslav. (The prince grasped the ring, as his murderers caught him.) Next to the portal by the chapel wall is placed the Renaissance **marble epitaph of Jiří Popel of Lobkovice** (died 1590). We can also see the chapel from the **western portal** (from the transept) decorated by statues of the Apostles St Petr and St Paul.

19. Opposite the St Wenceslas Chapel behind the transept is the **Hasenburg Chapel** built by Petr Parléř in 1396. We can enter it through a neo Gothic portal. It is situated on the ground floor of the large southern tower and originally it was as large as the Chapel of St Wenceslas. Nowadays its interior is smaller, since in the 19th century thick stonework was built around its inner walls to reinforce the foot of the large to-

The door to the coronation chamber in the Chapel of St Wenceslas

The Renaissance tombstone in the wall of the chapter library

The stained glass window depicting the Sending of the Holy Spirit in the Chapel of St Ludmila

wer. The stained glass window designed by Cyril Bouda depicts lying the foundation stone of completing the Cathedral. From the outside Renaissance tombstones of marble from Slivenice are fixed to the wall of the Chapel.

We can climb the look-out gallery of the tower at the height of 56 m via a spiral staircase with 287 steps passing by the bells and the clock. From the gallery we can view even the outskirts of Prague. Directly below the tower we can see the details of the roof and the stone decoration of the Cathedral.

20. The closed **capitular library** is next to the Hasenburg Chapel. A precious collection of manuscripts and old prints was kept here, which at present is sited in the rooms of the Archives of Prague Castle. On the outside wall of the library are installed Renaissance tombstones.

21. Next is the **Thun Chapel**. The classicist altar is decorated by a picture of Dead Christ with the angels by an unknown artist from the time of Rudolf II. From the corner of the chapel leads a door to the capitular library. The stained glass window was designed by František Kysela on the theme of the Psalm „Those who sow in tears shall reap in joy".

22. In the **Chapel of Christ's Tomb** we can be captivated by an early Baroque altar from 1674, the picture of St Mary Magdalene by Aurelio Lomi from 1600 and a picture of the Holy Family with the Angels by an unknown artist from the second half of the 17th century. The stained glass window with the theme of the Acts of Mercy was created according to a design by Karel Svolinský.

23. The Chapel of St Ludmila (Christening) is decorated with a stained glass window on the theme of the Descent of the Holy Spirit by Max Švabinský. By the same artist is the mosaic the Baptism of Christ. In the chapel a Baroque font and a picture „The Burial of Christ" by an unknown Italian painter from the 17th century are placed.

The stained glass window depicting the Sending of the Holy Spirit in the Chapel of St Ludmila

A cock - an attribute of the St Vitus Cathedral - on the Cathedral roof

We are leaving the Cathedral of St Vitus, a pearl of the Czech architecture. The building came out of the spirit of the Gothic and we should understand it as such. Also about it are true the words written on the gate of the French Abbey Saint Denis, the cradle of the Gothic style: „You who want to praize the beauty of the gates, do not amire the stone and the cost, but the work. The work shines with beauty, however, let the beatifully shining work enlighten the spirit, so that after having been enlightened, it could reach the real ligh where Christ is the real gate. Through mass, the spirit is heightened, though weak, to the truth, freeing itself from all earthly and entering the light.“

Fourth walk:

THE OLD ROYAL PALACE

The Old Royal Palace, the Romanesque palace with fortification towers, a chapel and the southern tower gate to the Castle

The eastern side of the *third courtyard* is enclosed by the building of the Old Royal Palace. From the outside it does not differ from the palace buildings on the southern side of the courtyard, since even its facade with a decorated balcony comes from Pacassi's rebuilding the Castle.

The architectural development

The Royal Palace is marked by a lengthy architectural development. Its foundation is the Romaneque palace of Prince Soběslav I, built after 1135. Its long building of a rectangular ground plan fulfilled the function of a fortification wall on the south side and therefore it was reinforced by pentagonal towers. On the eastern side the Chapel of All Saints was adjacent to the Palace, it was consecrated in 1185. The Palace was partly extended (by a transverse wing at the wester end of the Palace) and rebuilt by Přemysl II Otakar (from 1253), however nearly nothing was preserved.

A large reconstruction started at the time of Prince Charles (the later King and Emperor Charles IV) after his return to

Bohemia in 1333. He chose as the foundation of his seat the preserved lower part of the Romanesque building, which he extended on the north side by a row of arcades, thereby he gained a sufficient space for a prestigous hall upstairs. This determined the present width of the Palace. He also extended the building to the west and included into it the then separately standing tower of the Romanesque fortifications with the closed southern gate. Oriels were built on the polygonal Romanesque towers; one of them was used as a home chapel. Charles' rebuilding stressed mainly the official purpose of the Castle, whereas the residential premises were relatively modest.

Charles' son Wenceslas IV stressed the residential function of the Palace. He had two vertical wings built at the eastern end of the building (the larger north wing and a narrow south wing running up to the moat wall) and some rooms, till then with flat ceilings, equipped with vault-

1 - the Eagle Fountain
2 - the Palace vestibule
3 - the Green Room
4 - the Small Audience
   Hall
5 - the Romanesque
   tower (the former
   southern gate)
6 - the Vladislav Hall
7 - the Ludvík wing
8 - the viewing gallery
9 - the viewing terrace
10 - the Theresian wing
11 - the Church of All
    Saints
12 - the entrance to the
    room of the New
    Land Rolls
13 - the Diet
14 - the Riders Staircase
15 - the rooms of the New
    Appeals
16 - the entrance to the
    Gothic floor of the
    palace from the end
    of the Riders Staircase
17 - the northern palace
    court
18 - the entrance to the
    Romanesque floor
    of the palace

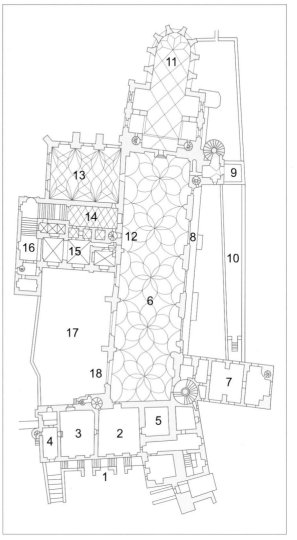

The Old Royal Palace, the ground plan

ing. The vaulting of the rooms required lowering the level of the floors, as a consequence of which the floor based on the vaulting of the Romanesque basement disappeared. Charles's arcades on the north side of the Palace were walled up. The most interesting work of Wenceslas' modifications from the style viewpoint was the Sloupová síň (Pillar Hall) in the western part, two floors above the former Romanesque southern gate. Also the newly built Church of All

The Gothic palace after the rebuildings of Charles IV and Wenceslas IV

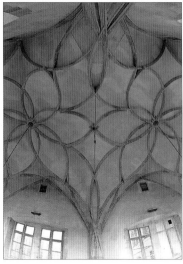

The curvilinear vaulting of the Vladislav Hall

Saints was consecrated, which, however, lost its direct connection to the Palace and became the seat of the newly established chapter.

After the Hussite Wars the Palace remained abandoned for a long time, it was rebuilt and renewed by King Vladislav Jagellon after 1483. First he had a small audience hall built and then he had the large Vladislav Hall, the work of Benedikt Ried built on the site of the throne hall of Charles IV and the adjacent rooms. Also Ried's Jezdecké schody (the Riders Staircase) and the south wing, built for Vladislav's son Ludvík, are worth noticing.

The Palace was modified significantly last time under Emperor Ferdinand I Habsburg after 1541, when the whole Castle and the Small Quarter were stricken by fire. The Sněmovna (the Old Diet) and later the Church of All Saints had to be rebuilt, the wing of the Nové zemské desky (New Land Rolls) was extended.

At that time the Palace was not probably used as the ruler's residence, since he built west of the Old Palace new palace buildings. However, the Old Royal Palace remained the seat of the country's administration.

At the rebuilding of the Castle under the rule of Empress Maria Theresa the western facade of the Old Palace was modified, to be in harmony with the other palace buildings in *the third courtyard*; above the entrance to the Palace a portico with a balcony was built. At that time in front of the southern facade of the Palace the so called Theresian Wing was built, connecting the Ludvík wing with the newly reconstructed Home for Noble Women. At the time of the reign of Josef II the Old Palace ceased to fulfil even the administrative function and in the 18th and the 19th centuries it was used only occasionally for coronation ceremonies and assemblies.

The entrance to the Old Royal Palace from the third courtyard   *The Eagle Fountain*

Seeing of the Palace

The seeing of the Palace usually starts from the *third courtyard* by entering the late Gothic and Renaissance floors and ends by seeing the rooms of the Gothic and Romanesque Palace under the present level of the *third courtyard*. We can enter the Romanesque and Gothic floor through the arcade of the northern palace yard.

West wing

Via the stairs encircling the small Baroque **Orlí kašna** (Eagle Fountain; complemented by Plečnik's small fountain) we enter the **Palace vestibule** (originally the Small Hall). Its right wall is created partly of the stonework of Soběslav's castle tower, turned red by the Castle fire in 1541. From the middle of the 16th century till the middle of the 18th century the room was used by the Czech Chamber, the central financial office of the realm. It had originally Gothic vaulting, which was

removed in the 18th century. On the left we enter the **Zelená světnice** (Green Chamber), whose late Gothic vaulting was also removed. Here used to be a hall where Charles IV presided over minor court cases. From 1512 the chamber was used for sessions of the royal and parliamentary court. The coats of arms of the members of the royal court from the 18th century are depicted on the walls. During the time when the representatives were in session this was also a meeting room for the nobles. The ceiling fresco of the Judgement of Solomon was brought here from the Old Chancellery.

Above the Green Chamber Emperor Ferdinand I Hapsburg had his residential rooms, and therefore he used it as his audience chamber. Here on Maundy Thursday he carried out the ceremony of washing the feet; together with other dignitaries he personally extended hospitality to 13 poor old men and then with the assistence of the Trident bishop he washed their right feet, wiped them and kissed them. This act was intended to

The Green Chamber

The windows in the Vladislav Hall from the outside

bring to mind Christ's humility and also to express the idea that the Emperor walked in his footsteps.

Next to the Green Chamber are two smaller rooms accessible from the stairs. The first of them is the **Small Audience Chamber**, incorrectly called Vladislav's bedroom. It was built under the rule of King Vladislav Jagellon and it has a fine late Gothic vaulting with polychrome ribs. On the corbels are sculptures of the emblems of Bohemia, Moravia, Silesia and Luxembourg, in the front the King's monogram W and the Polish eagle with a crown are carved. The walls of the chamber are decorated with the coats of arms of the highest Lords Chamberlains from the 16th century. The second room was used by the royal court; the coats of arms of the members of the court from the 16th and the 17th centuries are portrayed on its walls and vaulting.

Vladislavský sál

(The Vladislav Hall) Back through the Green Chamber and the Palace vestibule we enter the Vladislav Hall, at its time the largest vaulted secular space in Central Europe. The hall was built during the reign of King Vladislav Jagellon between 1492-1502 according to plans of the architect Benedict Ried. It is 62 metres long, 16 metres wide and 13 metres high and stands in place of the Gothic chambers of Charles IV's palace. It was vaulted with daring late Gothic **curvilinear vaulting**; the vaulting pressures of its five sections are led into large pillars, which by the walls go through two floors downstairs. From the pillars run the vaulting ribs which create in the middle of each section a six petal rose.

In the late Gothic time ribs no longer performed their load bearing function and they were completely freed from any structural purpose. It was their easthetic function that was stressed: the curvilinear ribs crossed one another, regularly and freely creating on

The Vladislav Hall

the ceiling elaborate star-like ornamentation. (The ribs of the Vladislav Hall, however, have partly the load bearing function.) The reddened stone wall by the entrance is a remnant of the Soběslav fortification tower, burnt at the fire in 1541. At that time also the tent five section roof above the Vladislav Hall burnt down (it was replaced by a simple ridge roof), the vaulting itself, however, survived.

The unusually large **rectangular windows** have a Renaissance adaptation from the outside. One of them, dated by 1493, belongs probably to the oldest examples of the Renaissance style in Central Europe. The hall itself, with Gothic vaulting, is close to the Renaissance by its appearance; the typical Gothic overtopping is missing, and though the hall is very large, it is adapted to human size by its proportions. The **eastern face** of the hall bears the monogram of King Vladislav Jagellon (the letter W) and on its sides are the emblems of the Czech and the Hungarian kingdoms; the number 29 under the Czech emblem denotes the number of the King's reign in Bohe-

The first room of the Czech Chancellery

mia, the number 10 in Hungary, related to the year 1500 inscribed in the middle. The hall was originally heated by two fireplaces; the remnant of one of them is visible after entering the Ludvík wing, the other used to be next to the portal to the Old Diet. **The wooden floor** comes probably from the time of the coronation of Emperor Leopold II in 1791, when a large feast was held here. Three of the **tin chandeliers** are original from the 16th century, the remaining two are modern replicas.

The hall was used mainly for official purposes. It served as a venue for banquets and audiences, for coronation feasts and balls and sometimes for the sittings of the council. It was also frequently used for knight tournaments. In 1527, two days after his coronation, King Ferdinand I earned himself admiration in one such tournament. In the period of Rudolf II antiquarians and antique dealers traded here, and the court engraver Jiljí Sadeler had a stall here. Since 1918 (the first Czechoslovak Republic was established) the hall has been used for important state occasions, especially for presidential elections.

The Ludvík wing

Through the portal in the southwest corner we enter the Ludvík wing built by Benedict Ried for Vladislav's son Ludvík Jagellon. On the same level as the Vladislav Hall are the two **rooms of the Czech Chancellery**, during absence of the King the highest administrative authority of the realm. The first room, decorated with late Gothic ribs with remarkable consoles, was used by officials of lower rank. The green tiled stove come from the 17th century (like the stove from the next room).

We will be captivated probably by a plastic model of Prague Castle, documenting the development of its fortifications from the 12th to the 15th century. Here we can see clearly the layout of the late Romanesque fortifications, hidden under the late Gothic and Baroque rebuildings. In a showcase are placed the facsimiles of three documents summarising briefly the beginning, the development and the end of the uprising of the Czech Estates against the Hapsburgs. The first of them is the facsimile of the Imperial Charter of Emperor Rudolf II from 1609 confirming the religious freedom in the Czech Kingdom. The document was depreciated (shorn) by Emperor Ferdinand II Hapsburg after the defeat of the uprising of the Czech Estates in 1620. The second is the text of the Confederation of the rebellious Estates against the Hapsburgs (who violated the provision about religous liberty) from 1619 and the third is the facsmile of the Renewed State Order from 1627, by which the Hapsburgs strengthed legaly their power after the defeat of the uprising of the Czech Estates in 1620.

The late Gothic vaulting of the first room of the Czech Chancellery

The second room of the Czech Chancellery is more significant for the Czech history. It was used by the governors administrating the country during the absence of the king. One can enter it through a portal with the crowned initial „L" (Ludvík Jagellon). The late Gothic ribs of this room are removed from the vaulting. On 23 May 1618 the representatives of the dissatisfied Czech Estates came here and after staging a brief trial „according to the old law" threw the representatives of the pro-Austrian Catholic side - the governors Jaroslav Bořita of Martinice and Vilém Slavata of Chlum - out of the eastern window into the castle moat. Together with them the secretary Fabricius was also thrown out. All three landed on a rubbish heap, from where they managed to escape into the safety of the Lobkovic Palace.

By this second Prague defenestration (sometimes called the third, the first was in 1419, the second, often neglected was in 1483) the uprising of the Czech Estates and the Thirty Years War started actually. The English writer Jerome Klapka Jerome viewed the Prague defenestrations from the more humorous side, he concluded that „Prague could avoid half of her problems, if the windows were smaller and therefore less tempting". „Since then", writes Jerome Klapka, „in Prague also other important issues were dealt; from the fact they were settled without violence we can infer they were decided in the basement. I feel that the window as an argument always seriously tempted true Prague citizens." The governors were later richly rewarded by the Hapsburgs and even the secretary Fabricius was not left empty handed, as he was elevated into the ranks of the nobility with the title „von Hohenfall" meaning Fabricius of the High Fall.

Protected by glass in the room is interesting evidence that the habit of scribbling and writing on walls is very old: in the 17th century someone wrote here with charcoal the sentence „I enjoy her favour".

A detail of the entrance to the second room of the Czech Chancellery

The entrance to the second room of the Czech Chancellery

One floor lower are the rooms of the **Czech Chamber**, the highest financial office of the country. Between the floors the **Court War Council** had its rooms in the period of Rudolf II. It was the highest imperial military office. These rooms are not opened.

Through the spiral late Gothic staircase we ascend one floor higher and after passing a small room enter the **Světnice Říšské dvorské rady** (Room of the Imperial Council). This office, administrating the matters of the whole Hapsburg Empire, had its sessions here at the time of the rule of Emperor Rudolf II. In the period after the Battle of the White Mountain during the land assemblies here was a council room of the high clergy. Here the sentence on the 27 noblemen, participants of the uprising of the Czech Estates, was read. They were executed on 21 June 1621 on Staroměstské (Old Town) Square. The rebelion of the Estates started on the floor below by throwing the governors out of the window, and ended by the cruel sentence pronounced only a few metres above the place of the defenestration. The interior is purely Renaissance, lit through large windows with a lookout at Prague. On the walls hang 12 portraits of the Hapsburg rulers and on the left a copy of Velasquez' picture of the Spanish King Filip IV. The furniture in the room and the tiled stove come from the 17th and the 18th centuries

Viewing places

From the right side of the Vladislav Hall it is possible to walk onto the viewing places above the southern gardens of the Castle. The entrance by the Ludvík wing leads onto the **viewing gallery** and its decorative vaulting with small fake ribs is worth noticing.

From the gallery leading along the whole south front of the Vladislav Hall one can see the Renaissance details of its windows. One can be captivated by the view over the roof of the Small Quarter houses and the distant

The spiral staircase to the chamber of the Imperial Court Council

The chamber of the Imperial Court Council

view over the whole Prague basin. Directly under the gallery is the narrow Theresian Wing and behind it there is the Garden *Na Valech*. The view westwards is screened by the Ludvík Wing, whose facade belongs among the first consistently Renaissance ones in Bohemia.

We return from the gallery and enter again the Vladislav Hall, now at its eastern end. Through the next entrance we walk out onto the **viewing terrace**, which was built on the lowered part of the vertical southern wing from the period of Wenceslas IV.

From the terrace new views over Prague and the garden *Na Valech* are opened. Also the two memorials on the sites where the governors thrown out of the window of the Czech Chancellery fell are visible. Next to the terrace an open granite spiral staircase is built, a work by Plečnik's pupil Otto Rothmayer, enabling the connection between the Old Royal Palace and the Theresian wing.

Theresian wing

The narrow Theresian wing connects the Ludvík wing with the Home for Noble Women (lying east of the Old Palace and the Church of All Saints). It was built in the period of the reign of Maria Theresa between 1766-68. On the lower floors were offices, registries and flats. The highest floor served as a passageway; in 1931 it and the ridge roof were taken down, since it screened the view from the town of the facade of the Vladislav Hall. After the reconstruction in 1993 the wing has been used for exhibition purposes, one can enter it either from the north palace yard, or from the Garden *Na Valech*.

At building the Theresian wing the staff of the offices on the Gothic floor of the Old Palace (that means under the Vladislav Hall) complained that they would not have enough light for work. However, the director of the building office exaplained to them in his extensive reply that the building was carried out on the order of the Empress and that the distance of the

The Church of All Saints

The rooms of the New Land Rolls

building site from the windows of their offices was sufficient. Moreover, the fact that they would lose a pleasant but diverting view of the city should only double their effort at work.

The Church of All Saints

From the eastern part of the Vladislav Hall we will go up a few stairs to the Renaissance portal by the Italian architect Giovanni Gargiolli and after going through we get onto the gallery of the Church of All Saints. The church was built by Petr Parléř on the site of the Romanesque palace chapel consecrated in 1185. Its vaulting belonged, it is said, to the best of Parléř works, unfortunately, it was destroyed during the fire in 1541. The renovation of the Church was performed only in 1580 at the expense of Rudolf II's sister, Queen Elizabeth, widow after the French King Charles IX. At that time the Church was extended up to the front of the Vladislav Hall and gained lower Renaissance vaulting. Short time before 1600 the above mentioned Gargiolli por-

tal was built into the eastern wall of the Vladislav Hall. The main altar of the All Saints Church is a work of the Baroque painter Václav Vavřinec Reiner from 1732. In the northern chapel is sited the altar with the Baroque tomb of St Procopius, whose remains were transferred to Prague in 1588 from the Sázava Monastery.

Chambers of the Nové zemské desky

(New Land Rolls) The spiral staircase in the northern wall of the Vladislav Hall leads into the four chambers of the New Land Rolls.

The Land Rolls were books into which the decisions of the Diet and ownership changes of real estates were recorded which were performed with the approval of the Diet. These records had the status of laws. They were established in the second half of the 13th century and were originally kept (up to 1541) on the Gothic floor of the Royal Palace in the

Maquettes of the volumes of the Land Rolls

*The entrance to the Diet;
in the background
the Renaissance platform*

chamber of the Old Land Rolls. At the Castle fire in 1541 most of them burnt down, which King Ferdinand I Hapsburg used for denying some older Estate privileges whose records were not preserved. In 1783 the activity of the office of the Land Rolls ended, and from 1796 they began mere land registers. The last records into them were performed in the middle of the 19th century.

The exhibits here evoke the activities of the Land Rolls office, display the office furniture and illustrate how entries were made into the Land Rolls. The walls are decorated with the coats of arms of the Land Roll Clerks from 1561 to 1774. The coat of arms of the Lord Bohuslav of Michalovice was whitewashed, as he was a participant of the Estates rebelion from the years 1618-20, executed in 1621. We can see the Czech inscription saying that „nothing will be read or written for anybody, unless paid in cash money in advance" and the Latin inscription „Iuste iudicate filii hominum" (Judge justly, human sons). In the second chamber stand the original **carved cabinets** from the period of Rudolf II in which **copies of Land Rolls** are kept. Their covers clearly show that the administrative books from earlier times were not numbered but were identified by colour and decoration on the spine. In the third chamber among others stands the oldest cabinet of Prague Castle, which was made in 1562. Next to the New Land Rolls chambers is the Baroque **Crown Archives**, closed for the public, built by Kilián Ignác Dientzenhofer in 1737. Originally the directors of the Land Rolls office were sitting here, in the 19th century the space was adapted into a safe depository of the Crown Archives where the most important documents of the Czech Kingdom and between 1867-68 also the Czech Coronation Jewels were kept.

Old Diet
We go downstairs again into the Vladislav Hall, passing by the portal of the Riders Staircase, we turn into the next door in the

The Diet

north wall of the Hall and here we are in the room of the Diet, which is in the vertical wing from the period of King Wenceslas IV. Under the reign of Vladislav Jagellon it was rebuilt by Benedict Ried, however, in 1541 it was destroyed by the Castle fire with the exception of the peripheral stonework. The Renaissance architect Bonifác Wolmut performed the renovation, who, out of piety to his late Gothic predecessor, applied late Gothic ribs, which however, he „stuck" only decoratively to the Renaissance barrel vaulting with lunettes.

The Diet served to the supreme body of the Czech medieval justice, the Supreme Court, whose sentences were recorded into the Land Rolls. The sessions were often fierce, mainly before the War of the White Mountain, however, the Estate representatives often preferred pleasant refreshment to duty. The warning of Václav Vilém of Roupov adressed to the „delegates" during the reign of Frederick of Falc still sounds appropriate today: „Gentlemen, Gentlemen. Please wait a moment. I guess that Gentlemen are hurrying to have breakfast, but look that you do not breakfast away your country."

The furniture in the Diet is from the 19th century and gives an idea of how proceedings in the Diet were carried out after issuing the Renewed State Order in 1627, which limited strongly the rights of the Czech Estates, that revolted against the Hapsburg ruler between 1618-20. The king sat on the throne, on his right the archbishop, on the bench behind him other prelates. Along the walls sat the highest officials and judges of the land, the benches in the front were reserved for the nobles and the knights, whereas the representatives of the most humbled Estate - the royal towns - stood in a gallery by the window and they altogether had only one vote. One can be captivated by the beatiful **Renaissance gallery** of the secretary with a direct entrance into the chambers of the New Land Rolls. **The portraits** hung on the walls depict Empress Maria Theresa, her husband

The vaulting of the Riders Staircase

The Riders Staircase with the entrance in the shape of a donkey's back

Stephen of Lothringen, Emperors Josef II, Leopold II and Franz II. The neo Gothic tiled stove come from 1836.

Jezdecké schody

(The Riders Staircase) We leave the Vladislav Hall via the **Riders Staircase**, which begin by the portal sited between the chamber of the New Land Rolls and the door to the Diet. The staircase was reserved for ariving knights on horseback who came to tournaments held in the Vladislav Hall. Probably at this place was also the main entrance to the throne hall of King Charles IV. The first part of the staircase leads through the space of a former open balcony which was rebuilt and covered with a Renaissance roof. On the left is the entrance to the offices of the New Appeals where between 1727-83 the Court of Appeal (of the whole kingdom) had its sessions. The rooms are not open. Through the **late Gothic portal** in the shape of donkey's back we get to the staircase itself with wide low

steps, above which is the outstanding **late Gothic vaulting** by Benedict Ried. We can turn to the right and come out to *Jiřské Square*, or go down the stairs into the rooms of the Gothic and Romanesque Palace.

Gothic floor of the Palace

The Gothic floor is approximately on the same level as the northern palace yard. The first room of the Gothic Palace after entering from the Riders Staircase is the **Chamber of the Old Land Rolls**. According to tradition it comes from the period of Přemysl II Otakar. The heavy vaulting of the chamber is carried by two low cylindrical pillars. Here the Land Rolls were kept up to the Castle fire in 1541, when a major part of them burnt down. Later the room was used by the Castle wardens, who were allowed to sell beer from taps in the neighbouring room under the staircase; therefore the room is also called the Tavern. Then we go through the **Arcade Corridor** from the

The Gothic floor of the palace near the entrance from the Riders Staircase

The Gothic hall with the remnants of a Romanesque room

time of Charles IV. Ten arcades were closed even at the time of Charles' son Wenceslas IV, at present three arcades are opened into the palace yard. We enter the **Gothic Hall** vaulted by vaulting from the first half of the 14th century. During the modifications in the 1930s the floor was removed, so that one could see **the remnants of a Romanesque living room** with a fireplace in a corner. This Romanesque room was filled up, when the vaulting of the originaly flat ceiling hall was built; its floors had to be lowered and the Romanesque storey downstairs became uninhabitable. In the Gothic Hall are also preserved the remnants of a hot air heating furnace, probably from the 15th century. Next to the hall is the **Charles Chamber** which was created of three original rooms. At the time of Charles IV it had a flat ceiling, the Gothic vaulting comes from the time of his son Wenceslas IV. Along the south peripheral wall wecam see large pillars which one floor above bear the massive vaulting of the Vladislav Hall. The floor

tiles are copies made according to the original patterns from the Emperor's time.

A part of the Charles Chamber was used in the 16th and 17th centuries for sessions of the Court of Appeal; also the leader of the rebellion in Chodsko, Jan Sladký called Kozina, was tried here. In the room are placed **models** of the Royal Palace, the early Romanesque Princely Castle and the Princely Castle after the Romanesque rebuilding of Prince Soběslav II. On the walls hang copies of the portraits of Charles IV and his wives from the sculptural gallery in the internal triforium of the Cathedral of St Vitus.

Next is the chamber of **the Old Registry**, in which were the registries of the bookkeeping department of the Czech Chamber. Throung the Gothic enterance in the west wall, which comes from the period of Přemysl II Otakar, it is possible to enter the **Pillar Hall of Wenceslas IV**, the most remarkable room of the Gothic floor of the Palace. The hall was built

The Charles Hall

around 1400 and it is vaulted by narrow profiled ribs. The vaulting pressure is led into two cylindrical pillars. The shape of the consoles and connections of the vaulting ribs are intentionally irregular, which corresponded to the style liberation in the period of Wenceslas' rule. Later the depository of the Court Rolls was sited here, in the 18th century this hall served as a refrigerator and a pantry. Via a few steps we enter the **Chamber of the Court Rolls**, vaulted by Renaissance vaulting carried by the middle pillar. It served as the depository of the Court Rolls of the Royal Court and later as a pantry.

Romanesque floor of the Palace

Through the western arcade by the north palace yard we enter the Romanesque floor of the Palace. On the right is the ground floor of the **former southern gate**, built after 1135 as a part of the Romanesque fortifications of the Castle. When crossing the wooden bridge we pass by the **space with the remnants of the original fortifications**; the earth mound was reinforced inside by a wooden construction and from the outside by a stone wall built without using mortar. Next is the elongated **hall of the Romanesque Palace**, built from 1135. Nowadays the hall is 50 metres long, in the past, however, it was divided into smaller rooms. It is vaulted with barrel vaulting and additionally (during the Gothic rebuilding of the Palace) reinforced by brick vaulting strips. Through the semicirle vaulted portal we can enter the **bottom floor of the Romanesque Palace Chapel of All Saints**, where during the second World War the Czech Coronation Jewels and some precious objects of the St Vitus treasure were kept (enclosed in the wall).

In 1547 the Castle basement was used as a prison for burghers after the defeat of the rebellion against Ferdinand I Hapsburg. Later here were wine cellars. The cellars under the Church of All Saints belonged to the dean of

The Pillar Hall of Wenceslas IV

The exit from the Royal Palace: the decorative door knocker

The room of the Court Rolls

that church. So that the wine barrels could go through the narrow vaulting, in 1739 on the dean's command the foundations and the buttress were partly hewn out, as a result of this operation the newly repaired vaulting was damaged, however, the barrels could get in its place.

We are leaving the Old Royal Palace, du-ring the visit of which we got from the present time to the period of its beginning. We say our farewells to it with the verses of Jaroslav Seifert, so much appropriate for the character of this one time alive, however at later times deserted, monument of the Czech magnificence: „And Its Majesty dust is slowly sitting down on the deserted throne."

Fifth walk:

THROUGH VIKÁŘSKÁ STREET TO THE CONVENT OF ST GEORGE

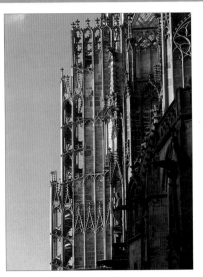

The northern side of the Cathedral of St Vitus

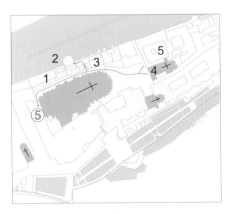

1 - the Vikárka Restaurant
2 - the Powder Tower
3 - the Mladota House
4 - the Basilica of St George
5 - the Convent of St George

Vikářská Street

Along the north side of the St Vitus Cathedral leads *Vikářská Street*. Probably, it has its origin in the period of Charles IV, after the seat of the St Vitus Chapter, called **the Monastery of the Prague Church**, was demolished. The Chapter House was adjacent to the north nave of the Romanesque Basilica of St Vitus and had the lay-out typical of monasteries with a square paradise courtyard, surrounded by a cloister.

The grey substance of the Cathedral of St Vitus evokes the impression of steepness from the narrow street; we are going directly under the Gothic pinnacles and gargoyles having the likeness of fantastic creatures and demons.

The first three houses on the north side of the street have uniformly modified facades: They are the house No 40/8 (with the sign of the St Vitus Chapter) and two houses of the Vikárka Restaurant.

The moat of the northern fortification with the Powder Tower

In the past: At this place after 1559 the bricklayer master Oldřich de Savosa, later the Emperor's architecht Ulrico Avostalis had its house, then here was the house of the „distillers", at the end of the 17th century called „lichtkomora" (light chamber), since at the time when the Eperor's court stayed in Prague, in it lived the Emperor's „chamberlain above light". In the 16th and the 17th centuries here used to stand also a house of rifle makers in which lived the workers of the near iron foundry. This has been standing north of this place since the Renaissance period in place of the former moat and from the years 1791 it was used for stabling horses. There is evidence about a few other houses on this site.

The House **Velká Vikárka** (Large House of the Vikars; No 39/6) gave the name to the whole street. It used to be connected with the Cathedral of St Vitus by a corridor removed during the rebuilding of the Cathedral. Later Emperor Rudolf II gained Vikárka by barter, under Empress Maria Theresa it became again the property of the Chapter and capitular vicars were accommodated in it. The next house called **Malá Vikárka** (the Small House of the Vicars No 38/4) had a similar history. On the ground floor of the Large Vikárka in the first half of the 19th century a tavern was established, which expanded gradually into the other rooms. The Czech writer Svatopluk Čech placed here the scene of his short story „The Trip of Mr Brouček into the 15th Century". Between 1964-65 both Vikárkas were rebuilt to be used by the Vikárka Restaurant, which since 1990 has also been using the reconstructed premises of the former foundry. Under a part of the long elevated ramp from which lead the present stairs into the restaurant is preserved massive stonework of the foundations of the north tower of the St Vitus Cathedral from the period of Vladislav Jagellon, who tried to complete the Cathedral.

The original Vikárka stood a little to the west and had Romanesque foundations. At first it was in property of the St Vitus Chapter. Emperor Rudolf II gained it together with other build-

113

The exhibition in the Powder Tower   *The exhibition in the Powder Tower*

ings and had it pulled down. The name Old or Large Vikárka was transferred then on the following objects, which are called this way even now.

Through the passageway between the Small Vikárka and the western part of the Mladota House we enter a small yard. The commemorative inscription on the facade reminds us that between 1518-34 at this place lived Benedict Ried, the most important architect of King Vladislav Jagellon.

From the yard we get to the open part of the moat of the northern fortifications. It is dominated by the large round **Prašná věž** (Powder Tower), called Mihulka (in the Middle Ages the name mihulka was often given to towers which by their roundness reminded cyclostomous river and sea vertebrates lampreys - in Czech mihule). This artillery bastion, the largest one at the Castle, was built at the end of the 15th century by Benedict Ried as his first commission for Vladi-

slav Jagellon. The bottom floor of the tower was built into the slope below the level of the moat wall and it was equipped with small loopholes for lighter fire arms. Above the massive vaulting of the basement a huge mound was raised to the height of 4.5 m, damping the tremor of the heavy bastion artillery on the ground floor. The ground and the first floors are vaulted with cupola vaulting. They are equipped with larger loopholes for artillery and airing holes and slide wooden shields. The top floor has a flat ceiling, originally ended by an open platform ecirled by a ledge wall, later it was roofed.

However, the defence ability of the tower was never used in practice. In the Renaissance it was also used as a bell maker's foundry, in which Master Tomáš Jaroš also worked, who cast the Singing Fountain in the Royal Garden and the largest St Vitus bell Zikmund. During the period of Rudolf II the tower was used as an alchemist's laboratory and a foundry.

The Mladota House

The New Deanery

During the Thirty Years War here was a store for gunpowder, after which the tower and the nearby Prašný most (Powder Bridge) received their names. At the end of the Thirty Years War because of carelessness of the Swedish garrison occupying the Castle an explosion happened, which damaged the tower seriously. In 1754 it became property of the St Vitus Chapter, that used it as a store and the dwelling for the sextons.

The exhibition in the cellar, ground floor and both upper floors of the tower documents the development of the arts and crafts at the court of Emperor Rudolf II. Among the exhibits it is worth noticing the detailed model of the achemist's laboratory, a copy of Rudolf's tin burial coffin and a small model of the Powder Tower illustrating its military function. The visit to the Tower belongs definitely between one of the most interesting excursions at Prague Castle.

Mladota's House (No 37/2), the former capitular deanery, is the most conspi-cuous building in *Vikářská Street*. Originally two (or more) houses stood here, and even at present the house has two distinctively separate parts; through the lower, western one, the above mentioned access to the Powder Tower leads. At first the houses belonged to the capitular deanery, later the Lords of Rožmberk acquired them. After the Hussite Wars the houses changed their owner up to 1483, when the St Vitus Chapter gained them again. In 1590 the old Rožmberk House was demolished and in its place a capitular school was built, in the neighbourhood (in the lower, western part of today's house) the house of choir singers and bell ringers was built. The dean Adam Ignác Mladota of Solopysky had the building modified into the present early Baroque palace form in 1705, probably according to the design of Giovanni Santini. The builder's sign is inserted into a triangular tympanum. In the eastern part of the ground floor is preserved the space of the former capitular library with vaulting decorated between 1724-26

1 - the western entrance
2 - the main nave
3 - the northern side nave
4 - the southern side nave
5 - the northern tower
6 - the southern tower with the Chapel of the Virgin Mary on the ground floor
7 - the crypt
8 - the tombstones of the Přemyslide princes
9 - the Chapel of St Ludmila
10 - the southern portal
11 - the Chapel of St John of Nepomuk
12 - the southern arm of the convent cloister

The Basilica of St George

with wall paintings of Jan Vodňanský. The canons of the St Vitus Chapter are depicted here in ideal portraits, on the ceiling an allegory of God's wisdom is portrayed.

Jiřské Square

We are entering *Jiřské Square*, which in the early Middle Ages used to be the main Castle space. It used to be larger than today, since the St Vitus Choir and the transversal wings of the Old Royal Palace did not take up its place. Also the houses along the north wall were missing. Probably in this square used to stand the stone princely throne, probably the Fountain of St George was sited here. It was later transferred to the *third courtyard*.

The western side of the square is enclosed by the large back of the St Vitus Cathedral; it is possible to distinguish the Choir and the ring of Choir chapels. On the northern side, outside the northern fortification of the Castle, used to stand several houses making up a continuous row with the houses in Vikářská Street. In their place today stand three neo Gothic houses, two smaller (united by the same facade), originally belonging to the residence of the canons and the **New Deanery** (No 34/4) by the architect Josef Mocker, with a statue of St Wenceslas at the corner.

The southern side of the square is created by the Old Royal Palace, the Church of All Saints and the circular portico of the **Ústav Šlechtičen** (Home for Noble Women), about which we will learn more in the following walk through *Jiřská Street.*

Basilica of St Jiří (St George)

On the eastern side of *Jiřské Square*, opposite the back of the St Vitus Chapter, stand the Church and Convent of St George.

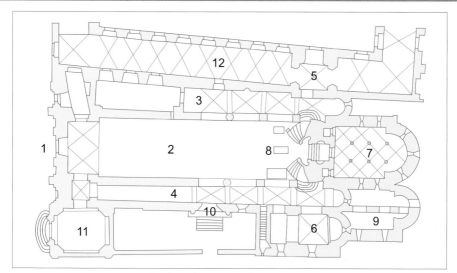

Basilica of St George, the ground plan

Building development of the basilica

The present appearance of the **Basilica of St George** is a result of several building periods. Originaly a one naved church was founded about 920 by Prince Vratislav I as the second oldest Prague church. It was consecrated in 925, when the remains of the Czech martyr, Princess St Ludmila, grandmother of St Wenceslas (died 922) were deposited there. In 979, in connection with founding the convent (in 973) the church was extended and rebuilt; a short three naved basilica was built with three apses on the east and a west and an east crypt and galleries above the side naves. The building was characteristic by its block closeness, typical of the Ottonian pre-Romanesque style. The importance of the early medieval church is supported by the fact that even the Přemyslide rulers - Princes Vratislav I, Boleslav II, Oldřich, Jaromír and probably Boleslav I were buried in it. The following re-building was carried out in 1142, after

the Castle was besieged and partly burnt down by Konrád of Znojmo. The church was extended to the west to nearly to-day's area, next to the apses of the side naves two towers were built, under the presbytery a three naved crypt was built.

The southern tower was built by the Chapel of the Virgin Mary, till then standing separately, the northern tower was included into the convent cloister in the Baroque period. When looking at the towers in front of the entrance, we will learn that they do not have the same width. The narrower, northern tower was called Eva according to a north Italian custom, and the wider, souther tower, built so that it could shade Eva, was called Adam.

In the first half of the 13th century the Chapel of St Ludmila (raised by one floor in the period of Charles IV) with the tomb of the saint was built next to the northern side of the choir. On the western side a portico was built, on whose site in the middle of the 14th century a new

St George is fighting with the dragon,
the relief of the tympanum of the southern entrance

The southern entrance
of the Basilica of St George

western front was built by the Parléř foundry. Between 1657-80 the facade was modified in the style of the early Baroque, the Chapel of St John of Nepomuk at the southwest corner was built in the high Baroque.

Exterior of the basilica

The typical brick red early Baroque facade of the **west front** is divided by pilasters; both corner pilasters are ended by obelisks, above the next two stand the sandstone statues depicting the founder of the Church Prince Vratislav I and the founder of the Convent beatified Mlada. The low triangular gable is decorated with a stucco relief of St George fighting with the dragon. The view of the west front is complemented by both white **towers**, standing by the eastern apses of the side naves. They have a stone helmet, under which are two rows of Romanesque windows with a small-arch frieze above them. In the south the symetry of the front is violated by the Baroque Cha-

pel of St John of Nepomuk with a bell Baroque roof and a statue of the saint on the ledge of the entrance. The **south front** faces *Jiřská Street*. At its beginning we can see the side wall of the Baroque Chapel of St John of Nepomuk, then there is Romanesque stone masonry, into which an early Renaissance portal leading to the south nave of the basilica is built. The entrance was created by the foundry of Benedict Ried around 1515, probably in place of an older Romanesque entrance. In its tympanum is placed a copy of the relief of St George fighting with the dragon (the original is in the National Gallery). The slanted view from above the relief is divided by panels with flowers, the entrance pillars are grooved. In the extraordinary view of the **end of the basilica** (also from *Jiřská Street*) both towers dominate. The Romanesque apse of the main nave is decorated by a small-arch frieze, the end of the St Ludmila Chapel in front of the southern tower is Gothic. Between this chapel and the Home for

The end of the Basilica of St George

Noble Women used to be a gate enclosing the street by drawing bars.

The interior of the basilica

is Romanesque and we are impressed by its strict monumentality. The main nave with a flat ceiling is separated from the narrow vaulted side naves by walls, into which an arcade is built. On the upper floors above the side naves are galleries, open into the main nave by a row of windows. The open western loft is separated from the main nave by a Baroque grill.

On the southern wall of the **main nave** is hung a picture with the main theme „The Martyrdom of St Ursula and 11,000 Christians Virgins" by Hans Burgkmaier from the 16th century. On the northern wall hangs the picture of the Assumption of the Virgin Mary by Jan Jiří Heintsche from the end of the 17th century. Three gravestones in the eastern part mark the burial site of the Přemyslide family, discovered by archeological excavations.

On the right is sited a limestone tomb with a wooden house-like cabinet from the 15th century. The remains of the founder of the church, Prince Vratislav, are kept here. The tomb in the middle with the original tombstone contains the remains either of Prince Boleslav II, or more probably, of Prince Oldřich. The tomb on the left, encirled by a Baroque grill, covers the remains of the other member of the family.

Behind the tombstones is a symetrical Baroque staircase leading to the square **choir**, on whose vaulting are preserved remnants of a Romanesque painting of Heavenly Jerusalem from the beginning of the 13th century. In the apse of the choir is preserved a part of the painting of the Coronation of the Virgin Mary from the end of the 16th century. To the south side of the choir is adjoined the **Chapel of St Ludmila**, separated by a Baroque marble balustrade with a forged grill. The body of this saint was transferred to the church after her murder

The main nave of the Basilica of St George

The Romanesque windows between the main and the northern nave of the basilica

at Tetín in 925. Charles IV had the stonemasons from the Parléř foundry make a tomb (standing in the middle of the chapel) in which the remains of the saint have been kept to this day.

We descent via the staircase to the easter **crypt** from the 12th century, built under the choir. It is vaulted by a system of crossed vaulting supported by pillars with cubical heads. On the altar in the axis of the crypt stands a casting of an extaordinary valuable Romanesque tympanum with the Madonna on the throne among angel (the original is in the National Gallery). On the altar by the south wall is sited a stone statue called Vanitas (an allegory of Vanity). It is a naturalistic portrayal of the decay of a human body with lizards and snakes in its entrails.

Legends say that this statue portrays the girl Brigita who was murdered out of jelaousy by her lover. When the body was found and he confessed what he had done, his last wish

before the execution was to get a chance to portray her body as a proof of his repentance. The legend is probably based on the story of the Italian stonemason Bernard Spinetti, who was sentenced to death in 1748 for an attempt to murder his lover, the daughter of the royal gardener Zinner. The penalty, however, was changed on the execution site to the obligation to sweep Prague streets with a ball fastened at his foot for three years. In fact, the statue is older by nearly 200 years.

From the space of the **northern side nave** leads a arched portal to the cloister of the St George Convent. In the eastern apse from the 10th century on the altar rests a torso of a Pieta, probably a work of the Parléř foundry from the second half of the 14th century.

Let us go into the **southern side nave**. In its eastern apse from the 10th century stands a wooden late Gothic statue of St Bartholomew. In front of the apse to the side nave is adjoined the space under the southern tower - originally the

The apse of the choir of the St George Basilica (on the left)
and the Chapel of St Ludmila (on the right)

separate **Chapel of the Virgin Mary**. Probably here used to stand the original tomb of Princess St Ludmila. The vaulting is decorated by the painting of Heavenly Jerusalem, the apse with the painting of Christ with a Halo on the Throne (Maiestas Domini) with angels and the Apostles. The altar is decorated with an original late Gothic relief of the Adoration of the Magi. Through the southern side nave we are returning to the western entrance to the church. On the right side of the nave is placed a small exposition of the results of the archeological excavations of the Basilica and Convent of St George, in the south wall are fixed several gravestones of the St George abbesses.

At the western end the **Chapel of St John of Nepomuk** is adjoined to the southern side nave, it was built by Ferdinand Maxmilián Kaňka. The cupola of the chapel is decorated by a high Baroque fresco of the Apotheosis of St John of Nepomuk by Václav Vavřinec Reiner.

The fresco opens seemingly in the typically Baroque way the view from the Chapel higher into another, saint space. Also the other paintings come from the same artist.

Convent of St George

The Convent of St Jiří was founded in 973 as the first convent in Bohemia. It was a Benedictine convent and it was Mlada, the sister of Prince Boleslav II the Pious who became their first abbess. The original convent consisted of a small building without a cloister. After the death of Abbess Mlada in 995 the Chapel of the Virgin Mary (later of St Anne) was built above her grave. In 1142 at the siege of the Castle by Konrád of Znojmo the Convent burnt down and between 1145-51 it was renewed and one floor was added by Abbess Berta, considered its second founder. It was rebuilt in the early Gothic period, when a cloister was built.

*The Gothic tomb with the remains
of St Ludmila*

*A double flight staircase into
the basilica choir*

In the Middle Ages in the convent used to be a scriptorium (a workshop of scriveners), in which many illuminated manuscripts, musical compositions, and many craft works were written or made. The abbesses of the convent often came from the rule's family or from prominent noble families. From the time of Charles IV the convent obtained the privilege that at festive coronations its abbess together with the archbishop could put the crown on the head of the queen. After closing the convent the right was transferred to the head of the nearby Home for Noble Women.

After the fire of the Castle in 1541 the convent was rebuilt in the Renaissance style; the eastern arm of the cloister was newly built. The last extensive reconstruction was carried out on the upper floors between 1657-80 in the early Baroque style. The Gothic cloister was closed and east of it a Baroque cloister was established. East of the new cloister another small yard and a cloister were built. However, under Josef II in 1782 the con-vent was closed and used as an artillery barracks and a prison for priests. Since 1975 in it there has been a permanent exhibition of the **collection of the Czech Gothic, Mannerism and Baroque art of the National Gallery.**

In the basement of the convent are sited the exposition of the Romanesque art and a part of the Gothic art, for instance the outstanding Gothic cycle of the pictures of the Master of the Vyšebrodský Altar and selected pictures by Master Theodoric. On the ground floor there are exhibited an extraordinary precious cycle of the Master of the Třeboň Altar, works of the fine style (namely pictures of Madonnas) and late Gothic works (among others there are works of the Master of the Rajhradský Altar, the Master of the Litoměřice Altar). On the first floor are sited the exposition of the Mannerism art of the period of Emperor Rudolf II (for instance Hans von Aachen, Bartolomeus Spranger, Adrian de Vries) and the Czech Baroque and Rococo art (the painters Karel Škréta, Petr Brandl, Jan Kupecký, Václav Vavřinec Reiner, Norbert Grund, the sculp-

The statue of the Virgin Mary above the entrance to the Convent of St George

The Romanesque windows of the southern tower of St George

tors Matyáš Bernard Braun, Ferdinand Maxmilián Brokoff and others).

Nowadays the convent is an extensive austere Baroque building with a paradise yard and with another inner courtyard. From the eastern arm of the cloister one can enter the convent **Chapel of St Anne.** Under its floor the foundations of the Romanesque Chapel of the Virgin Mary were discovered. In the glazed niche are placed the presumed (but in fact much younger) remains of the first abbess of the convent Mlada, wearing the order robe and decorated by a silver face mask. In the chapel are exhibited the St George altar, a pannel painting from the 15th century and the original of the three part limestone relief whose copy we saw in the south nave of the basilica. In the glazed showcase are placed the staff and the crown of the St George abbesses.

Sixth walk:

THROUGH JIŘSKÁ STREET TO GOLDEN LANE AND THE OLD CASTLE STAIRS

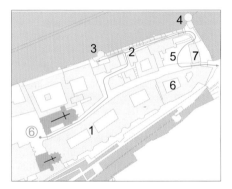

1 - the Home for Noble Women
2 - Golden Lane
3 - the White Tower
4 - the Daliborka Tower
5 - the Residence of the Highest Burgrave
6 - the Lobkovic Palace
7 - the Black Tower

Jiřská Street

The most important street axis of the southern half of the Castle is *Jiřská Street* leading from Jiřské Square to the eastern gate of Prague Castle. Into *Jiřské Square* the circular portico of the **Home for Noble Women** is opened, whose extensive building makes up two thirds of the length of the south side of *Jiřská Street*. Originally here used to stand the Rožmberk Palace, built in the first half of the 16th century and rebuilt several times. In 1600 Emperor Rudolf II gained the palace from Petr Vok of Rožmberk in exchange for the palace in *Hradčanské Square* (the present Schwarzenberk Palace). Later the object was again rebuilt. The last rebuilding into the Home for Noble Women was carried out between 1753-55 under the leading of Nicola Pacassi. An extensive building with three coutryards, the Chapel of the Virgin Mary and a garden on the southern slope was the result of the rebuilding. Also the deanery of the Church of All Saints and the Church itself, previously logically connected with the Royal Palace, were incorporated into the object. During the rebuilding the towers with the onion-like cupolas were taken down. They used to

The Home for Noble Women from the Garden Na Valech

stand on the original Romanesque towers and enlivened the Castle silhouette in a picturesque way. The main entrance led through the above mentioned pillar portico decorated with sculptures by Josef Klein.

The Home, in fact a charity institution for impoverished noble women, was established under the auspices of Empress Maria Theresa, who also participated in its ceremonial opening. The significance of the institution was heightened by the fact that after closing the St George Convent the right to crown the empress was transferred to its abbess. After establishing Czechoslovakia in 1918 the institute was abolished and the building was used up to the 1990 by the Home Ministry. At present it is used as an administrative building by the Office of the President and the Administration of Prague Castle.

The opposite side of *Jiřská Street* is shaped at first by the southern facade of the Basilica of St George and the rear building of the Convent of St George (see the previous walk). At the very beginning of

the street it is worth noticing the old marking of streets, Czech and German, painted on the facade of the Baroque Chapel of St John of Nepomuk (belonging to the St George Basilica). On the eastern facade of the same chapel a false window is painted, a typical expression of the Baroque illusionism.

Nearly in the middle of *Jiřská Street* we turn left to *Zlatá ulička u Daliborky* (Golden Lane at Daliborka). The lane creates something like a small square at this place. The houses here were built on lots bought from the St George Convent. (The Convent tried to buy them back later, since „the smoke from their chimneys displeases the whole convent".)

On the right side stand three originally Renaissance houses with fronts both facing *Jiřská Street* and *Golden Lane at Daliborka*. The largest of them is the **House Podybnikovský** (No 10/12). It has a Renaissance sgraffito facade and was built in 1561 by the court wheelwright Jan Milpoch. At the be-

Portico of the Home for Noble Women

The old street marking

ginning of the 17th century it was the property of Hans von Aachen, the court painter of Rudolf II. **The house** No 9/10 with a late Baroque facade from 1765 stands in place of the Romanesque Church of St John the Baptist destroyed during the fire of the Castle in 1541. **The House at St Florián** (No 8/8) from 1561 has a Baroque facade from the years 1710-12. Painted Renaissance ceilings are preserved inside. It is separated from the area of the Residence of the Highest Burgrave by the stairs connecting *Jiřská Street* with *Golden Lane at Daliborka*. The houses on the left side of *Golden Lane at Daliborka* are adjoined directly to the Convent of St George and are built alongside the Romanesque wall. The houses are these: the **House U modré koule** (At the Blue Ball, No 32) built in the second half of the 16th century by the „rifle maker and locksmith of His Imperial Majesty" Jiří Schmidthammer. The next **house** No 31 was built in 1562 by Oldřich Hagle, the baker of Archduke Ferdinand of Tyrol, the **House U kamenného stolu** (At the Stone Table, No 30) was built in the second half of the 16th century by Markus Rumpolt, the personal cook of Archduke Ferdinand of Tyrol. The north facade of these three houses faces *Golden Lane.*

Golden Lane and the northern fortifications of the Castle

We turn through the passageway between the House At the Stone Table and the next **house** No 11 to the most famous part of *Golden Lane.* The Lane is exceptional by its picturesqueness. There are many legends about it, according to which it was a residence of alchemists and a scene of many mysterious stories. The reality is, however, different. The lane came into existence on the site of the former moat of the northern Castle fortifications; on the south side it is bordered with houses whose facades are created by the Romanesque wall, on the north side behind the small houses towers the top of the moat wall built in the late Gothic by Benedict Ried. Achemists never lived here, in the 16th century, however, goldsmiths probably

Golden Lane

lived here, for the original name of the lane was Zlatnická (Of Goldsmiths'). In 1566 the Castle captain mentioned in his report 18 provisional houses, which were pulled down probably in the period of Rudolf II at the repair of the walls in 1591. Then the members of the Castle guard were accommodated in the lane according to the privilege of Rudolf II from 1597.

The lane was originally only one metre wide, since houses stood on both sides. Hygiene was rather difficult: there was only one privy for the whole lane. Cooking was done on open fires, so there was a constant threat of conflagration. Later the lane became a refuge for the poor. Its romantic spell was not appreciated until the 19th century. In the 20th century several well known personalities lived there. In winter in 1917 Franz Kafka had his study in the **house No 22**, and as did in the **house No 12** Jiří Mařánek, the writer of historical fiction, and where František Halas, Jaroslav Seifert, Vítězslav Nezval and other writers used to meet. According to the writer Gustav Meyrink, author of the famous novel about Golem, in the lane

exists the House At the Last Lantern, which cannot be seen by a human eye. In it the threshhold between the visible and the invisible worlds is hidden, which is the foundation stone of the mystical hidden town Sfér created by the esoteric order of the Asian brethren. In the **house No 14** used to live the Prague fortune teller Madame de Thebes, her real name was Matylda Průšová, who was killed during the War by the Gestapo for he prophesies about an early fall of the Third Empire.

We enter the **house No 24** standing nearly opposite the entrance to *Golden Lane*, and we get via the stairs into the long **defence corridor** sited on the moat wall of the late Gothic fortifications. Into the north wall of the corridor are built small loophole windows, into which rotating wooden drums are inserted with a slot for blunderbusses. In the late Gothic period such loopholes provided for the castle riflemen the highest possible protection against the fire of enemies. In the corridor is sited a very interesting exhibition of old weapons and armours and exhibits of period clothing. At the eastern

The moat wall of the northern fortification in the late Gothic style

1 - the level of the present Golden Lane
2 - the wall archs, to which the houses of
**   riflemen were built**
3 - the defensive corridor

end of the corridor one can try shooting at a target by a medieval crossbow.

At the western end the defence corridor leads to the first floor of the **White Tower**. It was built at the end of the 15th century by Benedict Ried as a part of the northern Castle fortifications. In 1585 the prison from the old White Tower was transferred here. In the basement used to be a dungeon, under which was another prison having the form of a narrow, completely dark pit. On the ground floor used to be a torture chamber. The two upper floors are equipped with loopholes and were used by the Castle riflemen.

Imprisoned in the tower were the achemist Edward Kelley, an adventurer who arrived at the court of Rudolf II from England, Rudolf's chamberlain Filip Lang and his successor Kašpar Rucký from Ruda, who hanged himself with the rope from the strongbox from which he had been stealing. Before their execution in the Old Town Square in 1621 the rebelious Czech noblemen Václav Budovec of Budov and Kašpar Kaplíř of Sulevice were imprisoned here. The Old Town prosecutor Martin Fruwein from Podolí, who was also imprisoned here, escaped during the journey to his interrogation, on to the roof of the tower and jumped to his death. Afterwards also his head, though posthumously, was severed from his neck and his body was quartered. Nowadays on the two upper floors of the tower are sited shops of replicas of historical weapons and tin figures. In the adjacent part of the defence corridor it is worth noticing the late Gothic privy (toilet) and also the exhibiton of medieval torturing instruments: we can see a rack, a wooden donkey with a sharp back on which the offenders were seated, an iron virgin, a Spanish foot and further instruments of the right of torture.

We return from the White Tower to *Golden Lane*. In the westward direction we can come to the moat **terrace above the Stag Moat**. On the other side of the *Stag Moat* we can see in *the Royal Garden* the southern facade of the Great Ball-game House and in the very east the building of the Royal Summerhouse.

From the terrace we come back to *Golden Lane* and go through it up to its eastern end. We go down the staircase of the **house No 12** onto the **terrace of the late Gothic fortifications** between the Daliborka Tower and the Black Tower. From the terrace one can see the lower part of the *Stag Moat*, directly under the terrace is the *Garden Na Opyši*.

The famous Tower **Daliborka** comes from 1496. Its builder Benedict Ried placed it on the slope above the Stag Moat,

Golden Lane

The terrace of the late Gothic fortification in front of the Daliborka Tower

which enabled its defenders very efficient shooting along the Castle fortifications. It was higher originally by two floors and connected to the White Tower by a defence corridor. Up to now five floors have been preserved. One can go down onto the fourth of them via a staircase covered by a high wooden ceiling. This floor was reserved for the Castle riflemen and it is lit by four small loopholes for blunderbusses. The transverse beams served for supporting weapons. The ceiling is missing, only the beams remained of it, and therefore from there one can see the present top floor, also without a ceiling, open to the roof. The basement is accessible via a small passage in the wall. It is vaulted by a massive five section vaulting and has four cells in the wall, into which cannons were placed. In the floor is a circular opening to the dungeon, on the vaulting one can see the pulley by means of which the prisoners were hauled down into the dungeon. Under the dungen is another deeper prison, accessible only through a hole in the ceiling.

The tower is called after the first of its prisoners, Dalibor of Kozojedy, who in 1496 took advantage of the uprising of his neighbour's serfs and welcomed them into his service. According to a legend he learned to play the violin in prison so that he could earn his own living. In fact however, in 1498, when he was thrown into the dungeon, violins were not known in Bohemia. The misunderstanding came obviously from the exchange of the word skřipky (violin) for the torturing instrument skřipec (the rack), on which the condemned was stretched and tortured till he „played" (i.e. talked). However the fact remains that many prisoners had to take care of their own living.

Jiřská Street again

From Daliborka we come back onto the terrace of the late Gothic fortifications, from where we come to the courtyard of the area of the **Nejvyšší purkrabství** (Residence of the Highest Burgrave). The two

The fortification near the Daliborka

The Residence of the Highest Burgrave

storey Renaissance main building is ended by Renaissance gables, nearly in the middle of the southern front a staircase tower is attached. At present the area is used for occassional exhibitions, also the **Museum of Toys** is sited here.

The highest Burgrave of the Czech Kingdom was the highest country official who represented the King, when he was not present. In his palace up to 1783 the Burgrave Court had sessions and in the adjacent courtyard even executions were carried out. Probably the oldest part of the palace is the preserved part of the Romanesque tower built by the northern wall of the Castle. In the 1330s the Palace of the Burgrave served as a temporary residence of Prince Charles (the later King and Emperor Charles IV) at the time when the Royal Palace was being rebuilt. During the fire of the Castle in 1541 the building burnt down and it was rebuilt in the Renaissance style by the Italian architect Giovanni Ventura. Between 1961-63 the object was reconstructed for the needs of the House of the Czechoslovak Children; some parts were demolished and

replaced by modern buildings. A part of the interiors was preserved in the original form, a part was newly equipped. (Their decorations were partly influenced by the ideological requirements of various artistic committees. The censorship interferences were dangerous even for the outstanding statue The Youth by Miloš Zet, standing outside the palace. According to the decision of a censorship committe this statue of a nude boy was deprived of the genitals, which were given back to it only after the shame at the ceremonial unveiling the statue.) In one of the buildings of the area lived the poet Jaroslav Seifert for a short time.

A part of the Burgrave Residence area is also the **Black Tower** coming from the Romanesque fortifications of the Castle. Originally (till the middle of the 13th century) the eastern Castle gate used to go through it. Under Charles IV its roof was gilded and it was called Golden, it got its present name after the fire which blackened its masonry.

The eastern gate to Prague Castle and the Black Tower

The Black Tower

The gate to the area of the Residence of the Highest Burgrave

In the 16th century a debtors prison was in the tower. Compared to the criminal prisoners the debtors were regarded as „superior" prisoners. They could bring their own quilts, have visits and write letters. They still had to provide their own food, perphaps by begging. At one time paradoxically the creditor himself had the responsibility for supplying food and if the prisoner starved to death, the creditor had to fast as a punishment. In 1573 the nobleman Bavor Rodovský of Hustiřany was imprisoned here, an adventurous figure of the Rudolfine Prague. He busied himself with alchemy and in prison translated foreign documents, which he donated to his patron Vilém of Rožmberk. In the light of his situation it is surely a testimony to his sense of humor that when he wrote the dedication in his work he used the words „Given at Prague Castle". Apart from alchemist tractates he wrote a treatise giving 35 reasons why one should drink a spirit which he himself made and called „Eau de vie". However, the book that made him most famous was „Cookery, a book about varied foods."

The Residence of the Burgrave is separated from *Jiřská Street* by a wall, in which is a **gate** decorated from the outside by four stone coats of arms belonging to the Highest Burgraves Adam of Valdštejn (on the left), Jaroslav Bořita of Martinice (on the right), Jan Josef of Vrtba (down in the middle) and Karel Egon of Fürstenberk (up in the middle).

Opposite the area of the Residence of the Highest Burgrave at the end of *Jiřská Street* stands the **Lobkovic Palace**, an extensive complex of buildings around two inner courtyards. In the second half of the 16th century it belonged to the Krajíř family of Krajek, from 1554 to the Pernštejn family, and from 1627 to the Lobkovic family. In the 1570s the Renaissance palace was extended, gained the present Baroque form between 1651-68, when it was rebuilt by Carl Lurag for Prince Václav Eusebius of Lobkovice. Two halls and a chapel on the level of the first floor were preserved in the original form. Both the entrances are bordered by

The coat of arms of the Lords of Šternberk
on the wall of the Highest Burgrave Residence

The eastern gate in the late Gothic style;
a barbican on the site of the present open space
in front of the Old Castle Stairs

pilasters ended by ionic heads with veils. Nowadays the Palace is used by the National Museum for the permanent exhibition the Monuments of the National History, for occasional exhibitions and concerts.

Jiřská Street is enclosed by the Renaissance **eastern gate** to Prague Castle with a preserved small Gothic gate for pe-destrians. Outside the entrance to the Castle originally used to be a moat and a protruding Gothic fortification - a barbican. In the gate itself are preserved the pulleys which served for lowering the drawbridge. Nowadays in place of the barbican is a small open area by which the *Old Castle Stairs* begin. However we are standing on the place which was dealt in the Introductory walk of this guide book.

Seventh walk:

FROM THE GARDEN AT THE BASTION TO THE STAG MOAT AND ACROSS THE POWDER BRIDGE TO THE NORTHERN FOREFIELD OF PRAGUE CASTLE

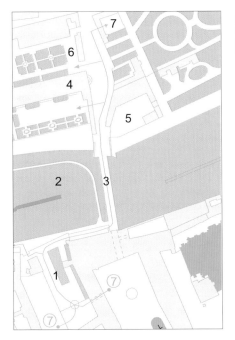

The fourth courtyard and the Garden At the Bastion

To the left from the main (west) entrance to the Castle behind the bar gate in the vicinity of the Archibishop Palace there is the so called *fourth courtyard*, in fact it is rather a small yard, adjacent from the ouside to the northern protruding part of the *first courtyard* and to a part of the western wing of the *second courtyard*, with which its is connected by a passage. It is only the height level which separates this courtyard from the higher lying Garden *At the Bastion*.

West of this place used to lead the first Castle moat, the natural Hradčany furrow, across which led a bridge, by which used to stand the first gate to the Castle. The moat was filled only during the rebuilding of the Castle under Maria Theresa in the second half of the 18th century. Later the main

1 - the Garden At the Bastion
2 - the Upper Stag Moat
3 - the Powder Bridge
4 - the Riding School

5 - the Stable Court
6 - the Riding School Court
7 - the Lion Court

The fourth courtyard, in the background the Garden At the Bastion

route connecting *Hradčany Square* with the Powder Bridge led through this place. The park in front of the outer entrance to the Spanish Hall was founded in 1861 in connection with the preparations for the (not realized) coronation of Emperor Franz Josef I as Czech King.

We come to the Garden *At the Bastion* from the *fourth courtyard* via a remarkable **circular staircase** by Josip Plečnik. is also the author of the present form of the garden, which he modified in 1930. The first geometrically regular part of the garden is created by yew trees inside circular stone bordering, the areas inside are sprinkled with white gravel. The second less strict part is enlivened by solitary trees, the most interesting of them from the botanical viewpoint is the weeping form of pagoda tree. There are also the foundations of a **bastion** from the period of the last Přemyslides, which was used in the late Gothic period as an artillery base for bombarding the west forefield of the Castle.

The foundations of the Přemyslide bastion were discovered in front of the Rococo entrance to the Spanish Hall. According to the recommendation of the committee for historical monuments Josip Plečnik was to leave them open and freely accessible, which however interfered with his original conception of the lay-out of the gardens. He fulfilled the recommendation in this way: He placed a pergola with overhanging flowers on the uncovered foundations and led the access to the bastion via separate stones placed in the distance of one step between them. This created the impression of a Japanese garden, which otherwise was not close to Plečnik's Classicist aesthetic feeling.

An ashlar stone wall separates the garden from the garden of the Archbishop Palace. The Restaurant At the Bastion going through the wall does not belong to Plečnik's conception of the garden and it was built between 1957-58. In the north the garden is bordered by the impressive Plečnik **ballustrade** above the *Stag Moat*.

The Plečnik pergola above the Přemyslide bastion

Stag Moat

One can descend into the upper *Stag Moat* via Plečnik's stairs in the north-western corner of the garden. Its roughly worked stones are in contrast with the Classicist garden and thus symbolically suggest the descend from the antique brightness into the mythical Underworld.

The Stag Moat is in fact a deep ravine, through which the Brusnice stream flows. It goes along the whole length of the Castle and the northern forefield of the Hradčany Town, where in the west it continues as the *Novosvětský příkop* (New World Moat). Until the end of the Middle Ages it provided the Castle with a perfect, natural fortification, though without any doubt artificially modified. With the development of artillery the moat lost gradually its millitary significance, and therefore it could be spanned by a bridge, which was later called Prašný (The Powder Bridge). Then above the northern slope the northern forefield of

the Castle and the extensive *Royal Garden* were established.

There was an attempt to found a garden also in the moat itself, which however could not succeed in the shady and humid environment near the Brusnice streem. In the vicinity of the Daliborka Tower at the eastern end of the Castle in the moat a brickworks was founded, where bricks as well as decorative terracotta parts for the Pernštejn Palace in *Jiřská Street* were made. From the time of Emperor Rudolf II the moat was used also as a deer park, from which the present name comes. The game rearing was not without problems; the sparcely overgrown slopes provided little food, which had to be brought, and moreover the Castle inhabitants frightened the deer by throwing waste into the moat (for this reason not because of the defence reasons the wall in *Golden Lane* had to be hightened). Deer was kept here till 1743, when it was completely slaughtered and eaten by the French troops occupying Prague.

The ballustrade above the Stag Moat

The Statue The Night Watchman in the Stag Moat

When in 1770 the Powder Bridge was replaced by a mound, the *Stag Moat* was divided into two parts, the upper one and the lower one. During time tall trees grew in it, and so the *Stag Moat* became and has remained until now a unique piece of free nature inside the city. Later the Brusnice streem was regulated and a part of it flows through pipes. Into the eastern part of the lower moat after 1832 a bend of *Chotkova Road* was included, a new access road to Prague Castle. In the upper moat a bear park was founded in 1920, where bears were kept that President T. G. Masaryk obtained as a gift from the Czechoslovak legionnaires. Above the north slope Josip Plečnik built a viewing terrace, a favourite spot of President Masaryk. Fortunately, the plans to use the *Stag Moat* for building a road and a tram track were not carried out.

An old water tunnel decorated by a small fountain leads to the upper *Stag Moat* below the Šternberk Palace. A little further on is sited a statue of a Night Watchman by František Úprka donated to President T. G. Masaryk as a birthday gift, and at the west end the moat is enclosed by tennis courts. In the lower moat is placed an obelisk by Pavel Janák erected in remembrance of the victims of the May Uprising Against Fascism in 1945. In the 1950s an access route was led from the bottom of the Moat into the bunker built under the Castle. The upper *Stag Moat* is open for the public, the opening of the lower moat (probably from the *Royal Garden* and *Chotkova Road*) is being prepared. It is planned that both moats (in the future perhaps connected by a passageway in the dividing mound of the Powder Bridge) will remain an open natural area without any unnecessary interventions.

Powder Bridge

One can come from the Garden *At the Bastion* along the front of the northern

---

137

The Stag Moat

wing via **Plečnik's Bridge** above the slope of the *Stag Moat* to the Baroque **Pacassi Gate**. It was built into the northern wing of the *second courtyard* at the time of the rebuilding of the Castle under Maria Theresa. (Deeper in the passageway to the *second courtyard* one can see the remnants of the Renaissance gate.) We, however, turn to the left and cross the *Stag Moat* via the **Powder Bridge** to the northern forefield of Prague Castle. It has not been a real bridge but a mound since the time of Maria Theresa, from which a unique view of the Cathedral of St Vitus and the massive late Gothic fortifications of the Castle with the Mihulka Tower is opened.

The bridge was built between 1534-40 in connection with the founding of the *Royal Garden* above the northern slope of the lower *Stag Moat*. In 1541 it was seriously damaged by a fire, but already in 1545 it was completed again. It was covered and had two floors; the wooden passage on the lower floor served for the

common use and the upper passage to the ruler, who did not wish to be disturbed. It ended 12 feet in front of the gate, from where it was completed with a drawbridge.

The bridge was not well kept; in 1549 the Latin poet and preacher Simon Fagullus Boček even fell through it and died as a result of his fall. From 1564 when the Royal Summerhouse was being completed, a covered wooden passageway led from the private exit from the bridge to the Summerhouse so that the ruler could walk from the Castle to the Summerhouse protected against the weather. Later the bridge was repaired several times. In 1742 during the French occupation of Prague the roof of the wooden bridge was covered by a layer of fresh dung, which protected it against fire.

In 1757 during the Prussian siege of Prague, the bridge was set on fire by a bomb and seriously damaged. Therefore a few years later (1769-70) it was replaced by the present mound. The five stone pillars, however, remained preserved in the

The Gallery of the Riding Room

The garden on the terrace of the Riding School

mound, though their upper part was demolished in 1987 at the building of a collector. The separate pillars and the stonework of the barbican are marked by different colours of the paving. The remnants of the drawbridge by the Pacassi Gate were removed in 1876 (even in 1854 a so called wolf pit was was dug out in front of the bridge because of greater safety).

Northern forefield of the Castle

Behind the Powder bridge used to be a barbican with a guard room, further on is the Street *U Prašného mostu* (At the Powder Bridge).

On the left we can see the **Baroque Jízdárna** (Riding School) built between 1694-95 to a design by Jean Baptist Mathey. Some time later a narrow gallery was built next to the Riding School, which faces the street only by blind windows, whereas the real arcade windows on the opposite side served as a viewing

place of the summer Riding School. The building of the Riding School with the narrow gallery was converted into exhibition premises in 1949, in place of the summer riding school garages were built. The garage roofs were modified in 1952 by the Castle architect Pavel Janák into a garden viewing terrace called **the Garden On the Terrace at the Riding School**. This garden designed in the style of Baroque gardens is the youngest garden at the Castle and provides us with an unusual view over the *Stag Moat* of Prague Castle and Hradčany.

In 1723, behind the Riding School a huge **wooden theatre** was built, where on the occasion of the coronation of Charles IV an opera „Constanza e fortezza" by Jan Josef Fux was staged. The stage designer was the famous creator of stage sets, the architect Giuseppe Galli Bibiena. The extensive scenic backdrops fastened to rotating boards like pages in a book, introduced the feeling of space with the ideal Roman architecture, gardens and military encampements. The stage design of this production has never received proper recognition for its unique contribution to Prague's theathrical history.

Opposite the Riding School, on the right side of the street is the **Stable Courtyard** (No 49/2). It includes also the house of a bricklayer foreman (in the past there lived the administrator of the Ballgame House), the Small Ball-game House converted under Emperor Leopold I in 1680 into a theatre, at the end of the 18th century into stables and during World War II into garages. A part of the object is also a Renaissance house, originally the theatre of Emperor Rudolf II, which was connected by a covered passage with the passageway leading from the Powder Bridge to the Royal Garden. The preserved part of this passage leads between the **house of the gardener** (No 50/6) and the former Small Ball-game House. Behind the stable courtyard is sited the main entrance to the Royal Garden, whose visit will be the theme of the next walk.

Further on on the left side of the street (behind the Riding School) we can see the gate leading to the **Riding School Courtyard**. From the end of the 16th century here used to stand a carpenter yard established in place of a vineyard. Later stables, residential and out-buildings were built here. The hunter's house (at present the seat of the fire unit) and a stable with a smithy (at present workshops and stores) were preserved.

West of the Riding School Courtyard lies a place one time called the Smaller Royal Mountain or the Smaller Kingdom (probably because King Vladislav Jagellon bought the vineyards here). The plots were united by Emperor Rudolf II in 1594 into the so called *New Garden*, where he had a pond established and in 1601 had „several rooms for large birds" (perhaps eagles) built. In 1604 at this place he founded a **pheasant pharm.**

The Renaissance House of the gardener

For rearing pheasants the so called pheasant chamber was built, in the pond swans, later geese and ducks, were kept. From 1650 also partridges were kept here and the house for „large birds" was adapted for the attendant of the pheasants and partridges. Also a pond from the 16th century has been preserved, into which water was brought by wooden pipes from the ponds in the village Liboc and which was also a source of water for general use for the Castle. The pheasant farm became twice a camping site of the armies of occupation (in 1649 the Swedish and between 1741-42 the French camped here) and it was always damaged and the birds eaten. In the second half of the 18th century Karel von Cramerius hired the pheasant farm, who here and also in other lands founded mulberry tree plantations for keeping the silkworm.

On the west the *Lumbe Gardens* are attached to the pheasant farm, founded after 1852, when the Prague surgeon Karel Lumbe began to buy small gardens

The gate to the Riding School court

and vineyards above the western end of the upper *Stag Moat* and in the *New World Moat*. In 1925 the Office of the President bought these gardens from Lumbe's heirs and established garden centres in most of them.

On the right side of the street we notice the building of the **Lion Court**, built under Emperor Rudolf II between 1581-83 by Ulricho Avostalis in place of a wooden court founded by Emperor Ferdinand I Hapsburg.

Around the court stood a gallery for spectators, in heated pens apart from lions three leopards (the gift of the Russian Tsar Fiodor I, son of Ivan the Terrible), a tiger (the gift of Ferdinand Medici, the Duke of Florence), an orang-utan and other wild animals were kept here. In the orchard behind the court allegedly parrots used to sit on branches fastened by golden chains so that they could not fly away. Emperor Rudolf II had a special care taken of the lion with the name Mohamed (the gift of the Turkish sultan)

that according to Kepler's horoscope had the same star constellation as the Emperor himself. The fact is that the Emperor died only a few days after the death of his favourite lion. Later the Lion Court had less animals, often only one bear was kept. The story about a lady who dropped a glove into a cage with lions and about a gentleman who brought it back, was put into verses by Friedrich Schiller.

The keeping of predatory beasts was ended in the Lion Court before the middle of the 18th century. Between 1967-72 the essentially Renaissance object was converted into a restaurant with a garden in place of a free range of the beasts.

The western forefield of the Castle was enclosed in the Street *At the Powder Bridge* by the gate through which led the path to the **Mariánské šance** (Mary's Fortification), a part of the massive Baroque fortifications of Prague. Together with the watchhouse it was pulled down in 1791 in connection with extending the

The roof of the Lion Court

A detail of the decorative grill of the entrance to the Royal Garden

road at the preparations for the coronation of Emperor Leopold II. Today there is the street *Mariánské hradby* (Mary's Walls) with a tram traffic leading to the Small Quarter or in the opposite direction to Pohořelec Square to the Strahov Monastery.

However, we can stay in Prague Castle and see its gardens.

Eighth walk:

THROUGH THE ROYAL GARDEN

The Royal Garden

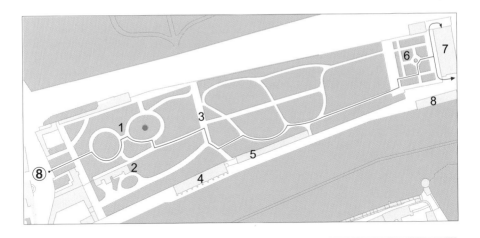

1 - the terrace with the ballustrade
2 - the Presidential Villa
3 - the central place
4 - the Great Ball-game House

5 - the orangerie
6 - the giardinetto
7 - the Royal Summerhouse
8 - the fig house

The grill gate to the Royal Garden

The sculptural decoration of the ballustrade

Our walks through the Prague gardens will lead mainly through the decorative gardens, especially through the park (a garden with trees) and the flower garden. These gardens were created according to the style requirements and the principles of the gardening art in various periods. They appeared at Prague Castle first at the beginning of the Renaissance. However, much earlier in the Castle vicinity existed productive gardens, an orchard, a flower garden and a herb garden (growing medicinal herbs and spices). According to a legend the oldest productive garden connected with the Castle is the **Vineyard of St Wenceslas** near the present *Old Castle Stairs*, we have already mentioned in the introductory walk of this guidebook. Even nowadays Prague Castle has a productive garden; it is the garden centre in the Lumbe Garden above the upper Stag Moat.

Royal Garden

The oldest and the largest decorative garden of Prague Castle is the *Royal Garden* founded in 1534 by Ferdinand I Hapsburg above the northern slope of the Stag Moat. The main entrance to the garden leads from the west from the Street *At the Powder Bridge*, the rear (east) entrance leads from the Street *Mary's Walls* to the Royal Summerhouse. The north gate from the Street *Mary's Walls* is usually closed.

On the site of the garden used to be vineyards which the Emperor gradually bought from their owners (he promised to give each year a barrel of wine to the Convent of St George for the vineyard). The building of the garden continued slowly at the beginning, however the garden grew gradually and acquired a Renaissance appearance. Many valuable plants and trees and shrubs were planted in it; from 1563 tulips were grown here, for the first time in Europe,

The ballustrade with a fountain

even before their spread to the Netherlands. The Emperor got their bulbs from Constantinopolis. In greenhouses, an orangerie and a fig house tropical plants were planted; citruses, pomegranates and figs were grown here. At that time (and during nearly the whole 17th century) foreign fruits and vegetables were sent from the Royal Garden onto the Emperor's table in Vienna. The governor Ferdinand of Tyrol took great care of the garden, in whose service was also the significant Italian physician and botanist Petr Ondřel Matthioli, the author of the famous Herb book. Also Emperor Maxmilián II and namely Rudolf II liked the garden. Damage was caused to it during the Thirthy Years War, it reached a new bloom in the last quarter of the 17th century. In the 1730s and 1740s it was changed into a Baroque garden in the cooperation of the gardener František Zinner Jr, the sculptor Matyáš Bernard Braun and the architect Kilián Ignác Dietzenhofer.

The garden was seriously damaged at the beginning of the reign of Empress Maria Theresa; during the French-Prussian occupation in 1741 perhaps only three dozen carefully chosen grown pineaples saved the garden from destroying, since the then gardener gave them to the Prussian general Püller accommodated in the Royal Summerhouse and then he commanded his soldiers to spare the garden.

At the end of the 18th century and mainly at the beginning of the 19th century the ornamental Baroque flowerbeds were being abolished and the garden began to be changed into an English park. At present three garden styles can be seen in the garden: a Renaissance garden in the giardinetto by the Royal Summerhouse, a Baroque garden in the flowerbeds in the western part and an English park in most of the eastern part.

The main entrance, the **bar gate** with gilded details, was established in 1742 in place of the former Poultry Court. From

A Baroque niche with a fountain

The Presidential Villa viewed from the southern tower of the St Vitus Cathedral

the gate between the Lion Court on the left and the Renaissance houses of the Stable Court on the right leads a short avenue of shaped chestnuts, nowadays domesticated in Bohemia, but one time regarded as foreign. This entrance part, decorated with Baroque flowerbeds, is enclosed by a **terrace with a ballustrade** and Baroque sculptures of playing children and lions coming from the workshop of Matyáš Bernard Braun from the 1730s. Nearby both ends of the ballustrade grow two valuable specimen of magnolia. On a lower lewel below the terrace is sited a circular fountain and behind it are grown beeches and in the southeast direction is a Chinese metasequoia. In the period of Rudolf II here used to be a skittle alley. Left of the terrace stands an **Empire greenhouse** from 1820, on the right the **Presidential Villa**.

The central wing of the Presidential Villa is created by a Baroque pavilion, originally the core of a greenhouse built in 1731 by Kilián Ignác Dientzenhofer. The greenhouse was completely destroyed by the Prussian bombardment of Prague in 1757, only its middle part remained, rebuilt in 1791 into a summerhouse with an upstairs. Between 1947-49 side residential wings were built next to it.

Approximately in one third the garden is divided by the so called **middle place**, bordered by a low wall and grown lime and chestnut trees. From 1604 here used to be a playground for ball games. The dominant of this place is a Baroque niche with a fountain decorated by an early Baroque statue of Hercules fighting with a dragon, a work of Jan Jiří Bendl from 1670. From there you can see the Royal Summerhouse directly.

On the right side stands the Renaissance **Great Ball-game House** built between 1567-69 by the architect Bonifác Wolmut.

At the time of its origin the Great Ball-game House was the third building in Prague Castle designed „For the noble sport of bend-

The top of a Baroque niche,
a detail with the initials
of Emperor Leopold II

The Great Ball-game House

ing the body". A leather ball was used here, only sometimes a bladder, or a game with rackets and a shuttlecock was played, a predecesor of the present badminton. In the Baroque period it was rebuilt into a stable and a riding school, in the period of the rule of Emperor Josef II (from the 1780s) it became an army store, at the end of the World War II it was seriously damaged by artillery bombardment. The reconstruction was completed in 1952 by the architect Pavel Janák.

The Great Ball-game House is a typical example of the Renaissance architecture influenced by the Italian models. The greatest care was taken of its long northern front, whereas the southern front directly above the slope of the *Stag Moat* has only a facade with illusively worked ashlar stones. The northern side is divided by massive sandstone semipillars whose heads bear the heavy main beam. The walls with the built-in large arches of the windows, are decorated by a rich sgraffito decoration - both ornamental

and figural. On the sides of the archs below the ledge are always painted two allegorical figures symbolising the elements, virtues and arts. A rarity is, that between these allegorical figures the restorer has included in the 1950s two girls with a sickle and a hammer, an allegory of „The socialist five year plan" declared by the Communist regime. The interior of the Ball-game House was divided during the last reconstruction into the middle hall and two vestibules, the ferroconcrete vaulting is a copy of the damaged original Renaissance vaulting. At present the building is used for occasional exhibitions, concerts and festive meetings.

In front of the Ball-game House is placed the **sculptural group of Night** by Matyáš Bernard Braun from 1734; its opposite, the sculptural group of Day, was destroyed by the Prussian bombardment in 1757. The narrow space of the **shooting range** was attached to the Ball-game House in the longitudanal axis in the west di-

*The Allegory of the five years plan
on the facade of the Great Ball-game House*

Water flows from the figure of a piper placed on the top of the fountain, it falls on the upper bowl supported by figures and from there it falls on the lower bowl. We can hear the noise of the drops falling on the bell-metal „singing" best just under this bowl.

Behind the Renaissance giardinetto stands the noble architecture of the **Royal Summerhouse**, the purest Italian Renaissance building north of the Alps.

Emperor Ferdinand I Hapsburg had the Summerhouse built according to the design of Paolo della Stella. It was built between 1538 to 1560. By 1550 the ground floor and the arcade gallery including the rich relief decoration were completed. The first floor was built by Hans Tirol and Bonifác Wolmut after 1552, the unique roof covered by copper plates was built before 1560. After 1648 the Summerhouse was plundered by the Swedish, however, the decision of Emperor Joseph II became fateful for it; he gave it into the use of the army in the 1780s. An artilery laboratory was founded here. After moving it away in connection with the coronation of Ferdinand V as Czech King the military administration left the house, and so it could be renewed in 1863 (the monumental inner staircase was built, which changed the character of the ground floor considerably). Further modifications were carried out between 1928-30 and 1952-55.

rection, which was converted into stables at the time of the coronation of Charles VI in 1723. In the east the orangerie was adjoined to the Ball-game House, which in the period of Rudolf II served for growing oranges and mainly lemons, which at that time were pickled into salt and regarded as a medicine. In the 1950s a part of the orangerie was converted into a greenhouse.

From the middle place to the east lies the **English Park**; among its most interesting trees are a tuliptree, a Turkish hazel, a ginkgo.

The eastest part of the Royal Garden is made by a typical **Reanissance giardinetto**. It was built by Pavel Janák according to a model of the significant Renaissance architect Sebastian Serli in place of the original giardinetto, removed in 1820. In the middle of the giardinetto stands the famous **Singing Fountain** cast according to the model of Francesco Terzio by Tomáš Jaroš between 1564-68.

The Summerhouse is wrongly called Belvedere, this name was transfered on the Summerhouse from the demolished Belvedere built by the Černín family on the near Letná slope. The name coming from the Romanticism is acceptable: The Summerhouse of the Queen Anne, the beloved wife of Emperor Ferdinand I Hapsburg, who gave to his husband fifteen children. The royal pair is portrayed on the western front (facing the giardinetto) in the relief between the se-

The Royal Summerhouse
The lower part of the English park and the Renaissance giardinetto

cond and the third arch of the arcades (from the left side): The Emperor is giving a rich fig twig to his wife. The building meant as a recreation place with a ball room on the first floor served in the period of Rudolf II also as an astronomical observatory; from whose gallery together with the Emperor the court astronomer Tycho Brahe observed the stars.

The building is surrounded by arcades with rich figural and ornamental relief decoration drawing on themes from mythology, history, and from hunting and genre subjects. The remarkable Renaissance roof was designed in the shape of a ship's hull turned upside down and covered with copper plates.

This new construction solution of roofs was really inspired by building ship keels. It was introduced into architecture by the ship builder Philibert L'Orme, whose book „The instructions how to build cheaply instead of stone and brick vaultings, wooden vaultings" is owned by the State Library in Klementinum (it is

one of the three preserved copies). The keel system was applied to the Summerhouse probably thanks to Queen Anne, who admired it during her visit to Paris.

On the ground floor of the Summerhouse (Belvedere) are two halls with the original Renaissance vaultings and a monumental staircase. The first floor consists of a single hall with a wooden panel ceiling in the style of barrel vaulting. The walls are decorated by paintings from the 19th century on the themes from the Czech history. At present the Royal Summerhouse serves mainly for exhibitions.

In front of the northern front of the Summerhouse stands a **statue of Victory** by Jan Štursa, on the slope below the Summerhouse we can see the remnants of the **fig house** (originally with a roof that could be dismantled) built in the second half of the 16th century. An interesting view opens for us over the *Stag Moat* of the eastern part of the north-

The Singing Fountain

Emperor Ferdinand I Hapsburg and Queen Anne, the relief on the facade of the Royal Summerhouse

ern fortifications of the Castle with the Daliborka Tower.

In the past the *Royal Garden* continued even behind the Summerhouse, where was originally a tilt-yard for tournaments of knights, later a pen for timber.

Between 1833-41 this part of the garden was separated by the governor Karel Chotek for a public park, later called *Chotkovy sady* (the Chotek Park). We went through its corners, however, in the introductory walk of this guide.

Ninth walk:

THROUGH THE SOUTHERN GARDENS OF PRAGUE CASTLE

The decorative bowl in the Garden of Eden

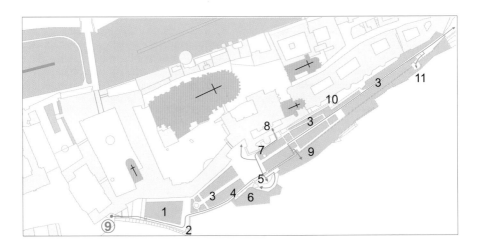

1 - the Garden of Eden
2 - the Mathias Pavilion
3 - the Garden Na Valech
4 - the louk-out pavilion
5 - the semicircular louk-out place
6 - the Hartig Garden

7 - the obelisks
8 - the southern court
   of the Old Royal Palace
9 - the Alpine rockery
10 - the Bellevue Pavilion
11 - the Moravian Bastion

It is possible to enter the gardens on the southern slope from three sides: from the east through the gate (near the end of the *Old Castle Stairs*), through the Plečnik Bull Staircase from the *thrird courtyard,* or through the main entrance from the west from *Hradčany Square* (from the end of the Castle Stairs). We choose the last possibility.

The western entrance to the gardens leads through the brick protective wall built between 1849-50 for fear of repeating the revolutionary upheavals in 1848. Josip Plečnik built into it an original **portal** supported by one Doric pillar. In this way he removed the impression of austerity and closeness which the wall evoked and by the small reminder of the Antiquity he suggested the contrast between the sunny southern gardens and the originally medieval walls of the roayl residence.

The entrance to the southern gardens of Prague Castle

The garden of Eden

Immediately behind the entrance we come onto a landing with a decorative sandstone statue in a niche. From here the **monumental stairs** become wider and lead down. The stairs make up a substantial part of the *Garden of Eden.*

In place of the *Garden of Eden* stood originally a protruding fortification of the Castle with mounds and moats. In 1547 Archduke Ferdinand of Tyrol became governor of the lands of the Czech crown. Above the southern slope of the Castle he built his palace residence called the New House of Archduke Ferdinand and later he decided to found a private garden below it for his own pleasure. In 1559 the western part of the moats was filled on his order (partly by rubble from the large fire of the Castle in 1541) and three years later, in 1562 the Archduke founded a terraced garden separated from the *Castle Stairs* by a wall

built by Bonifác Wolmut. At the turn of the 18th and 19th centuries the garden was slightly extended, in 1823 and between 1846-47 it was modified into an English park. After the formation of the Czechoslovak Republic in 1918 a decision was taken to convert the *Garden of Eden* (together with the Garden *Na Valech*) into a private space for the President. The Slovenian architecht Josip Plečnik began the work in 1920.

Into the **hall under the stair**s (at present used for occasional exhibitions) and into the so called Wine Cellars under the southern wing of the *first courtyard* leads a narrow flight of stairs along the southern facade. The entrance into the basement is emphasised by a square bowl of a black stone and a **small fountain** with a bronze gargoyle.

On the grassy surface under the monumental stairs in place of the original Baroque fountain stands a forty tons weighing **decorative bowl** hewn out of a single

The Mathias Pavilion

The statue of the Good Shepherd near the Mathias Pavilion

block of granite from Mrákotín according to the design of Josip Plečnik.

The bowl symbolising the earthly female principle was originally to be a contrast to the monolithic obelisk which was to stand on the monumental stairs. This obelisk (on whose top an eternal light and a statue of the Czech lion with the Slovak cross were to be placed) was to symbolise beside the state symbols also the heavenly male principle. Unfortunately, a monolith of the required height could not be get, and so after years of waiting Plečnik abandoned its erecting. The reminder of Plečnik's grand scheme became the smaller monolith subsequently placed in the *third courtyard* of the Castle.

In the southeastern corner of the garden, directly above the *Castle Stairs* we can see the **Mathias Pavilion** completed in 1617 for Emperor Mathias. The small cylindrical building with a pointed roof with Mathias' initials on the top has

a wooden Renaissance ceiling decorated by the 39 emblems of the lands of the Emperor's empire. The decorative painting on the walls was created by Josef Matěj Navrátil in 1848. The modification of the surroundings of the Pavilion is by Josef Plečnik, who also had the bronze statue of the Good Shephard by Josef Kalvoda from 1922 placed on the wall. Nearby grows a hundreds years old yew, the oldest tree in the Castle gardens.

The Mathias Pavilion is sometimes mistaken for the **Trumpeter Tower**, which was built in the garden by Ferdinand of Tyrol in 1562 as a small garden summerhouse. Under Rudolf II trumpets were blown here on various festive occassions and at midday at the time of the Emperor's lunch. It is said that in 1611, when Rudolf II fell ill, the trumpeters were blowing and singing the words of the Psalm Miserere Deus, however not because of Emperor's illness, as the passers-by believed,

The Baroque fountain in the Garden Na Valech

The look-out pavilion

but they wanted to recover their wages they had not got for a long time. In 1724 the tower was pulled down, because there was danger it could tumble down, and its foundations were covered at the Plečnik modifications to the Garden of Eden.

Not far from the Trumpeter Tower used to stand **Emperor's Bath**. In 1721 its equipment was found outdated and unsuitable for the temporary stay of Empress Elizabeth Christine on her way to Karlovy Vary. Therefore the three ells deep embedded tin bathtub was smelted and the material was used for the production of candelabra and chamber pots prepared for the coronation of Emperor Charles VI in 1723.

The Garden Na Valech

The *Garden of Eden* ends by the Mathias Summerhouse and further on along the southern front of the Castle runs the narrow strip of the Garden *Na Valech*.

The Garden *Na Valech* also lies in place of the filled mounds of the southern fortifications of Prague Castle. After the rebuilding of the Castle under Maria Theresa in the second half of the 18th century an avenue was founded here connecting the *Garden of Eden* with the bastion under the Black Tower at the eastern end of the Castle. Then on the mounds first gardens were founded, namely below the Home for Noble Women and below the Lobkovic Palace. The whole space was modified in 1861 into the form of an English park in connection with the prepared, however not carried out, coronation of Emperor Franz Josef I as Czech King. The present shape of the gardens is (except for smaller modifications) the work of Josip Plečnik.

At the beginning of the garden in the middle of a regularly divided flowerbed is placed a **Baroque fountain** from 1703, transferred here from the *Garden of Eden*, where it was replaced by the above mentioned decorative bowl, whose

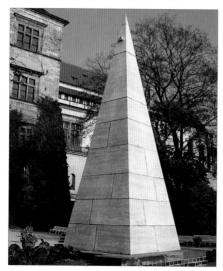

*The limestone pyramid in front
of the semicircular look-out place*

The Musical Pavilion in the Hartig Garden

robustness corresponded better to the scale of the monumental stairs. From the fountain the garden is divided along the whole lenth by a direct **viewing path** with large stretches of a lawn with grown trees. Among the botanical curiosities are mainly the pagoda tree, the Chinese metasequoia, the Paulownia, the catalpa, the weeping beech, the Turkish hazel and the tuliptree. The impressive panorama of Prague with the Small Quarter roofs and church towers and cupolas inspired Josip Plečnik to lower the protective wall and to modify newly its top. In this way he created a viewing terrace nearly along the whole length of the garden complemented by several viewing buildings. The first of them is the **Look-out Pavilion** also called the small belvedere. Its granite pillars are complemented by heads of white marble, and also the window sill plates between the pillars are of the same material. A little further to the east Plečnik placed a **semicircular look-out place** with a thin limestone pyramid on the remnants of the old bastion. From the look-out we can see the wide panorama of the Small Quarter, which is dominated by the copper cupola and the belfry of the Baroque Church of St Nicolas. However, we can also see the towers of the other Small Quarter churches, mainly of the Church of St Thomas, the Church of the Victorious Virgin Mary, the Church of the Virgin Mary and St Kayetan. In the background behind the row of the roofs we can see the slopes of Petřín. Unfortunately, the look-out place has not been preserved in the original form and it was rebuilt in the 1960s. The limestone pyramid itself reminds us probably intentionally by its whiteness and shape of the octagonal endings of the towers of the Basilica of St George. It stands directly on the line between the Bull Staircase from the *third courtyard* and the Baroque cupola of the Small Quarter Church of St Nicolas, with which the sharpness of the pyramid is in contrast. Directly under the look-out place one can see the garden of the Thun Palace modified into the form of an English park.

The Bull Staircase (on the left) and the protruding Ludvík wing of the Old Royal Palace

The obelisk of Vilém Slavata of Chlum

The Hartig Garden

From the terrace we can descend the *Hartig Garden*. From the historical viewpoint, the garden belongs to the Hartig Palace standing in Thunovská Street (No 184/20). It was built by Isabela Švihovská of Salm, who had the garden found together with the Musical Pavilion, rebuilt in Baroque after 1720 by the then owners from the Count Hartig family. The ground floor of the **Musical Pavilion** is open into the garden, the interior of the upper floor has a stucco decoration. From the very beginning musical productions were held in the pavilion, the present time continues in this tradition. Between 1965-68 the garden was attached to the gardens of Prague Castle, newly modified and decorated by six sandstone statues by Matyáš Bernard Braun transferred from the Štiřín Castle.

The Garden Na Valech again

We come back to the Garden *Na Valech* again. Nearby the Bull Staircase the Renaissance **Ludvík Wing** of the Old Royal Palace protrudes from the southern front of the Castle. Near the stairs is the western entrance to the **Theresian Wing** of the Royal Palace adapted for occasional exhibitions. From the other side of the Ludvík Wing one cannot fail to notice two **sandstone obelisks** marking the landing spots of the governors Jaroslav Bořita of Martinice (by the foot of the facade) and Vilém Slavata of Chlum (by the path in the garden) thrown out of the window of the Czech Chancellery during the second Prague defenestration in 1618. The Slavata obelisk is slighty embedded below the present level of the garden showing thus the then level of the inclined terrain. The lowered place is protected by the original Plečnik ballustrade of polished granite.

Both governors (and the secretary Fabricius

The gate and the stairs to the Apline rockery

for whom nobody built a memorial) were thrown out of a window in the eastern wall of the Ludvík Wing; probably it was a corner window, the second from the bottom. The fact that nothing serious happened to any of them durign the fall was considered a miracle by the Catholic side; according to a legend the Virgin Mary herself supported the governors by her heavenly coat. The rebellious anti-Hapsburg side explained their saving in a more sober way. The chronicler of the Uprising of the Estates Pavel Skála of Zhoř writes that the governors „fell on a rubbish heap, on which the janitors of the Czech Chancellery threw rubbish from the office and the second room where the officials usually sit. They threw rubish out of the window and therefore the place was not much hard, but it was ruffled as a heap of dung and soft." The chronicler was not probably far from the truth, though even a good luck and the inclined slope on which they landed played its role, as well as the bad bead of the rebellious lords who were shooting at them. Even at later times the place of the present Garden *Na Valech* served as a suitable dump, both for the

Castle inhabitants, and for the Small Quarter burghers, whose gardens reached up to the Castle mounds.

The semicylindrical tambour adjacent to the front of the Theresian Wing is a new transformer station which replaced utterly unsuitably the original Plečnik **aviary** built on the foundations of a late Gothic artillery bastion.

Between the transformer station and the Empire garden house, originally a guardhouse, is one of the foundation archs of the Theresian Wing converted into an entrance to the **southern court** of the Old Royal Palace. We notice the bottom part of the Palace facade with the preserved parts of the **polygonal towers** of the Soběslav Romanesque fortifications from the period after 1135.

We return to the southern wall of the garden, into which after a few steps eastwards a **small gate** is built, the entrance to the vineyard and the Alpine rockery founded by Josip Plečnik. The gate is de-

The Bellevue Pavilion with the Home for Noble Women in the background

corated on the top by a bronze female head, a copy of an unpreserved sculpture by Damian Pešan, a sculptor who often created details for Plečnik's architectural works and furniture designs. The sculpture of the wreathed maiden head was perhaps to remind one of the legendary Princes Libuše, who prophesied the fame of Prague. Also the view of Vyšehrad, the legendary residence of Libuše, corresponds to this interpretation.

On the elevated terrace below the Home for Noble Women stands Plečnik's **Bellevue Pavilion** with an impressively decorated ceiling, whose pillars remind us of the architecture of the Ancient Egypt. Plečnik placed **sculptures of angels - light-bearers** by Ignác Platzer from 1770 on the supportive wall below the pavilion. The sculptures stood originally in the *third courtyard*, where they were replaced by copies. Opposite the Bellevue Pavilion is sited **Samson's Fountain**, made according to Plečnik's design and decorated by an early Baroque statue of Samson

(correctly of Heracles fighting with a lion), which used to stand in the *first courtyard*.

The eastern part of the garden is ended below the front of the Lobkovic Palace by the **Moravian Bastion**. Plečnik had oval windows and a bar gate built into the brick wall on the foundations of the old bastion. Under the wooden pergola supported by sandstone pillars stands an oval granite table, at which President T. G. Masaryk liked to sit. The dominant of the bastion is a nearly 12 metres high slender monolith with a ionic head bearing a gilded ball with lighting depicted on it. From the viewing terrace one can see not only the Small Quarter roofs but also the Small Quarter palace gardens on the slope below Prague Castle.

Since 1997 it has been possible to enter some of the Small Quarter gardens directly from the Moravian Bastion and go down through them up to Valdštejnské Square in the Small Quarter. The walk through these palace gar-

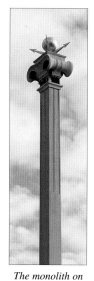

The floor of the Bellevue Pavilion

The monolith on the Moravian Bastion

The look-out at the top of the Old Castle Stairs

dens, however, will be a part of the next volume of our edition „From every side".

We come out from the Garden *Na Valech* to the eastern Castle gate into the space of the late Gothic barbican on the top of the *Old Castle Stairs*. At this place, from where one can see nearly the whole historic part of Prague, we leave Prague Castle.

(III)
The Hradčany Town

The Hradčany Town is a continuation of Prague Castle
by its silhouette and its whole long southern front faces the Prague basin,
which is enriched by the picturesque panorama
on the slope above the Small Quarter.

First walk:

THROUGH THE HISTORY OF THE TOWN

The garden wall in Loretánská Street

Perhaps up to the beginning of the 14th century a forest stretched as far as the present western gate of Prague Castle. Through the forest along the long Hradčany ridge a path passed around the Strahov Monastery and the Břevnov Monastery leading in direction of north western Bohemia. The area of Hradčany was separated from the Castle by a natural moat - the Hradčany furrow. Perhaps from the beginning of the 14th century a small settlement began to exist in the Castle neighbourhood, settled spontaneously by the serfs of Prague Castle (the people living in the Castle and its neighbourhood were called „hradčani").

In May 1310 a part of the future Hradčany near the western forefield of Prague Castle became a battle field. The troops of Jindřich of Lipá, Jan of Stráž and Vítek of Landštejn (supporters of the future King John of Luxembourg) compelled the army of King Henry of Carinthia to retreat to the Castle. The Castle was not conquered at that time only because the bridge over the Castle moat broke through under the weight of the attackers. However, in the same year John of Luxembourg gained control over the Castle and the whole kingdom.

In 1321 during the reign of John of Luxembourg, a feudal town was founded here on the initiation of the Castle Burgrave Hynek Berka of Dubá. The layout of the town was derived from the given situation; in fact, Hradčany creates an inhabited forefield of Prague Castle, which has a transit character. It is built up (including the large *Hradčany Square*) mainly along the road from the Castle to the Strahov Monastery. The built-up area is bordered on one side by the slope above the Small Quarter and on the other side by the *Stag Moat* and the *New World Moat*, through which the Brusnice stream flows.

The original town stretched only around the present *Hradčany Square*. It was surrounded by walls connected in the east to the Castle fortifications, in the west they run approximately on the site of *Loretánské Square*, in the north they led above the *Stag Moat* and in the south along the southern side of *Loretánská Street*. The Small Quarter was much smaller at that time and did not border on Hradčany directly. People entered the town through three gates, from the Small Quarter through the Gate

The Cathedral of St Vitus above the Hradčany roofs, viewed from the Hradčany fortifications

1 - Hradčany Square
2 - the Loretto
3 - the New World
4 - Pohořelec
5 - the Baroque fortifications
6 - the Strahov Monastery

WALKS:

① Through the history of the town
② Around Hradčany Square
③ From Hradčany Square to the Loretto and back
④ From Pohořelec to the Strahov Monastery

of St Benedict (on the site of the present *Townhall Stairs*), from the Strahov Monastery through the Strahov Gate (in the second third of the *Loretánská* Street) and from the Brusnice stream through the gate in the middle of today's *Kanovnická Street*. The road from Prague Castle led through its own western fortification.

The built-up area was not regular, planned, but natural, therefore Hradčany was never referred to as a „new" (intentionally founded) town. The courtiers of Charles IV, craftsmen and artists who participated in extensive building work in Prague Castle were accommodated here. Also the Church representatives, mainly the members of the St Vitus Chapter, whose house (called the Monastery of the Prague Church) had to be demolished during the building of the Cathedral of St Vitus, lived here.

From the second half of the 14th century the settlement extended to the west, mainly to the area of the present *Loretánské Square*. Between 1360-62 Emperor Charles IV had the border of the Small Quarter

The Toscan Palace in Hračany Square

extended considerably and the Strahov Monastery was included into its new fortifications. The fortifications of the Hradčany Town itself was sligtly extended, into whose range the area of the present *Loretánské Square* was probably incorporated. The fortifications along *Loretánská Street* now separated Hradčany from the extended Small Quarter, and therefore it lost its military purpose. Building work began also outside the walls; a small suburb was built below the Gate of St Benedict, the foundation of the lower part of the present Street *Úvoz*, and in 1375 the suburb Pohořelec was formed between the Strahov Monastery and the western fortifications of Hradčany.

At the beginning of the Hussite Wars - in 1420 - nearly the whole town was burnt down and houses were renewed only during the 15th century. The fire in 1541 was disasterous; it originated in the Small Quarter and also attacked Prague Castle and Hradčany, which burned down nearly completely at that time.

The fire was an incentive for new building activity of the aristocracy. At important places (mainly in *Hradčany Square*) the plots were united and the first Renaissance Palaces were built on them. Hradčany gradually became a town of the aristocracy and high Church dignitaries, but also a small colony of artists.

Italian artists called by Emperor Ferdinand I Hapsburg and his son, the governor Ferdinand of Tyrol, to the Renaissance rebuilding of the Castle began to come to Prague. The Czech aristocracy began to build Renaissance palaces a little later - only after 1564, when the Czech nobles went to Genova to welcome the new King Maxmilian II, who was to arrive by ship from Spain. Since the King delayed his arrival for the whole year, the lords had enough time to get acquainted with the Italian Renaissance architecture and to gain Italian craftsmen and artists into their services.

The importance of the town increased during the period of Rudolf II, who elevated Hradčany to the status of a Royal Town in

The Baroque fortifications of Hračany

The coat of arms of the Lords of Martinice on their palace in Hradčany Square

1598 (the so called Upper Prague Town). Hradčany remained a separate town up to 1784, when it became a part of the united Prague. After the Battle of the White Mountain in 1620 the burghers and craftsmen gradually moved out of the square into the side streets and the prestigious sites were taken by people who enriched themselves in the Thirty Years War and by the church. The character of the town was completed during the high Baroque by building church and secular objects, and it was slightly enriched in the Rococo period. Between 1653-1720 Hradčany (including the outskirts) was included into the new Baroque walls bordering the whole Prague. In the 19th century, however, the town was not changed from the architectural viewpoint, and thus it has preserved its unique character up to now.

Second walk:

AROUND HRADČANY SQUARE

The facade of the Archbishop's Palace with the archbishop's coats of arms

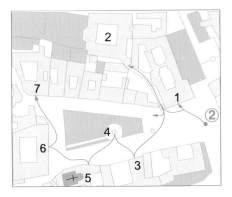

1 - the Archbishop's Palace
2 - the Šternberk Palace
3 - the Swarzenberk Palace
4 - the Column of the Virgin Mary
5 - the Monastery of the Barnabites
   with the Church of St Benedict
6 - the Toscan Palace
7 - the Martinický Palace

The architectural dominants of the elongate *Hradčany Square*, the proper core of Hradčany, are created by the wide front of the *first courtyard* of Prague Castle in the east, and on the opposite side by the front of the Toskánský Palace in the west. The open space of the square is made dynamic by a Baroque column of the Virgin Mary. The whole square evokes an aristocratic impression, as if the facades of the palaces and the houses were looking back into the past.

The square gained its aristocratic character only after the fire in 1541, when the plots were united and there was a radical rebuilding. At the time when the square still had the burgher character, in the eastern part used to stand meat shops and near by them a pillory. Here on August 22 1547 the representatives of the first anti-Hapsburg rebellion were executed - the commander of the Prague troops, the Knight Václav Pětipeský of Krásný Dvůr, the Knight Bernart Barchanec and the burghers Václav Jelení and Jakub Fikar from Vrat.

The Archbishop's Palace

On the northern side of the square, next to Prague Castle, one can be captivated by the Rococo facade of the large **Archbishop's Palace** (No 56/16) built in place of eight houses.

Lord Gryspek of Gryspek, the personal secretary of Ferdinand of Tyrol, the administrator of the Castle foundry and the secretary of the Czech Chancellery, began to build the palace in 1538. (As if his career anticipated the situation which was quite usual in Bohemia after one hundred years: the chronicler of the Uprising of the Czech Estates from the years 1546-47, Sixt of Ottersdorf wrote about him that „he came to Bohemia with an empty bag, and gained property worth many thousands by his unjust enterprise").

In 1562 the palace was bought for Antonín Brus of Mohelnice, the first Catholic archbishop in the country after the Hussite Wars in the first half of the 15th century. The Archbishop had the palace rebuilt in the Renaissance style during two years according to the plans of Hans Tirol. The gable on the northern side, the remnants of the sgrafitto in the court and the palace chapel remained preserved from the Renaissance building to date. At the end of the 16th century the palace was extended and between 1675-79 it was rebuilt in the early Baroque style according to the design of the significant architect Jean Baptist Mathey. The main marble portal and the wide superstructure come from this rebuilding. The present Rococo facade from 1764-65 is a work by Jan Josef Wirch.

The large archiepiscopal heraldic device of Jan Bedřich of Valdštejn is displayed in the middle of the facade. Church ranks were differentiated in heraldry by coloured hats above coats of arms and at the sides cords with knots or tassels. For instance archbishops had in their device a green hat with ten tassels, cardinals had a red hat with fifteen tassels and bishops had a green hat with five tassels.

The entrance to the Kolowrat House

*The courtyard wall
of the Schwarzenberk Palace*

In the palace are ornate interiors, especially the chapel and the picture gallery. Particulary fine is the cycle of French tapestries on the theme of the New Indies. The collection of glass and china is also very rich.

Left of the Archbishop's Palace nearly along the whole north front of the square there is a row of originally canons' houses. They have mostly Baroque fronts and they are marked by the coat of arms of the St Vitus Chapter (a golden stripe in the black background). Canons began to build houses here in the period of Charles IV, when their common house (called the Monastery of the Prague Church) was demolished because of the building of the Cathedral of St Vitus. Nowadays here stand: the **house** No 58/14, the House **At the Black Eagle** (No 59/13), the House of the **Metropolitan Chapter** (No 60/12), the House **At the Swans** (also the Losenovský Palace, in the past the Šternberk House, No 61/11), rebuilt in the 18th century. The last two houses are united by a rich Baroque stucco facade. The first of

them is the the House **Saxon-Lauenburk** (formely Rožmberský 62/10), built around 1596 for Petr Vok of Rožmberk. In the 14th century on this site stood the house which belonged till 1372 to Petr Parléř, the builder of the St Vitus Cathedral, who lived here till his death. The second is the **Kolowratský** House (No 63/9) with Renaissance frescos in the courtyard. Next is the **Martinický Palace**, which however we will visit at the end of this walk.

Through the passage in the left portals of the Archbishop's Palace we come in a small lane ended by the entrance front of the high Baroque **Šternberk Palace** (No 57/15). The Count Václav Vojtěch of Šternberk had the palace built between 1698-1707 according to the design of Giovanni Baptis Alliprandi and perhaps also Giovanni Santini. The four-wing building with an inner court belongs to the most significant palace buildings of the high Baroque. As far as its character is concerned, it is a garden palace with the main front facing the garden above the *Stag Moat*, which also the windows of the northern wing face.

Since 1948 in the palace has been sited the **collection of European paintings of the National Gallery**. We can see here fine paintings of old masters (for example Pieter Brueghel, Lucas Cranach, Hans Holbein, Albrecht Altdorfer, Albrech Dürer, Jacopo Tintoretto, Giovanni Battista Tiepolo, Petrus Paulus Rubens, José Ribera, El Greco, Francisco Goya).

A painting gallery used to be here even between 1821-71, at that time the palace was the seat of the Company of Patriotic Art Lovers. Between 1821-47 the National Museum had its seat in the palace.

We come to the southern side of *Hradčany Square* and stop at the **viewing ramp outside Prague Castle**. The view of the Prague basin is impressive from this place perhaps at any weather and at every day and year time. From the east the *Castle Stairs* lead here, decorated by a Baroque statue of St Philip Nereyský, from the west the Street *Ke Hradu* hewn out in the rock after 1639 leads onto the terrace. The character of the place (we have mentioned at a great detail in the Introductory walk of this guide) is completed by the sculptural group of Pieta and a modern statue of St Wenceslas nearby the torso of the former Chapel of the Virgin Mary of Einsiedel.

The first house on the southern side of the square is the Empire **Salmovský Palace** (also called Small Schwarzenberský, No 186/1). Its honour court, enclosed by a grill, imitates the *first courtyard* of Prague Castle at a smaller scale. The Palace was built between 1800-10 by Archbishop Vilém Florentin of Salm in place of the Renaissance houses which belonged in the past to the Berkas of Dubá and Sixt of Trausohn. The name of the builder was reminded by the crowned capital letter S on the gate grill (at present it is miss-

The Renaissance gable of the Swarzenberk Palace

ing). After 1811 Josef of Schwarzenberk gained the palace and had it joined to his palace next door.

In the middle of the square in front of the Salmovský Palace stands a remarkable **cast iron candelabrum** of the gas lighting from 1867. Is was made in the Komárovské Steelworks by Hořovice.

The dominant of the southern front of the square is the large building of the **Schwarzenberk Palace** (No 185/2) decorated with Renaissance envelope shaped sgraffitti. The palace was built on the site of four burnt down houses between 1545-63 by the Prince Jan Jr. of Lobkovice, the highest Burgrave of Prague Castle. The design was created by Agostino Vlach. The next owner, the Prince Jiří of Lobkovice, rebelled against Emperor Rudolf II, was imprisoned and the palace was confiscated from him. Petr Vok of Rožmberk gained the uncompleted object from the Emperor in 1600 in exchange for the Rožmberk Palace in the Castle

The cast iron candelabrum in Hradčany Square

The Column of the Virgin Mary in the middle of the square was built from 1726 (it was consecrated 10 years later) as an expression of thanks for the end of the plague which afflicted Prague eleven years earlier, and as a plea for averting next plagues.

The Hradčany burghers skipped the Building Office of the Castle at planning the construction and appealed to Emperor Charles IV directly, whom they reminded cleverly that the God-pleasing erecting of the column would surely ensure that he would be blessed with an heir. The Emperor got aquainted with the construction design at a great detail and after a number of comments he approved of it. (However, a plague epidemy did not avoid Prague - the last plague afflicted it in August 1773. Nor was heard the Emperor's wish and it was his daughter Maria Theresa who took over the rule after his death).

(the present Home for Noble Women). Petr Vok bequeathed the palace to Jan Jiří of Švamberk, from whose son it was confiscated after 1620. Not long afterwards the palace was given by Emperor Ferdinand II Hapsburg to Oldřich, Prince of Eggenberk and in 1719 it came over into the ownership of the Schwarzenberk family by marriage.

The Schwarzenberk Palace is one of the finest examples of the Prague Renaissance architecture; it is characterised by gables supported by lunette ledges and sgrafitto decorations. In the interior under the Renaissance painted ceilings an extensive collection of the **Military Museum** has been exhibited since 1947. The collection of fire arms (about 6000 examples) and the collection of army uniforms (5000 uniforms and kit parts) are especially valuable.

The authors of the sculptural decoration of the column are Ferdinand Maxmilian Brokoff and his pupils. On the central site stands a statue of the Immaculate Virgin Mary, around her are sited nine saints, St Wenceslas, Vojtěch, Vít, Elizabeth Durynská, Petr, Paul, Florian, John of Nepomuk and Charles of Boromea. The last of them replaced the originally planned St Norbert, the founder of the Premonstratensian Order and the Patron Saint of Bohemia. It happened so because the Abbot of the Premonstratensian Strahov Monastery refused to help out with money for the building, since he had exhausted himself financially by the completion of the Strahov Hospital. At first the Hradčany emblem was placed on the column, however, before the coronation of Leopold II as Czech King (in 1791) it was replaced by the emblem of the united Prague Towns, identical with the Old Town emblem.

Next to the Schwarzenberk Palace stands the **Monastery of the Barnabites** (No 184/3) with the **Church of St**

Benedict. The church was mentioned already in 1353. It was originally a parish church, in the 16th century it was also a guild church (it belonged to the stonemason guild, whose head was the builder of Prague Castle, Benedikt Ried), from 1626 it became the property of the Barnabite Order. The Barnabites built next to the church in the first half of the 17th century an early Baroque monastery building with one upper floor, modified in the 17th and 18th centuries. It stood on the site of the former presbytery and the house which belonged one time to the humanist poet Bohuslav Hasištejnský of Lobkovice. In 1786 the Barnabite Monastery was abolished, and six years later the Carmelite nuns gained the Monastery, who were forced before to leave their convent by the Church of St Joseph in the Small Quarter and go from Prague to Pohled by Havlíčkův Brod. The nuns brough with them the mumified body of the founder of the convent, the Reverend Mother Elekta. Between 1958-60 the Monastery was adapted for state guests. At that time on its external side in the direction to Hradčany a look-out pavilion decorated with sgrafitto was built out of the former castle tower. It can be seen best from the Street *Ke hradu*. After the fall of the Communist regime in 1989 the Carmelite nuns gained the object again.

Behind the convent the romantic *Townhall Stairs* descend into the Small Quarter *Nerudova Street*, which we mentioned in the introductory walk of this guide.

The western front of the square is created by the **Toskánský Palace** (No 182/5), which Michael Osval Thun-Hohenstein had built in place of five houses between 1689-91 according to the design of Jean Baptist Mathey. In 1718 the Toscan Dutchess Maria Anna bought the palace and it remained in the ownership

The column of the Virgin Mary

The gables of the Martinický Palace

of the Toscan dukes (coming from 1675 from the Hapsburg-Lotrine branch) up to the formation of the Czechoslovak Republic in 1918. The early Baroque facade is decorated above both pillar portals by the sculptural heraldic devices of the Toscan dukes and on the attic gable between the two roof penthouses by a row of statues of Antique gods by Jan Brokoff. At the corner towards *Loretánská Street* in a stucco frame stands a statue of Archangel Michael, the Patron Saint of the builder of this palace. Probably it is a work by Ottavio Most. Under the statue between the heraldic Thun-Hohenstein eagles is placed the Toscan coat of arms.

The next **Canons's Residence** (No 65/6) was built in place of two medieval houses. In the second half of the 14th century here used to stand the farmstead of Václav of Radeč, the director of the building of the St Vitus Cathedral and a forefather of the famous Field Marshal Radecký. In 1486 the Chapter dean Hanuš of Kolowrat had it rebuilt.

According to the tradition reminded by the picture on the facade, Jan of Nepomuk lived here. In the background of the picture the Charles Bridge is marked, from where the saint was thrown down. The next **Canon's House** (No 68/7) has two preserved floors of the Gothic basement. It was rebuilt in the Renaissance, and gained the present Baroque appearance in 1775.

Next to the Canon's House the narrowed *Kanovnická Street* leads to *Hradčany Square*. On the opposite side we are attracted by the corner **Martinický Palace** (No 67/8). The palace was built in the third quarter of the 16th century by Ondřej Teyfl of Kinsdor, from whom Jiří Bořita of Martinice bought it in 1583. His successor, Jaroslav Bořita of Martinice, was one of the two governors thrown out of the window at the Prague defenestration in 1618. After 1620 he had the palace extended, one floor built and the palace decorated by late Renaissance gables. Above the entrance he had the Martinice coats of arms placed - a water lily leaf with a star. The figural sgraffito on the front facade was discovered at the reconstruction between 1967-72 and it represents scenes from the Old Testament stories about Joseph. The facade in the courtyard is decorated by sgraffito depicting the life of biblical Samson (the third quarter of the 16th century) and the acts of Heracles (around 1634). Renaissance beam ceilings are preserved in the palace, the square palace chapel has a richly decorated Renaissance vaulting.

The palace stands on the site of four medieval houses, one of which was owned by Beneš Krabice from Weitmile, a chronicler of the period of Charles IV. Perhaps from here he observed the bustle in the square, and with displeasure he observed the new fashion excesses: „People imitate foreign manners like apes," he complained, „they wear shorter and shorter dresses, so brazenly that even their thighs and buttocks can fre-

The Archangel Michael
at the corner of
the Toscan Palace

The statue of St John of Nepomuk at the
gable top of the Chapter House

The Martinický Palace

quently be seen and so narrow, that they can hardly breathe." It should be added that these excesses just described were mainly displayed by men.

We will end the walk through the calm *Hradčany Square* at this place. When looking at its austerity one can hardly imagine the forest that once grew here, and the hardly believable reports of chroniclers saying that in winter 1276 packs of wolves were going through the forest and endangered the gates of Prague Castle.

Third walk:

FROM HRADČANY SQUARE TO THE LORETTO AND BACK

1 - the Hradčany Townhall
2 - the Martinický Palace
3 - the Hrzánský Palace
4 - the House with the Renthouse Restaurant
5 - the House at St Lucas (At the Black Bull)
6 - the ground plan of the former Chapel of St Mathew
7 - the Černín Palace
8 - the Loretto

Loretánská Street

From the southwestern part of *Hradčany Square* leads *Loretánská Street*, through which originally led the old path from Prague Castle to the Strahov Monastery and further to the west. On its left side towered the originall walls of the Hradčany Town. The houses standing on their sites are founded on a steep slope; they often have only one upper floor from *Loretánská Street*, whereas they have up to five upper floors from the parallel, however much lower lying street *Úvoz*.

The first building on the left side, immediately behind the *Townhall Stairs*, is the **Hradčany Townhall** (No 173/1). The first Hradčany townhall used to be sited in the presbytery by the Church of St Benedict in *Hradčany Square*. The present Renaissance building was built between 1601-04 in connection with the elevation of Hradčany to the status of a royal town (in 1598). On the Renaissance sgrafitto of its western part it

is possible to recognize the remnants of the imperial coat of arms and the picture of the Justice. On the portal we notice the Hradčany coat of arms and on the gate we can see the official standard of measurement, the Czech elbow (59.4 cm), where the customers of the nearby marketplace could test the honesty of the Hradčany merchants. After the uniting of the Prague Towns in 1784 the townhall was used as a residential building, on whose ground floor is a restaurant. However, an inn used to be here much earlier, as it was usual in most townhall houses, where it was permitted to drink beer and wine till late night to the benefit of the town treasury.

On the right side we pass by the side facade of the **Toskánský Palace** (No 182), in whose back part is an arcade, which testifies to the originally burgher character of the place. Next is the **Martinický Palace** (No 181/4) built between 1700-05 by Jiří Adam II of Martinice, the Emperor's ambassador to Rome and

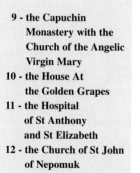

9 - the Capuchin
   Monastery with the
   Church of the Angelic
   Virgin Mary
10 - the House At
   the Golden Grapes
11 - the Hospital
   of St Anthony
   and St Elizabeth
12 - the Church of St John
   of Nepomuk
13 - the House of the Pages

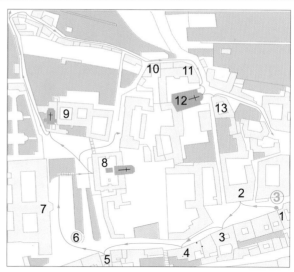

the viceroy of Naples. The author of the design is the Roman architect Carlo Fontana, the construction was run by the Milan architect Bartolomeo Scotti. The simple, but artistically noble high Baroque building with a typical high arbour on the roof belongs to unique evidence of the Roman architecture in Prague. In 1837 a military hospital was established here, later there were barracks of the Castle guard.

Loretánská Street becomes wider at this place creating a small square decorated by a cast iron candelabrum of the gass lighting from 1867. As if the ground plan of the square copied on a smaller scale the ground plan of *Hradčany Square*. Also the candelabrum, similar to the one in *Hradčany Square* supports this idea. The gradation of the ground plans, shapes and forms, the copying of the dominant places on a smaller scale, this all completes the genius loci of the old Prague.

Opposite the Martinický Palace stands the late Renaissance **Dietrichšten Palace**

(No 176/7) built by Kateřina Benigna of Lobkovice, the founder of the Prague Loretto. Next is the late Baroque **Hrzánský Palace** (No 177/9). This originally Gothic house used to be the property of Petr Parléř, the builder of the St Vitus Cathedral. In the second half of the 18th century it was rebuilt in the Renaissance style (the stone-lined portal and the remnants of the sgrafitto remained preserved). The palace belonged originally to the Kolowrat family, later to the Hrzán family of Harasov. At the end of the 18th century it became the seat of the Chapter Deanery of the St Vitus Cathedral and gained the present appearance. Between 1950-52 it was adapted into official rooms of the Czechoslovak Government.

The house has one upper floor from the *Loretánská Street*, on the side of Street *Úvoz* it has five upper floors connected by a winding staircase, which consists nearly of 700 steps. At the beginning of the 20th century the painter Ferdinand Engelmüller led a fa-

The Hradčany Townhall   The Martinický Palace

mous painting school in the palace, his bust can be seen in the court, where is also sited a Baroque fountain with a statue of Hercules. In the rear wing of the palace the painter Jan Slavíček had his studio. According to legends in the ground floor room (with the windows into the Street *Úvoz*) lived a hangman and next to his dwelling was a torture chamber. Rumour has it that from here leads a branched underground passage up to the Břevnov Markéta.

On the right side behind the small Street *U kasáren* is the **Trauttmannsdorf Palace** (originally Trčkovský; No 186/6). Its present Classicist shape comes from the first half of the 19th century. Between 1833-1918 here used to be a penitentiary, later a student hostel and at present here is a workplace of the Central State Archives.

Opposite the Trauttmannsdorf Palace stands the **house** No 179/13 with the Renthaus Restaurant. The view of the Prague panorama from the house terrace belongs to the most impressive. The commemorative plaque on the front reminds us that between 1937-39 and 1945-48 Alice Masaryk, a daughter of the President T. G. Masaryk, the co-founder and the first chairperson of the Czechoslovak Red Cross lived in the house. The next commemmorative plaque reminds us of the stay of the American writer Marcia Davenport (1947-48), the lady friend of Jan Masaryk. By the next **house** No 179/15 used to stand the **Strahov Gate** (Strahovská brána), a part of the original Hradčany fortifications. The narrow stairs between this house and the House **U kanónu** (At the Cannon) (No 103/17) lead down to *Street Úvoz*. Originally a narrow path used to be in their place, into which one could get from *Loretánská Street* through a small gate. Behind the House At the Cannon on the left side are three houses; passing the last of them, the House **U hodinářů** (At the Watchmakers, No 106/23) we come into *Loretánské Square*.

*The stairs from Loretánská
Street to Street Úvoz*

The front of the House At St Lucas in Loretánské Square

The opposite side of *Loretánská Street* is created at this place by the protective wall of the garden of the Trauttmannsdorf Palace, into which a small Chapel of St Barbora is built, the patron saint of the dying. It was exacly at this place that two robber knights were impaled on stakes. One of them crawled as far as the Barnabite Monastery in *Hradčany Square* where he died. The picture in the Chapel, many times repainted, comes from Václav Vavřinec Reiner and depicts a dying man to whom the priest is administering the last rites.

Loretánské Square

Loretánské Square, one of the most picturesque ends of Hradčany, was settled occasionally after 1370. The houses on its southern side directly continue the row of houses in Loretánská Street. The first of them (the only one in this row without an arcade) is the House **U sv. Lukáše** (At St Lucas) (in the past also **U černého orla** - At the Black Eagle; No 107/1), commonly called according to the famous pub here **U černého vola** (At the Black Bull). It is richly decorated by a painted Baroque stucco facade, on which stands out the plastic coloured picture of the Evangelist Lucas, the patron saint of painters, painting the Virgin Mary with Little Jesus. An attentive observer notices also the windows on the upper floor, painted on the facade. They are evidence of an interesting feature of the Baroque aesthetics - the effort to preserve symmetry in architecture, though at the cost of making fake architectonic articles and elements (gates, windows and similarly). The next House **U Drahomířina sloupku** (At Drahomíra's Column) has a Renaissance core, and is modified in the Baroque and the Classicist styles. Next is the House **U Deklamátorů** (At the Declamators) (also called **U Pešků** - At the Peškas; No 109/3), in which the significant Baroque sculptor František Ignác Platzer died (in 1787). The street ends by the **Trauttmannsdorf House** (No 110/4), which

The Černín Palace

faces Pohořelec by its narrow main front.

The name of the House At Drahomíra's Column reminds us of an old legend connected with *Loretánské Square.* According to it, Princess Drahomíra, allegedly the main enemy of Christianity, who had her mother-in-law, St Ludmila, murdered at Tetín Castle, passed by the Church of St Mathew here one time. The mass was served in the church at that time, the Princess began to blaspheme rudely, and she fell into the hell as a punishment. For a long time a fenced pit was shown in *Loretánské Square* - called Drahomíra's abyss. The legend was described on the sculpturally decorated column which stood till the first half of the 18th century between the mentioned House At Drahomíra's Column and the **Church of St Mathew.** Allegedly, the house was founded here by Prince Spytihněv at the beginning of the 10th century. According to the legend, the body of St Ludmila rested here, when it was being transported from Tetín to the Convent of St George. At the time of the

Hussite Wars it was destroyed and in its place two houses were built, one of which, the House **U zlaté koule** (At the Golden Ball) was a tavern of ill fame. Because the tavern displeased the pilgrims walking to the Loretto, the houses were pulled down in 1702 at a request of Count Heřman Černín. A new church was built in place of them in 1737 by František Josef Černín, the central building of which was decorated by frescoes by Václav Vavřinec Reiner. Unfortunately, it was closed in 1784 and seven years later demolished. Its ground plan is marked in the pavement at the beginning of the terrace by the Černín Palace.

The eastern side of the square is dominated by the massive bulk of the **Černín Palace** (No 101/5) standing on the site of two lanes of burghers' houses. The Imperial Ambassador to Venice, Humprech Černín of Chudenice and his son Heřman Černín had it built. The plans in the style of the Palladian Renaissance were worked out by the architect Francesco Caratti, who supervised the construction till his death in 1677. The large scale of the building refers to the Italian theatrical Baroque, untypical in Prague otherwise. The work on the interior decoration of the palace and the addition of an entrance portico (already in the high Baroque style) continued until 1720. The architect was Ferdinand Maxmilián Kaňka. The sculptor Matyáš Bernard Braun, the painter Václav Vavřinec Reiner and a number of other artists participated in the decoration of the interior. The palace has four wings and two courtyards. Two sala terrenas, orangeries and ponds belong to the vast garden of the French type.

Inside the palace on the ground floor there are glazed arcades. Through the centre of the inner courtyard runs an inner wing, in which the Baroque architect Ferdinand Maxmilián Kaňka built a monumental staircase between 1718-20. Its vaulting is decorated with a fresco on the theme The Fall of the Titans created by the painter Václav Vavřinec Reiner. The staircase leads into the main hall, which takes up two storeys of the building; however, it has never been fully completed. On the second floor of the north palace side there is a corridor called the Tapestry Gallery. It was also built by Ferdinand Maxmilián Kaňka and it was decorated with stuccos by Tomasso Soldati. On the ground floor the Baroque Circular Salon decorated with stuccos and paintings was established next to the arcades of the sala terrena. The ground floor chambers are decorated by ceiling paintings from the 17th century.

The high columns of the Černín Palace

The monumentality of the palace tempted the Prague inhabitants to wild fantasies. Apart from anything else it was being said that the massive walls were created, because Count Černín promised to pay the bricklayers according to how many cubic metres of walls were completed. In fact, the large scale was a requirement of the Baroque aesthetics claiming that a large number of windows and columns evoke an especially festive impression. Such an aesthetical requirement was, however, alien to Prague, and therefore the Černín Palace ranks among the few historical buildings which were never united with their neighbourhoods. On the contrary, the jealous reaction of Emperor Leopold I is typical. He tried to be equal to the building activity of his rival, the French King Louis XIV. Allegedly, the Emperor said that the Černín Palace is a „large barn with no gate". However, a diplomatic struggle was conducted for this „barn" a few years later: in 1741 Prague was conquered by the united French and Bavarian armies. When the French commanders wanted to demolish the palace in the next year and to place artillery batteries on its ruins, the Austrian Prince Charles of Lotringen threatened to blow up the palace of the Emperor Elector in Munich in retaliation. As a result of this tie situation, both buildings remined preserved.

The Černín family fell into debt through this costly undertaking and moved to Vienna in the 18th century. The palace remained uninhabited and later on it

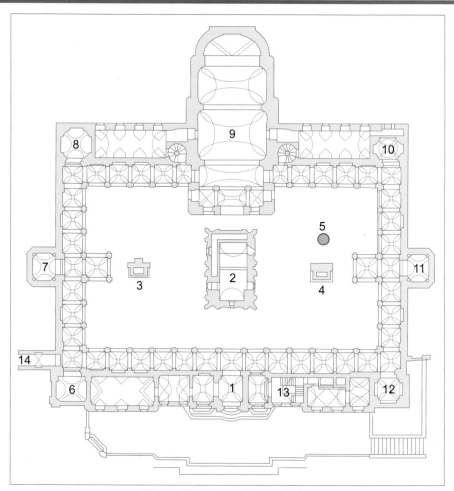

The Hradčany Loretto, the ground plan

1 - the main entrance
2 - the Santa Casa
3 - the fountain with the sculptural group
   of Christ's Ressurection
4 - the fountain with the sculptural group
   of the Assumption of the Virgin Mary
5 - the well
6 - the Chapel of St Anne
7 - the Chapel of St Francis of Seraphim
8 - the Chapel of St Joseph

 9 - the Church of the Nativity
10 - the Chapel of the Holy Cross
11 - the Chapel of St Anthony
12 - the Chapel of the Virgin Mary
    the Painful
13 - the staircase to the upper floor
    to the treasury
14 - the corridor (bridge) between the
    Loretto and the Capuchin Monestery

The front of the Hradčany Loretto

The Loretto bells

was leased as temporary accommodation for the poor. In the middle of the 19th century it was rebuilt into barracks and between 1928-32 it was adapted into offices and flats for the Ministry of Foreign Affairs. The original flat of the Foreign Minister in the rear wing is connected with the tragical death of the Minister Jan Masaryk, whose body was found below the windows. The circumstances of his death have not still been explained.

Opposite the Černín Palace stands the lower elongated **Small Černín Palace** (No 102/8), the former Černín Riding School. At present the U Lorety Wine Bar is opened in the Baroque house modified in the Classicism.

Hradčany Loreta (Loretto)

Our eyesight is attracted by the front of the famous pilgrim place - the Hradčany Loretto (No 100/7), which is a copy of the Italian Santa Casa from the Italian Loretto.

By the Loretto, or Svatá Chýše (Santa Casa) is meant the small building in which, according to a legend, lived the Holy Family in Nazareth. In 1291 (a short time before the Saracen invasion into Nazareth) the house was saved from the hands of the infidel miraculously: it was transferred to Dalmatia and from there it was transported to Italy near Ancona, into laurel woods of Lady Laureta. Since that time the house has been called the Laureta House, from which the name Loretto comes. After a few months the house was moved by the angels onto a nearby hill, where it stands now. The Pope Pius II founded a church above the house in 1461, where the house was kept as a relict. It was deeply venerated and

The sculptural group of St John of Nepomuk on the Loretto front

The stucco decoration of the Loretto Santa Casa

in the Baroque period replicas were built all over the Catholic world.

The Loretto's Santa Casa in Prague was built between 1626-31 at the cost of Kateřina Benigna of Lobkovice. Forty years later the place of pilgrimage was already surrounded by cloisters to which after 1740 an upper storey was built. In the first half of the 18th century also the entrance front was built and the Church of the Birth of Jesus was completed.

Before entering the pilgramage area we will mention the **Loretto carillon**.

A touching legend about the Loretto carillon has been told. Once at the time of a terrible plague in the near street *Nový Svět* (the New World) lived a widow who had many children. They were gradually infected with the plague and were dying. The caring mother put her child in the grave and had the Loretto bell rung as a death knell. After she had the knell rung for her last child she found out that even she was afflicted with the plague. When she was dying, she sighed: „I had the knell rung for all my children, but nobody will have the knell rung for me." At the moment, however, the Loretto bells began to play by themselves a touching melody.

The Loretto bells placed in the front tower from 1685 are best seen from the terrace in front of the Černín Palace. The carillon was ordered in 1694 by the Small Quarter citizen Eberhard from Glaukov from the renowned Amsterdam bell maker Claudius Fromm. The bellmaker selected for the Prague Loretto a total of 27 bells with a range of 2.5 octaves and a total weight of 14 hundred quintals. In Prague the bells were put together by the clockmaker Petr Neumann and consecra-

The Santa Casa in the Loretto courtyard

ted. The patron of the largest bell was Emperor Leopold I himself. They rang for the first time on 15 August 1695.

The carillon can be rung in three ways. The oldest and simplest is the straightforward tapping out of the melody by the metal hammers fastened to the bells. Also it can be used on the principle of the orchestrion - inside the clockwork mechanism a cylinder with pegs is installed which during the movement activates the rod which starts the striking of the hammers on the bells. Usually we can hear the Virigin Mary hymn „We Greet Thee a Thousand Times". The third method of playing originates in the Netherlands. The bells are connected to piano keys which can be played in a similar way to an organ. Some composers have even improvised on this keyboard including František Škroup and Ferenc Liszt.

The **front** of the Loretto comes from 1721-23 and is a work of Kilián Ignác Dientzenhofer (his father Kryštof Dientzenhofer participated in the plans). By building it the architects managed a difficult task to unite the whole complex of buildings which was built in the previous years. A typical Prague building was completed here, sensitively integrated into its environment and contrasting by its intimity with the official monumentality of the Černín Palace. The builders were Filip, Prince of Lobkovice and his wife Eleonora Karolina. The sculptor Jan Bedřich Kohl created their alliance heraldic device in red marble and placed it above the entrance. This sculptor is probably also the author of the other sculptural works: the group of St Felix and the Madonna on the northern corner, St John of Nepomuk on the southern corner and perhaps the statue of St Francis and St Anthony on the entrance sides.

*The towers of the Loretto Church
of the Nativity*

Ondřej Filip Quittainer embellished the ballustrade by Baroque statues of angels.

In the middle of the Loretto courtyard we can see the Santa Casa, built between 1626-31 by Giovanni Battista Orsi (he was sent by the Empress to Loretto two years ago to measure the building there and to build its replica in Vienna). The building of the Santa Casa was financed by Kateřina Benigna of Lobkovice, who was inspired by the Loretto in Mikulov. The Casa was only painted from the outside, in 1664 stucco reliefs were made on it.

The elongated northern side is decorated by the scenes of the Nativity and the Engagement of the Virgin Mary, the western side is decorated by the scenes of the Annunciation and the Visitation and the Coming to Bethlehem, the southern side is decorated by the scenes of the Nativity and the Adoration of the Magi, the eastern side by the scenes of the Death of the Virgin Mary and the Transportation of the Holy House to Dalmatia.

Allegedly, inside the Santa Casa a beam and several bricks from the original Italian Loretto have been incorporated. On the silver altar is a statue of the Virgin Mary of black ebony from the third quarter of the 17th century. One wall is intentionally damaged in one place: this imitates the damage in the original chapel, which was struck by lightning as punishment for blasphemers. Under the Santa Casa it the tomb of the founders and patrons of the Prague Loretto, the Lobkovic family. (Some members of the family even died in this saint place, the marble plaque in the Church of the Nativity marks the place where in 1858 František Josef, Prince Lobkovic died.)

The cloisters around the Santa Casa were built till 1664 and one storey was added by Kilián Ignác Dientzenhofer after 1740. The vaulting sections are decorated by 47 ceiling paintings on the theme of the Loretto litany. They were created in 1750 by Felix Antonín Scheffler. By the walls of the cloisters are sited altars with pictures of saints, protectors against various human troubles. Many female saints have the appearance of the noble women who contributed to the Loretto. Six chapels are placed around the cloister. In the northwestern corner is the Chapel of St Anne with a ceiling fresco of the Sacrifice of the Virgin Mary. In the middle of the northern wing is the Chapel of St Francis of Seraphim. On its altar is placed a painting of the Stigmatisation of St Francis by Petr Brandl, an outstanding work of the Baroque realism, distinct from the pomposity and intentional ecstaticness of the only average decoration in the cloisters. In the northeastern corner of the cloister is the Chapel of St Joseph decorated by a ceiling painting of Christ in the Temple.

In the middle of the eastern side of the cloister is a front of the **Church of the Nativity**. The church was built on the site of the original Chapel of St Anne. In

1722 Kryštof Dientzenhofer was called to the rebuilding, however he died in the same year. In the next year his son Kilián Ignác Dientzenhofer continued in his work. He also built the two belfries on the sides of the church. The final rebuilding and extending of the church was performed between 1734-37 by Dientzenhofer's foster brother Jan Jiří Aichbauer. The outstanding high Baroque building is complemented inside the church by equally exceptional decorations. The vaulting of the presbytery is decorated by a fresco of the Crucifixion by Václav Vavřinec Reiner from 1736, in the nave we can see the ceiling fresco of the Adoration of the Magi and the Adoration of the Shepherds by Jan Adam Schöpf from 1742. On the main altar is the picture of the Nativity by Jan Jiří Heinsch. The precious organ with a rich carving decoration comes from the first half of the 18th century.

In the southeastern corner of the **cloister** is situated the Chapel of the Holy Cross with a ceiling painting of the Virgin Mary and St Dismas, in the middle of the southern side stands the Chapel of St Anthony of Paduan. Visitors spend most time by the Chapel of the Virgin Mary the Painful in the southwestern corner. On the main Rococo altar is an exceptional statue of the Virgin Mary the Painful from the turn of the 14th and the 15th centuries. On the other altar is placed a famous statue of a crucified bearded saint woman, called St Starosta.

St Starosta, according to a legend a pious daughter of a Visigoth king, was to be married to a pagan. Starosta refused the marriage, since she made a vow to God. Through prayer she got help - miraculously, she sprouted a beard. The wedding was cancelled, however, her father, an enemy of Christianity, had her crucified. The saint is adored in various countries under different names, such as Kümmernis, Wilgefortis, Liberata, and she is always considered the patron of the poor and the afflicted, the

helper in the worst poverty, and there are many legends about her. For example, one of them is about a poor soldier whom she gave her shoe decorated with gold. When the soldier was falsely accused of sacrilege, even the other shoe went down off the saint's foot into the soldier's hands in the sight of the judges, which confirmed the innocence of the soldier.

In the strongroom on the first floor above the cloisters is the renowned **treasury** containing liturgical objects from the 16th to the 18th centuries. The oldest is the Gothic cup with enamelled pictures from 1510. The most famous exhibit, the diamond monstrance, was made between 1696-99 of heavily gilded silver, studded with 6222 diamonds from the wedding clothes of Countess Kolowrat. It was made by the goldsmiths Matyáš Stegner and Jan Khünischbauer according to the design of the Viennese architect Jan Bernard Fischer from Erlach. It weighs 12 kilograms (approximately 25 pounds), its base has the form of a rock on which the Virgin Mary stands with rays above her head. This dynamic work, influenced by the work of Lorenzo Benini, is one of the first sculptures which brought the principles of the radical Baroque into Bohemia.

Before leaving the Loretto complex we should add that between the World Wars unique musical festivals were held here in which rediscovered medieval compositions were performed.

The Capuchin Monastery at the Angelic Virgin Mary

The Loretto is connected by a coverd passage (bridge) on pillars with the **monastery building of the Capuchin Order** (No 99/6), the keepers of the Loretto shrine. The Hradčany monastery is the oldest Capuchin monastery in Bohemia. It was founded in 1600 by the General of the Order Lawrence of Brindisi (who was later sanctified). In 1602 the

*The Capuchin Church
of the Angelic Virgin Mary*

The neighbourhood of Černínská Street

church was consecrated, the monastery was built during the whole 17th and the first half of the 18th centuries. In 1944 the monastery was used by the SS command which established a prison in it, which was used during the two postwar years as an internation camp. In 1946-47 the monks moved in the monastery again, who, however, were moved out by force after the formation of the Communist regime in 1948. The monastery was given back to the Order only after 1990.

The monastery Capuchin **Church of the Angelic Virgin Mary** is a single nave structure without a tower; as in all Capuchin churches the Order's regulations stipulating the strictest simplicity were applied here. In the church we can see besides the original interior from the middle of the 17th century also the outstanding modern relief Stations of the Cross by Karel Stádník. We notice the main altar placed in the middle of the presbytery, as it is usual in Capuchin churches. Capuchin monks participated

in the Mass in the space behind the altar, separated from lay believers. In the right side chapel is kept an old Nativity scene created in 1700 by the Capuchin monk Kašpar. It is enlivened by wooden and straw figures with the faces made of gypsum and paper. Their appeal is heightened especially by the fact that the maker dressed them in real clothes impregnated with resin. This picturesque Nativity scene is the main reason why the Capuchin monastery is among the most popular at Christmas time.

A large garden with several other buildings belongs to the Capuchin Monastery. The monastery stood close to the town walls. It enabled the Capuchin monks during the night from 25 to 26 May to break part of the walls and to let the imperial army led by Albrecht of Valdštejn into the town. The half-year long Saxon occupation of Prague ended in this way. Short time afterwards, in 1646, the badly built walls fell and were poorly repaired. The Swedish general Königsmarsk took advantage of it in 1648, who by a quick attack and with the help of treason seized the Small Quarter, Hradčany and Prague Castle during the night from the 25th to the 26th July. The Swedish occupation meant irretrieveable loss not only by the plundering but also by the trasportation of valuable objects of art into Sweden. In 1757 Prague was bombed from the Hradčany slopes by the Prussian artillery. The cannon balls which fell on the monastery were fixed into the facade of the Capuchin church and they can be seen best from the corner of *Černínská Lane* and *Loretánské Square*.

Opposite the church stands **Christ's figure** showing the stigmata with the spear and the sponge soaked in vinegar.

Černínská Lane

After leaving *Loretánské Square* and passing by the Capuchin monastery we enter the small *Černínská Lane*, bordered on one side by the garden of the Černín Palace and on the other side by the Capuchin garden.

Loretánské Square can also be left via Kapucínská Lane starting behind the passage (bridge) connecting the monastery with the Loretto and ending in the second third of the Lane Nový Svět (New World). The building on the right side (No 214/2) comes from the end of the 19th century. A court martial and a military prison were established in it. The memorial plaque reminds us of the tragical period of the Communist terror, when in the so called Hradčany Little House here the military intelligence service, the army parallel to the secret state police, had its inquisition rooms. Many political prisoners were inquired and tortured here, many of them paid to the Communist terror with their lives.

In the middle of *Černínská Lane* we pass by the **house** No 97/5 with a folk statue of St John of Nepomuk from the middle of the 17th century (transferred here from

The House At the Golden Grapes in Nový Svět Street, a detail of an oriel

Southern Bohemia). Next is the House **U zlatého bažanta** (At the Golden Pheasant, No 95/7), behind which we find ourselves at a small place below the walls of the Baroque fortifications of Prague - in the crossroads with the Lane *Nový Svět* (the New World). The last house in *Černínská Lane* is the House **U raka** (At the Crawfish, No 93/10) made up of two separate buildings from the period before the middle of the 18th century. They were originally used as butchers' cowsheds, they were adapted for residential purposes at the end of the 18th century. The writer Jakub Arbes placed the plot of his novel „The Miraculous Madonna" into the house. (Behind the house are the stairs leading to *Jelení Street*, on whose right side are the *Lumbe Parks*, nowadays belonging to Prague Castle.)

Nový svět

We come into Lane *Nový svět* (the New World), one of the most romantic spots of

The crossroads of Černínská Street (on the right) and Nový Svět

the Old Prague. This part of Hradčany was formed only at the end of the 16th century on the outskirts of the town along the road leading from the Hospital Gate in *Kanovnická Street* to Střešovice. The lane acquired its final form after building the Capuchin Monastery in the first half of the 17th century. The houses in the quiet, at one time poor quarter evoke an extraordinary picturesque impression and can remind some people of Golden Lane. Apart from two, all houses stand on the southern side of the lane (mainly on the monastery land), whereas most of the northern side is bordered by a wall, behind which stretches the green surface of the *New World Moat,* through which the Brusnice stream flows.

It is worth mentioning at least the names of the houses. On the northern side are the House **U zeleného křížku** (At the Green Cross) (No 89/24) and the House **U zlaté hvězdy** (At the Golden Star) (No 87/22); probably they both were built according to the designs of Ignác Palliardi, on the former is a remnant of the first Czech-German marking of street names. On the southern side we pass by the House **U zlatého slunce** (At the Golden Sun) (No 92/27) and **U zlatého pluhu** (At the Golden Plough) (No 90/25), where the well-known violinist František Ondříček was born (died in 1922). The House No 88/23 has no name and originally was connected with the House At the Golden Plough. Next is the House **U bílého lva** (At the White Lion) (No 86/21), the House **U zlatého beránka** (At the Golden Lamb) (No 85/19), the House **U zlatého čápa** (At the Golden Stork) (No 84/17), the House **U zlatého keře** (At the Golden Bush) (83/15), the House **U zlatého stromu** (At the Golden Tree) (No 82/13), the nameless House No 81/11, the House **U sv. Michala** (At St Michael) (No 80/9). Between both ends of *Kapucínská Street* stands the House **U zlatého žaludu** (At the Golden Acorn) (No 79/7) also called Šmicerovský. At the beginning of the 18th century it belonged to the family of the stuccoer František Santini Aichl, the brother of the famous architect Giovanni Santini. Behind *Kapucínská Street* is the early Baroque House **U zlatého hroznu** (At the Golden

The Church of St John of Nepomuk

*The Chapel of the Hospital
of St Anthony and St Elizabeth*

the former **Hospital of St Anthony and St Elizabeth** (No 73/7). It was here probably in the 14th century, it was founded by Archbishop Jan Očko of Vlašim, however it fell out of use during the time of the Hussite Wars. The new hospital intended for retired employees of the Castle was founded in 1574 by Emperor Maxmillián II.

The hospital inhabitants had only one duty, to attend every day the requiem Mass celebrated for the soul of the Queen Anne in the St Vitus Cathedral. This requiem was established „for eternal times" by her loving husband Emperor Ferdinand I Hapsburg. The hospital inhabitants got from the royal treasury the fixly stated sum of 10 kreutzers a day for a living. The money was sufficient at the time of founding the hospital, however at the beginning of the 18th century it was quite insufficient. The complaints had no end, since it was impossible even to ensure the elementary foods and firewood. The finance officials took their time over „re-valuation" of the pensions even two hundred and fifty years ago.

Grapes) (No 78/5) with a corner oriel; here lived the composer Rudolf Friml, whose sister Zdena was courted here by the famous Prague song writer Karel Hašler. Next is the House **U zlaté hrušky** (At the Golden Pear) (also called At Abraham; No 77/3) and the last is the House **U zlatého noha** (At the Golden Griffin) (No 76/1), in which probably lived the Danish astronomer Tycho Brahe around 1600.

The hospital was rebuilt into the present form around 1735 by Kilián Ignác Dientzenhofer. In 1784 the hospital was closed and changed into a military hospital, later into a residential house. In the hospital court one can see the noble front of the hospital chapel. Next the hospital stands the **Church of St John of Nepomuk**, built between 1720-29 by Kilián Ignác Dietzenhofer for the neighbouring Ursuline Convent. It is one of the oldest church buildings by Dientzenhofer. The central layout going through the transcept, so much typical of his later buildings, is not complemented, however, it is marked by a large illusive fresco. This is a work by Vavřinec Reiner and depicts scenes from the life of St John of Nepomuk and his miracles. The top of the tower was modified in 1815. After abolishing the Ursuline Convent in 1784 the church was converted into a military

Kanovnická Street

At the end of the lane we turn right into *Kanovnická Street*. In it used to stand the Hospital Gate built before 1657 by the three Italian architects - Giovanni Battista Orsi, Domenik Caneval and Domenik Rosetti, who payed in this way for the rights of the Hradčany citizens. On the left side we pass by the early Baroque **Palace of the Hložek family of Žampach** (No 70/4), whose builder was the Prague Castle captain.

On the opposite side of the street stands

*The entrance to the Church
of St John of Nepomuk*

*The niche in the wall of the St Anthony
and St Elizabeth Hospital*

warehouse, in 1861 it was adapted for the military Protestant service and in 1902 for the military Catholic Mass. South of the church stands the **Ursuline Convent** (No 72/5). The Convent was founded originally in 1691 in the Small Quarter, however, in 1700 the Ursuline nuns bought the Hradčany House of the Counts Talmberks and in 1721 built new convent buildings in its place. The author of the design was Kilián Ignác Dientzenhofer. In the Convent was even placed a school for girls. Noteworthy was mainly the layout of the top floor with small luxury apartments for girls from rich noble families. After abolishing the Monastery in 1784 the buildings were converted into barracks.

The Ursuline nuns bough the Talmberk House among others thanks to the generosity of Kateřina Lamingerová, the wife of the well-known „Lomikar". Previously, the house was called At the Black Moor. In the Renaissance period it was owned by the Italian architect and stonemason Paolo della Stella, later it was the residence of the Spanish ambassadors to the court of Emperor Rudolf II.

Next on the right, behind the crossroads with the Street *U kasáren*, stands the Renaissance **Dům pážat** (House of the Pages) (No 69/3), originally a Gothic building. In 1587 the house was bought from Kateřina of Lokšany (the wife of Jiří of Lobkovice) for the pages of Emperor Rudolf II.

Along the side facade of the Renaissance **Martinic Palace** (No 67) on the left we come back to *Hradčany Square,* where we end the walk.

Fourth walk:

FROM POHOŘELEC TO THE STRAHOV MONASTERY

The sculptural group of the Pieta at the top of the staircase of the St Elizabeth Hospital

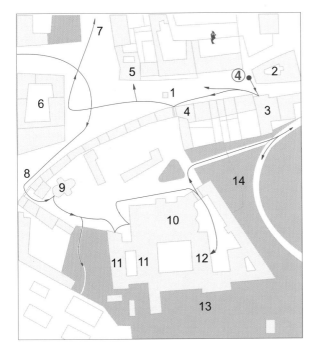

1 - the sculptural group of St John of Nepomuk
2 - the Trauttmannsdorf House
3 - the Hospital of St Elizabeth
4 - the House At the Green Tree
5 - the Dermatini Palace
6 - the barracks
7 - a path to the Baroque fortifications
8 - the entrance gate to the Strahov Monastery
9 - the Church of St Roch
10 - the Church of the Assumption of the Virgin Mary
11 - the monastery library
12 - the monastery
13 - the monastery garden
14 - the abbot's garden

The roof of the Trauttmannsdorf Palace

Pohořelec

Pohořelec Square *was founded in 1375 by the vice-Burgrave of Prague Castle, Aleš of Malkovice as a Hradčany suburb. It stretched outside the old Strahov Gate (in* Loretánská *Street) along the route to the Strahov Monastery and further to the west. In the Baroque period it was incorporated into the large fortifications of Prague.*

Because this quarter lay in the direction of the easiest access to the Castle, it was often stricken by war. In 1420, during the fights of the Hussites with King Zikmund, Pohořelec was burnt down. It was renewed in the 15th century, however it was completely burnt down in 1541 during the fire of the Small Quarter and Hradčany. It suffered in a similar way during the French occupation of Prague in 1742. Pohořelec had to experience fire at the time of its foundation, since its name is original. (Compare the name with the Czech word „hořet" (burn). There is also an explanation deriving the name of the square from the Czech word „hora" (mountain), i.e. the Hradčany ridge).

The preserved houses are completely of the Renaissance origin, rebuilt in the Baroque period. The Hradčany Town was engaged in a lawsuit with the Strahov Monastery for the southern side of the square. The Strahov Premonstratentians won the years-long suit by the decision of Emperor Rudolf II in 1603. From that time the southern part of Pohořelec was under the administration of the Strahov Monastery.

In the square at Christ's figure showing the stigmata, execution were carried out of people falling within the jurisdiction of Hradčany, mainly of people of lower birth. Nowadays in the middle of the square stands the Baroque **statue of St John of Nepomuk** transferred here from the corner of *Hradčanské Square* and *Kanovnická Street*.

The eastern side of Pohořelec is enclos-

that time it was usual to gather all sick into one large ward.

The original Strahov Hospital used to stand from 1623 at the western end of the square, however, it was demolished during the building of the Baroque fortifications of Prague. A Latin commemorative plaque has been preserved of it, placed above the entrance to the new hospital.

We should be aware that the medieval hospital or home for the old had a different function than modern hospitals. The main motive for their founding was not the care of the physical illnesses, but the spiritual service and comfort to the afflicted. In spite of this, the patients got in hospitals also the elementary medical treatment. The life of the patients was not comfortable. If they could, they had to work, and they often walked and begged. A burgher could pay in advance a place in a house for the old, even then there existed a prototype of „social insurance".

The House At Two Golden Stars

ed by the narrow front of the corner **Trautmannsdorf House** (No 110/26), which widens by the long side wings into *Loretánské Square* and *Úvoz* Street. The house is also called the *Wide Court* because of its vastness. It has an interesting entrance and roof gables from the 17th century. Till 1636 it belonged to the Trčka family of Lípa, then to the Trauttmannsdorfs. Here used to be an inn with stables and a brewery. Between 1885-86 here lived the painter Mikoláš Aleš.

On the southern side of the square (at the end of Street *Úvoz*) is the front of the **former** Strahov **Hospital of St Elizabeth** (No 155/15), founded in 1668 by the Strahov abbot Vincenc Frank. Its facade is adorned by a double flight of stairs with a sculptural group of the Calvary from 1726. Inside leads a long corridor on whose sides are preserved a few of the former hospital cells for the poor and the sick. The existence of separate cells was a relatively considerable comfort, since at

Of the houses in the southern front of the square (belonging to the Strahov Monastery) it is worth mentioning the House **At Two Golden Stars** (No 152/3) with a housesign above the windows and a fresco of the Virgin Mary in a cartouche on the front, the House **At Three Red Lion Heads** (No 151/4) with a picture of three lions, the House **At the Golden Plough** (No 150/5) with a painted housesign, the **House** No 149/6 with a remarkable roof ledge on consoles. The House **At the Golden Tree** (No 147/8) has a staircase connecting *Pohořelec* with the *Strahov Courtyard* (leading directly to the pub of the Strahov brewery). Above the entrance to the staircase is placed the sign of the Strahov Monastery. The House **At Three Golden Roses** (No 144/11) has on its front a glazed picture of St Norbert in a rich stucco frame. Above the roof one can see the battlements of the protective

The Dermatini Palace

wall of the Strahov Monastery. The House **At the Blue Star** (No 143/12) is decorated by a sculpture of the Madonna with little Jesus. In the House **At Three Lilies** (No 139/16) used to be the pub of Antonín Jitrnička in the 19th century. The house is mentioned in a legend about a girl who came here to dance because of her passion from the bed of her deceased mother.

The northern side of the square consists now of only four houses. The first in the direction from *Loretánské Square* is the **Šlik Palace** (No 111/25), modified in the Classicist style, later called the Municipal House. In the 19th century here used to be a municipal orphanage and a school. In the house in 1848 Josef Boleslav Pecka-Strahovský was born, a poet and a pioneer of the Socialism. The next House **At the Kundratics** (No 112/24) has a sober, but noble Baroque facade. Next is the former **Strahov presbytery** (No 113/23) with a painting of the Virgin Mary and the coats of arms of the Strahov abbots. This house was originally called At the Golden Lion and in the 18th century it was used as an inn. It was bough for the parish and modified by the Strahov Monastery in 1773. The corner with *Keplerova* Street is created now by the **Demartini Palace** (also the Kučera Palace or the House At the Golden Ship, No 114/22) with a charming Rococo facade. It belonged to an Italian family of chimney sweepers, the Demartins, who gained the priviledge „to sweep the imperial chimneys" under Emperor Rudolf II. A later occupier, the Imperial officer Jan Kučera, was well known for his friendship with Ludwig van Beethoven. Behind the Dermatini Palace used to stand four houses, which were demolished in connection with building *Keplerova Street.*

The western side of the square is created by the large neo Renaissance building of the **barracks** (No 121/21), behind which led the Baroque fortifications. Its front

The military cemetery below the Hradčany fortifications

The gravestone of General Schilke in the military cemetery

with Corinthian semicolumns has a gable with a clock on its top.

Along the southern side of the barracks leads *Dlabačov* Street, in which used to stand the new **Strahov Gate**, a part of the Baroque fortifications of Prague. Between the northern side of the barracks and the modern school building (No 1118/2) at the corner of streets *Parléřova* and *Keplerova* stood the **Kurz House** till 1593. In 1599 Emperor Rudolf II bought it for the astronomer Tycho Brahe, who lived here till his death in 1601. The astronomer Johannes Kepler used to be present during his astronomical observations. Both astronomers are reminded by the sculptural group by Josef Vajce from 1984. At the place around the present tram stop used to stretch a pond of the Strahov Monastery, used for watering monastery horses.

Now we can come to the southwestern corner of the square and come through the main gate into the area of the Strahov Monastery or we extend our walk by

nearly a kilometre and make a visit of the preserved parts of the Baroque fortifications of Prague.

Turning to the Baroque fortifications

We turn from *Pohořelec Square* to *Keplerova Street*. Along the **Savoy Hotel** (No 219/6) and four next houses and along the garden wall of the Černín Palace we come into a narrow park sited (like the whole *Keplerova Street*) on the top of the former Baroque fortifications. Directly below the park leads the Hradčany Lane *Nový Svět*, evoking the same picturesque impression from above as when we visited it directly in the previous walk. From the fortification mound an unexpectedly beatiful view opens up of the Hradčany roofs, the Capuchin Monastery by the Loretto, the Loretto Tower and the tower of the St John of Nepomuk Church. From here the St Vitus Cathedral makes a unique impression especially at twi-

The park near the Hradčany fortifications

between the former **Bastion No X of St Francic Borgiash** and the **Stone Bastion No XI** Emperor Joseph II founded in the 1780s a small **military cemetery** for the Prague artillery regiment. The most ostentatious tomb is that of General Wenzel Schiepke, the Knight of Blumenfeld, whose coats of arms is carved out upside down to signify that the general was the last of his family. Also the artillery brigadier, mathematician and geodesist, Josef Jüttner, the author of a detailed Prague street plan, is buried here. This seldom visited place is an example of a decaying but still picturesque spot on the outskirts of the historic Prague.

We walk on through the nature along the Baroque walls southwards and pass by a star shaped kerb of the mass grave of the Prussian artillerymen who died in 1866 in occupied Prague.

light, when the rays of the setting sun touch it. It seems as if the Cathedral were emerging from the greenery of the Hradčany gardens and glowed itself with sublime light.

A few metres further, on the site of the former bastion No XI the park widens and is planted with mulberry trees. (Mulberry trees were planted on the site of the Prague walls mainly in the 19th century, when their fruit was popular. Also the silkworm was kept here, and Prague became a small centre of the silk industry.) In the park is placed a statue of the Belarus physician, botanist and printer Francisko Skorina, the founder of the Belarus and Lithuanian typography, who lived in Prague for a longer time in the service of the Archduke Ferdinand of Tyrol and printed here the Old Testament in the Cyrillic.

We cross *Keplerova Street* and at the end of the park go down below the external side of the fortification mound. Here,

On the way we can see various elements of the bastion fortification system - mainly the protruding brick pentagonal bastions with reinforced edges, but also smaller complementing fortification elements, such as small gates for quick counterattacks and the remnants of the moat. The Baroque fortifications were built after the Thirty Years Wars experience, when Prague was occupied several times. Therefore after its end the military command of Prague decided to build a unified belt of the walls around the whole city. The fourteen kilometres long fortifications with nine gates and thirty bastions were built between 1653-1730 according to the designs of the military engineer Count de Conti. Thus Prague was enclosed in a sturdy shell, which surrounded it nearly by the end of the 19th century. Only after demolishing the walls, on whose site streets and parks were founded, Prague could develop into a modern city.

We come from the park outside the walls into *Hládkov Street*, where we continue to the left (to the east) till we

The Strahov Monastery from the Street Úvoz

come in *Keplerova Street* near its end into *Pohořelec*.

Strahov Monastery

We enter the Strahov Monastery throught the Baroque gate decorated on the top by a statue of St Norbert, the founder of the Premonstratensian Order. We stop in the *Strahov Courtyard* in front of the column with a Baroque statue of the saint.

St Norbert of Xanthe experienced a deep conversion to faith in the summer in 1115. A miracle helped him in this. When he was on his way to a merry festivity, lightning struck in front of him. Norbert fell off his horse and heard a voice urging him to abandon his wrongdoing and do good. In 1120 he fulfilled the order by founding a monastery, known as Premonstratensian after the valley Premontre. Premonstratensians monasteries spread quickly across the whole Europe and became guardians of medieval culture. Norbert became archbishop of Magdeburg,

and was buried here later. In 1582 he was sanctified. Because Magdeburg was taken over by Protestants, in 1627 his body was transferred to Doksany and from where it was transferred with a procession and all due ceremonies to the Strahov Monastery. Here the remains of St Norbert were buried and he became a patron saint of the land. (The legend of St Norbert is often depicted and commemorated mainly in Premonstratensian monasteries. An unsubstantiated theory has been suggested that the legend about the lightning influenced the Czech inventor of the lightning conductor, the priest Prokop Diviš, brought up in the Premonstratensian Monastery Louka near Znojmo.)

History of the Monastery

The Strahov Monastery was founded in 1140 on an important country route leading to the Castle. The founder was Prince (and from 1158 King) Vladislav II himself. He was prompted to found the monastery by his friend and advisor, Jindřich Zdík, the Bishop of Olomouc

1 - the Church of the
    Assumption of the
    Virgin Mary
2 - the estate
    manager's house
3 - the prelature (the
    abbot's residence)
4 - the monastery
    building with the
    Paradise Court
5 - the Summer
    Refectory
6 - the Theological Hall
7 - the Philosophical
    Hall

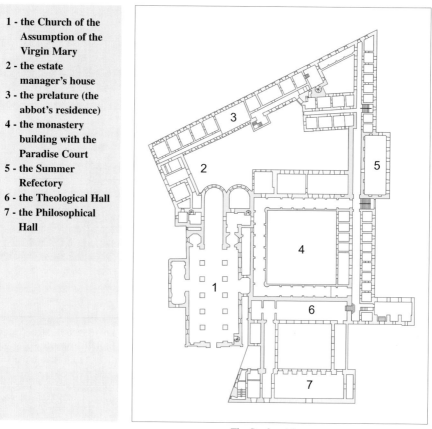

The Strahov Monastery,
the ground plan of the central monastery part

and a diplomat, who just had returned from the pilgramage into the Holy Land. At first Zdík tried to form a Czech variant of the Order of St Augustin and appointed Blažej as abbot of the new Order. The activities of the Czech canons were not successful, and therefore Zdík called from Germany members of the newly founded Premonstratensin Order. The first abbot was called Gezo and came from Rhineland's Steinfeld.

The Premonstratensian Monastery flourished thanks to Vladislav's favour and soon became a famous centre of learning with a well-known library. The king himself and his wife Gertruda of Babenberk and Bishop Zdík frequently stayed here and were buried here. Then the Strahov Monastery exceeded by its size even the residence of the ruler at Prague Castle. It was the largest Romanesque building in Bohemia, and perhaps in the whole Central Europe. Important delegations used to be accommodated here, the Monastery refectory was used till the time of Přemysl II Otakar as a Diet. The originally Romanesque group of buildings

The entrance gate to the Strahov Monastery

The Church of St Roch in the Strahov courtyard

was damaged by fire and warfare several times, and so was frequently rebuilt. It burnt out completely in 1258, but it was soon renewed. In 1360 it was incorporated into the town walls of the Small Quarter and thereby it was better ensured against attacks. It was modified partly in the high and late Gothic periods, the extensive Renaissance rebuilding was carried out between 1614-29 under the abbot Kašpar of Questenberk, when the cloisters of the Paradise Court were completed and the prelature was built. The Monastery suffered during the Thirty Years War, mainly at its end in 1648, when valuable spoils of works of arts, manuscripts and old prints were transported from there to Sweden. During 1682-98 it was modified in the Baroque style according to the design of Jan Baptista Mathey. During the Renaissance and Baroque rebuildings heated rooms were established instead of the common bedroom (dormitory) and the warming-up room, and the Monastery lost its stronghold character. It was seriously damaged

in 1741 during the liberating of Prague occupied by the French troops. New damage was caused by the Prussian bombardment of Prague in 1757. The Monastery gained the present form by further modifications, in 1783 a new monastery library was built. In 1950 the monks were expelled by the Communist regime and the Monastery with its renowned library was adapted for the needs of the Museum of the National Literature. After 1989 the Premonstratensian Order came back here.

It is worth noticing the complex monastery water supply system, interesting from the technical viewpoint, designed even before the beginning of building the monastery and built with it simultaneously. Water was brought from rich springs on the Petřín slopes by its own gravity, and it was lead through several canals into the monastery buildings and the fountain. If flowed from the fountain into a pond in the middle of the Paradise Court, where fish were kept, a favourite fast meal. At the end of the 17th century the water system was rebuilt. An underground tunnel was dug out, into which the Petřín springs were led. Also the sewer tunnels were dug out. Other tunnels were driven in the second half of the 17th century.

Strahov courtyard

Left of the entrance is the **Church of St Roch** coming from the beginning of the 17th century. Emperor Rudolf II dedicated it to St Roch, the protector against plague sores, to express his gratitude for his living through the plague epidemy in 1599. The church has a cross groundplan and is built in a remarkable combination of the Gothic and the Renaissance, probably according to the design of Giovanni Mario Filippi. In 1784 it was closed, in 1882 it was newly consecrated. Since the second half of the 20th century it serves as an exhibition hall.

The front gable of the Church of the Assumption

Right of the entrance are the out-buildings. Behind them leads a path to other agricultural buildings and the monastery garden, closed for the public. However, we can visit the famous Peklo (Hell) Restaurant (No 132), whose name reminds us of the original division of the monastery garden into the upper (Heaven) and the lower (Hell) parts. A number of agricultural buildings borders the northern side of the *Strahov courtyard* behind the Church of St Roch. The most important of them is the former **Strahov Brewery** (No 135). A brewery was in Strahov even in 1400, however at a different place. The present building was built in 1629, beer was brewed here till the beginning of the 20th century and it was sold in an adjacent, later demolished, tavern.

The Church of the Assumption of the Virgin Mary

We are approaching the abbey Church of the Assumption of the Virgin Mary. The church is in its core a three naved Roma-

nesque basilica from the 12th century built parallelly with the monastery. It was vaulted in the period of the early Gothic, between 1601-05 it was rebuilt in the Renaissance style according to the design of Giovanni Bossi de Campione. Then both towers by the western front were demolished and two new towers were built on the sides of the presbytery, which were considered the protectors of the altar, as it began to be usual in Catholic (anti-Reformation) churches. Between 1630-31 the church was extended to the west; from that period the late Renaissance western portal is preserved. The church acquired the present Baroque appearance between 1742-58 during the rebuilding carried out by Anselm Lurag. In 1992 the church was elevated by Pope John Paul II to the status of Basilica minor, which is a title given to the most significant Catholic churches.

The inner decoration of the church is mainly Baroque coming from around 1750. The vaulting is decorated by eight large and 32 small frescos with scenes on the motives of the Loretto litanies and the litanies about the Immaculate Conception. Above the arcades of the side nave in beatiful stucco cartouches are placed 12 wall paintings depicting the legend about St Norbert. By the wall of the choir stands a memorial of the church founders, Prince Vladislav II and Bishop Jindřich Zdík, who are buried in the church at an unknown place. From the left side nave it is possible to enter the Chapel of St Ursula. Here on the main altar the remains of St Norbert are kept. On the altar opposite the entrance are placed the remains of St Ursula. From the right side nave one can enter the Chapel of the Virgin Mary of Passau, decorated on the vaulting by a picture of the Battle of Lützen by Siardus Nosecký. In the chapel is buried General Gottfried of Pappenheim, who died in 1632 as a result of his wounds in this battle. His name found its way into the Czech proverb „We know our Pappenheimers". The organ from 1746-80 was played by Wolfgang Amadeus Mozart during his Prague sojourn.

Strahov library

In front of the western front of the church is the Classicist building of the Strahov library, which was rebuilt during 1783-86 out of an early Baroque barn. The gilded portrait medallion of Emperor Joseph II was placed on the facade probably as an expression of thanks that the monastery (that opened providently its rich collections for the scientific public) was not abolished by the enlightened Emperor. The idea of opening the collections was pushed through by the abbot Mayer, a member of the Free Mason Lodge At Tree Crowned Columns.

In the entrance exhibition on the upper floor are displayed some documents concerning the founding of the monastery and the building and development of the library. Here are also placed facsimiles of the most significant manuscripts and old prints from the rich funds of the Strahov library. The Strahov library contains over 130 thousand volumes including manuscripts and early prints printed before 1500. The oldest manuscript is the Strahov evangeliary from 860. Next is the **Room of Curiosities -** a prototype of present historical and scientific museums. The collections were collected here from the end of the 18th century. From the room we can visit the **Philosophical Hall**. The hall is 32 m long, 10 m wide and 14 m high. It goes through two floors and is decorated by a fine ceiling painting by Antonín František Maulbertsch from 1794. The most significant painter of the Viennese Rococo, then 70 years old, depicted here the theme of the Struggle of Mankind to Find the Real Wisdom. He points out how philosophy and sciences improve themselves parallelly with religion and find the way to the greatest wisdom in Christianity. (Among others even the French encyclopedists are painted here looking towards heaven afraid that they will be buried by the falling boulders.) Around the hall stand richly decorated Baroque cabinets transferred here from the abolished Premonstratensian Monastery Louka near Znojmo. The size of the already completed hall was modified according to the cabinets. The building was heightened and some of the windows were walled up and one wall was newly built. The rebuilding was completed in 1792. In the hall are about 50,000. volumes, all old and modern scientific literature. In the middle of the hall we can see a cabinet inlaid with nacre containing ten volumes; it was given to the monastery by Maria Louisa, wife of Napoleon I, who visited Prague in 1813.

From the Room of Curiosities leads a **corridor** connecting the Philosophical Hall with the Theological Hall. A similar

The front of the Strahov library

corridor connects both halls from the other side.

In the corridor continues the exhibition of curiosities, we can be captivated by a model of a warship from the 16th century, collections of weapons and precious stones. Here are also kept collections of the law, medical and pharmaceutical literature. Also the dendrological library from 1852 is worth noticing; it contains 68 volumes describing the trees growing in Bohemia. Each volume is dedicated to one tree, its wood and bark are used for the cover and the spine.

At the end of the corridor we can visit the **Theological Hall**, the older official room of the Strahov library. The hall was established between 1671-79 by the architect Giovanni Domenik Orsi from the initiative of the abbot Jeroným Hirnheim, a significant thinker and theologist. Onto stucco cartouches of the Baroque barrel vaulting Siard Nosecký painted pictures with themes related to bibliology. He painted himself with a pa-

lette in his hand in the third section between the windows. In the Baroque cabinets are kept numerous theological publications, manuscripts and first editions. The oldest manuscript is a parchment evangeliary from the 9th century. The prohibited books were kept in two small barred bookcases above the entrances. In the hall are placed Holland globes from between 17th - 19th centuries, we can be captivated by a compilation wheel (rotary desk for books) from 1678 and the late Gothic statue of Evangelist St John holding a book in an interesting medieval binding in his hand.

Monastery buildings

We come out of the monastery library into the courtyard and along the abbot church we come to a gate built into a wing of the high Baroque **building of the estate manager**. We enter the **monastery court**, whose left side is created by the **House of the Prelates** (the Abbot's residence), rebuilt between

The end of the Church of the Assumption viewed from the monastery court

a fresco „Isaac Blessing Jacob". On the ground floor of the western wing are preserved two Romanesque rooms, above them on the upper floor is the **Theological Hall**, originally the monastery library. The southern flight of stairs is extended eastwards by the building of the **Summer Refectory** built around 1690 according to the designs of Jean Baptist Mathey. In the first half of the 18th century the high refectory hall was decorated by rich stuccos and on the whole vaulting by a large fresco of the Heavenly Feast by Siard Nosecký.

Strahov picture gallery

On the first floor of the cloister is the famous Strahov picture gallery. It was founded in 1836 by the abbot Jeroným Zeidler and its collections contain above 1000 pictures, of which only a small part is exhibited. The exhibition provides a survey of the art from the 14th to the 19th centuries. There are many Gothic works (the Strahov Madonna from the 14th century, the paintings of the late Gothic Master of the Litoměřice Altar etc.), later styles are represented by works by Bartolomeo Spranger, Karel Škréta, Petr Brandl, Václav Vavřinec Reiner and others. The picture gallery is complemented by collections of crafts, mainly by liturgical objects from between 14th - 19th centuries.

Strahov Garden

We enter the *Strahov courtyard* again and after passing by the sculptural group of the beatified Heřman with the Madonna by Jan Antonín Quitainer we come to the eastern gate leading into the *Strahov Garden*. The garden stretches across the slope up to the Small Quarter Hospital of the Merciful Sisters and has mainly an orchard character. Only its top part from the beginning of the 17th century, called the Abbot's Garden is embellished by flower beds. At the beginning of the 17th centu-

1680-98 according to the design of Jean Baptist Mathey. On the upper floor of the House of the Prelates is the abbot's dining room and private chapel from 1743 decorated with frescos by Siard Nosecký. On the right side of the courtyard opposite the House of the Prelates stands the **monastery building itself**, originally a Romanesque object from 1142-82, standing around the Paradise court with a large pond in the middle. The present appearance of the monastery is Baroque, however numerous remnants of the Romanesque building remained preserved, including double shafted windows and two complete rooms. The eastern monastery wing is created mainly by the **Capitular Hall** from the 12th century, rebuilt after 1742. It is decorated by a ceiling fresco of the Healing the Lame Man by Siard Nosecký. From the Capitular Hall we can come into the **Winter Refectory** (a dining room) decorated with a stucco Baroque vaulting and

The house of the estate manager with the entrance to the monastery court

The view of Prague from the slopes of Strahov Monastery garden

ry an architecturally designed monastery garden was founded south of the monastery buildings, which was modified in the Baroque style between 1682-1700 according to the design of Giovanni Baptist Mathey.

The monastery garden has three parts: the flower garden in front of the sala terrena, the middle ornamented part and the eastern part with a look-out terrace and a **summerhouse** from 1661, decorated with frescos of the personified elements by Antonín Stevens. In the summerhouse the view of the Vltava Marian Streams was painted, which were made navigable thanks to the Strahov Abbot Kryšpín Fuk. The top part of the monastery garden, one time stretching up to the Petřín hillside, was called „Paradise", whereas the lower part of the slopes near the monastery was called „Hell".

On the slopes of the *Strahov Garden* below the House of the Prelates we can have an extraordinary impressive view of the Prague basin with the roofs of the

Small Quarter in the foreground, Hradčany and Prague Castle on the left side, and the *Petřín* hill on the right side. We can come through *the Look-out Path* to *Petřín*, in the opposite direction to the Hradčany Street *Úvoz*.

We notice a **statue of the Virgin Mary**, placed on a high column on the edge of the monastery garden above the path to *Petřín*. It is a modern copy of a statue of the Virgin Mary, Queen of Peace. The original stood on a Baroque column erected in 1652 in Staroměstské Square. In 1918 this artistically valuable column was pulled down by an enranged mob, since it was considered wrongly the symbol of the Hapsburg oppression of the Czech nation.

Our walks through the Hradčany Town end at the *Louk-out Path*. We can compare our impressions for instance with the experiences of the French writer and thinker Albert Camus, who wrote down: „I was losing myself in the splendor of the Baroque churches and tried to find home there ... I was wandering along the Vltava crossed over with stormy weirs. I spent long hours in the great Hradčany Town, a deserted and quiet quarter." Or will it be more suitable to increase our impression with the words donated to Prague by the poet Oskar Wiener? „She is beatiful. Tempting like a woman, indefinite like a woman in blue veils of twilight, in which she hides herself under blossoming slopes, girt by the steel belt of the river, sprinkled with the smaragds of copper copulas."

(IV)
Where one can sit, eat and drink

Final walk

After tasting the Krušovice beer you will be greatly delighted

The Genius loci of Prague is created among others by the perfect harmonious joining together of the thousands years old work of the nature and the hundreds years old creative human activity. Prague has its dominants emphasises by the spiritual and cultural foci. It overflows with life. It can intensify the charm, with which it affects a visitor, and it can let the charm live in distant views and memories. Numerous pubs, restaurants and wine bars can help a tired wanderer to take rest and to make the first classification of his/her impressions.

A thirst goes hand in hand with lengthy travel, but it is not water which gladdens best the parched throat of a wanderer. Even the personal physician of Emperor Ferdinand I, the scholarly Jan Kopp, writes: „And because not everywhere can good water be found, for this reason the human mind artfully invented a different beverage, which we call beer, and that is brewed from water, grains and hops ... our blessed Czech beer."

A liking for beer was great in Bohemia from old times, even one of the first strikes was caused by it. It was in 1399 when the elders of the guild of locksmiths withheld the celebratory refreshments and toast from their journeymen at accepting a new apprentice. In the end the masters had to yield and pay for the cost of celebratory beer from that time on. The journeymen had to promise in return that henceforth they would only drink after working hours.

Since we walked through royal places, we should also taste royal beer. It is the **beer from the Royal Brewery in Krušovice**, founded in 1581 by Emperor Rudolf II himself. Until now the Krušovice beer belongs among the most popular beers. At Prague Castle we can taste it for instance in the pleasant **Restaurant Lví Dvůr** (the Lion Court) in the Street *U prašného mostu* (At the Powder Bridge). We can sit here both in the pleasant interior, and in the garden on the site of the original range for predatory animals, which the melancholic Emperor Rudolf II used to come to observe here. You will not find predators here, the only danger for you can be the Krušovice beer

Pleasant pubs and wine bars can be found at many spots of historic Prague

itself, whose fine taste tempts to intemperance. You can also sit in evening hours in the Lion Court area in the **Arcimboldo Restaurant**, called after a favourite Rudolf's court painter with rich fantasy. We find here also the pleasant **Cattedrala Coffee-house**.

In the Hradčany Town, which Rudolf elevated to the status of a royal town, you can taste the Krušovice beer for instance in the **Café-Restaurant** (No 145/10), placed in a Baroque house in *Pohořelec* Square.

A person preferring the Pilsen beer can visit the **Restaurant U sv. Jana Nepomuckého** (At St John of Nepomuk) (No 60/12) in a Renaissance house in *Hradčany Square*. St John of Nepomuk is the patron of the seal of confession and silence, however, maybe good meal and drinkink make you talk pleasantly. In the next house with a splendid Baroque front we can visit the **Restaurant U labutí** (At the Swans) (No 61/11). In the pub there

you can compare the beers of both Pilsen breweries, Prazdroj and Gambrinus. The menu here will satisfy you too.

The best known restaurant at Prague Castle is the **Vikárka Restaurant** (No 39/6 and 38/4), whose salons you can find in *Vikářská Street* directly below the northern side front of the St Vitus Cathedral. The name reminds us that one time here used to be the residence of the St Vitus vicars. The pub was made famous by the popular Czech writer of the 19th century Svatopluk Čech, since he placed in it the scene of his popular novel about the Prague burgher Mr Brouček. The presidential residence is not far from here, and it is no wonder that this restaurant was several times visited by the first President of the Czech Republic Václav Havel. You can find refreshment also in the **restaurant** in the Garden *Na Baště* (At the Bastion).

A person wanting to get acquainted with a traditional Prague pub, can visit the

The Lion Court viewed from the Royal Garden

Square. In *Pohořelec Square* we can visit the **Sate Restaurant** with the Indonesian quisine. It is in the Baroque House U dvou zlatých hvězd (At Two Golden Stars) (No 152/3). In the *Strahov Courtyard* we can take a rest in the **Peklo** (Hell) **Restaurant** (No 132). It is not easy to get into the Peklo, since it is skillfully hidden from the sight of tourists behind the walls of the Strahov Monastery below the Petřín slope, and there is no sign that could lead us to the lovely restaurant.

After a good meal it is good to drink coffee for better digestion, and it is no wonder, we can find a coffee bar nearly in each street and at every corner.

The custom of drinking this beverage got to Prague from Vienna. Praque was besieged by the Turks in 1683 and after their defeat bags with till that time uknown berries were found in the camp. The first Prague coffee bar was founded as late as in 1714. However, before this coffee grains were sold in pharmacies as an exotic medicine. Another gastronomical novelty owes for its origin to the Turkish siege. The Viennese bakers began to bake rolls bent into the shape of the Islamic crescent in the joy over the defeat of the Turks. This custom was also adopted by other bakers.

pleasant **Restaurant Hradčanská Radnice** (the Hradčany Townhall, No 173/1) at the beginning of *Loretánská Street* near the end of the *Townhall Stairs*. The Hradčany councillors had a pub here from the beginning of the 17th century. Another famous beer, Radegast is drawn here to typical Czech meals. A well-known Hradčany pub is the **Restaurant U černého vola** (At the Black Bull) in *Loretánské Square*. Another delicious beer - Velkopopovický kozel is drawn here in pleasant environment.

The visitors to Hradčany can also come to the pleasant **Renthaus Restaurant** (No 179/13) in *Loretánská Steet*, where they can enjoy special meals of the Czech quisine and at the same time have a charming view of Prague from above. Good dishes are prepared also in the **Restaurant U císařů** (At the Emperors) (No 175/5). From *Loretánská Street* you can also enter the **Tosca Restaurant** (No 182), placed in the Baroque Toscan Palace, whose main front faces *Hradčany*

Directly at Prague Castle we can visit for instance the Coffee House **Black Tower Cafe**, accessible from the court of the Burgrave's Residence. Its English name should remind the customer that English was never spoken at the Czech Royal Court, though one could hear here besides Czech and German also frequently Italian and Spanish. English might have been spoken in the Castle only during the short rule of the Winter King Friedrich of Falc (1619-20), whose wife was Elizabeth Stuart. However, she brought to Prague rather French customs. The coffee house is named after the Black Tower, to which it is adjoined. We should remind you that in the tower used to be a prison

The Garden At the Bastion with the place of refreshment

The entrance to the Kajetánska Coffee Bar

for debtors. In the Lobkovic Palace in Jiřská Street we can visit the **Café Terasa**, three or four coffee bars are also in *Golden Lane*. During our walks through Hradčany we should also visit the peculiar **Literary Coffe Bar U zavěšenýho kafe** (At the Hung Coffee) in the side wing of the Hradčany Townhall (No 173) facing the *Townhall Stairs*. On the ramp in front of Prague Castle, at the end of Street *Ke Hradu*, we can visit the Coffee Bar **Kajetánka**, established in the preserved part of the former Baroque Chapel of the Virgin Mary of Einsiedeln.

We should turn from coffee and sweets to something heavier. Wine always belonged on the table of a Prague nobleman or burgher.

The patron saint of the Czech wine-growers is St Wenceslas, Prince of the Czech Land, however, it was Emperor Charles IV, who contributed most to the tradition of the Czech winegrowing. On 16 February 1358 he ordered the owners of the till then infertile lands in

the Prague neighbourhood to plant vine there. The Emperor's motivation was not only lithurgical purposes, since he had quite a secular fondness of wine. He found out at least twice, that drinking too much wine can be treacherous. For the first time, under the influence of wine he branded undiplomatically Queen Elizabeth, mother of the Hungarian King Louis and sister of the Polish King Kazimír as „not enough chaste". Unfortunately, it happened in the presence of the Hungarian delegation. King Louis threatened with war, that was averted at a grand feast in Krakow, where the offended rulers married the Emperor to Elizabeth of Pomerania, a relative of the offended Queen. According to a Hungarian legend King Louis took his revenge on Charles IV: When he arrived in Prague, he brought with himself a number of waggons loaded with Hungarian wine, whose effects nobody of Charles's subjects knew. The Hungarian King was giving wine to the whole town, and on the second day, at the time of the festive audience with the Emperor, the whole Prague was lying at Ludvík's feet. To prevent such a thing in the future, Charles IV ordered to

Nor does Prague Castle lack playfulness: a cat and a dog in the triforium of the St Vitus Cathedral

The entrance to the Kolowrat House gives evidence about the likings of its owners

plant vine also in Bohemia. Everybody could train in drinking wine, and so this dangerous Hungarian weapon was for ever rid of its edge.

We can taste wine in the previously mentioned restaurants and coffee bars. We would like to draw your attention to the pleasant **Wine Bar and Restaurant U Lorety** (At the Loretto), established in the Small Černín Palace (No 102/8) in *Loretánské Square*. You can hear the Loretto carillon not only from the garden in front of the wine bar, but also from its Baroque salons. At the crossroads of *Černínská Lane* and the picturesque lane *Nový Svět* (the New World) stands the Wine and Coffe Bar U Raka (At the Crawfish, No 93/10). The house, in which it is reminds us of the Czech folk timber houses. It is also interesting, that the Czech writer Jakub Arbes placed into it the scene of his novel the Miraculous Madonna. Further on in *Lane Nový svět* stands the **Wine Bar U zlaté hrušky** (At the Golden Pear) (No 77/3), which belongs to the local colour of this Hradčany spot.

The times have long been gone, when the English writer Lady Wortley Montague complained that she „brought her own bed with herself and did not find a place where to place it." The possibilities of accommodation are now numerous in Prague. From those in Hradčany we can mention the **Savoy Hotel** (No 219/6) in *Keplerova Street*. In *Úvoz Street* is the **Hotel U Krále Karla** (At King Charles) in the Baroque House **U tří červených růží** (At Three Red Roses) (No 170/4).

Naturally, we can refresh ourselves and have a rest and experience something not only in the territory of Prague Castle and Hradčany. It is sufficient just to go down into the Small Quarter, once a separate Prague town, founded in 1257 by the Czech King Přemysl II Otakar. The Small Quarter is famous for its palaces and palace gardens. The prevailing style is the Baroque, the whole quarter is dominated by the large Church of St Nicolas in Malostranské Square. Directly at its foot we can sit, for example, in the Malostranská (Small Quarter) Coffee Bar. Next to it, in Letenská Street is the

The last farewell to Prague Castle

famous brewery At St Thomas founded long time ago by the Augustinian monks. In Maltézské Square is the famous wine bar U Malířů. Lovely wine bars and restaurants are spread along the Vltava river and its arm called Čertovka. However, the Small Quarter has many more wine bars, pubs and restaurants. The Nebozízek Restaurant on the slope of Petřín is famous for the beatiful view of Prague. We can approach it from Pohořelec (from the Strahov Monastery) via the Strahov Path leading through the Petřín top and then we can take the cableway (one stop downwards). Walking through Petřín parks is pleasant and the view of the Gothic toothed Hunger Wall might evoke the need to sit and have a pleasant meal. A legend says that Emperor Charles IV had the wall built at the time of famine to provide living for the poor. The Nebozízek itself is originally an old farmstead with an interesting history. Its name comes from the winding paths leading to it and reminding us of the spiral of a drill. Friedrich Schiller stayed here during his visit to Prague.

From the Small Quarter we can have a nice walk across the Gothic Charles Bridge getting thus to the Old Town - the oldest Prague town, founded in 1232 (inhabited permanently since the 11th century). The Old Town lanes are full of hospitable places. Undoubtedly, we will stop in Staroměstské (Old Town) Square in front of the Old Town Townhall with the famous astronomical clock, which we can see also from the garden of the restaurant and wine bar U Prince (At the Prince). It is memorable by the stay of King Friedrich of Falc in it during his flight from Prague after the lost Battle of the White Mountain. Undoubtedly, the most famous restaurant in the New Town founded in 1348 by Emperor Charles IV is the brewery and restaurant U Fleků founded at the end of the 15th century and popular for its black beer.

Let us end the exhausting list of the places where one can rest. Perhaps intuition will tell us, which of them is the most suitable place for enriching our walks through Prague Castle and Hradčany.

KEY FIGURES OF THE CZECH HISTORY

Chronological
outline
of the significant
personalities
mentioned
in the book

Boňvoj I (about 852/57 - 888/89), a Czech prince from the Přemyslide dynasty. He ruled from about 882/84. The first historically substantiated Přemyslide ruler and the first Christian ruler of Bohemia. The husband of St Ludmila, a patroness saint of the Czech nation. Christened in Great Moravia around 882. His Christian orientation caused a pagan uprising, which was suppressed with the support of Great Moravia. The founder of the oldest churches in Bohemia (St Kliment in Levý Hradec, the Church of the Virgin Mary at Prague Castle). He founded Prague Castle by fortifying a hill above the bend of the Vltava.

Wenceslas (about 907 - 28 Sept 935), a Czech prince from the Přemyslide dynasty. He ruled from 924. A patron saint of the Czech land. A son of Prince Vratislav and Princess Drahomíra, who ruled during his minority. According to tradition very educated, he supported the spreading of Christianity, he himself excelled at piety. He had the remains of his grandmother Ludmila transported to Prague and founded the Rotunda of St Vitus at Prague Castle. He consolidated the power of the Přemyslide family in Bohemia. In 929 defeated by the German Emperor Henry the Fowler (the Czech side again had to pay a tribute to the Empire). He was assassinated in Stará Boleslav by his brother Boleslav I the Cruel, who then took over the power. Wenceslas's body was transported into the Church of St Vitus in Prague, which became the centre of St Wenceslas' cult. From the 10th century he was adored as saint, first in Bohemia, then in the neighbouring countries. From the second half of the 11th century the St Wenceslas cult had a key position in the ideology of the Czech state. (St Wenceslas was regarded as the heavenly ruler and defender of the Czech state, the Czech rulers were considered only his temporal deputies, who ruled in the name of his heavenly justice.) From the period of Charles IV the so called St Wenceslas crown became the symbol of the Czech state, to which the particular lands of the Czech crown were subordinated. St Wenceslas' cult is strong even in the latest history of the Czech nation.

Boleslav II (died on 7 Feb 999), a Czech prince from the Přemyslide dynasty. He ruled from 972. In 973 he founded the Prague bishopric and at the same time his sister Mlada obtained from the Pope the permission to found the first convent in Bohemia (the Benedictine Convent of St George at Prague Castle) and became its first abbess. Boleslav II completed the uniting of Bohemia under the Přemyslide rule in 995, when he conquered the seat of the competing Slavník family and had all present Slavníks murdered.

Vojtěch (around 957 - 23 April 997), a Czech bishop and saint from the Slavník family; a patron saint of the Czech land. He was elected the second Prague bishop in 982. In 988 he left for Italy because of the controversies at pushing through the ecclessiastic interests. In 992 after the urging of Prince Boleslav II he decided to return to Bohemia, where he founded the first monastery in the country in 993 (the Benedictine Monastery in Břevnov, now in Prague). After culminating the disagreement with the Czech nobility he left Bohemia again in 994. (In 995 the Slavník family, competing with the Přemyslide family, were murdered). In 996 he left for the Baltic region as a misionary, where he was killed in the next year by the pagan Prussians. He was soon adored as saint, his body was buried in Polish Hvězdno, which became the seat of the archbishopric. In 1039 the Czech Prince Břetislav I seized the body of St Vojtěch and transported it to Prague. St Vojtěch was buried in the St Vitus Church at Prague Castle.

Břetislav I (around 1005 - 10 Jan 1055), a Czech prince from the Přemyslide family. He ruled from 1034. He was called „Czech Achilles" for his bravery. He kidnapped his later wife Jitka from the Convent in Schweinfurt. During the rule of his father Oldřich he ruled in Moravia. In 1039 he invaded Poland and had the remains of St Vojtěch, a patron saint of the Czech land, transported from Hvězdno. He tried to gain the elevation of the Prague bishopric to the status of archbihopric, but he did not succeed. At the end of his life he issued an order about the right of succession according to which the rule belonged to the oldest member of the Přemyslide family.

Vratislav II (died on 14 Jan 1092), a Czech prince and king from the Přemyslide dynasty. He ruled from 1061, the first Czech king from 1085 (as Vratislav I). A son of Břetislav I. In 1063 he established the Olomouc bishopric as a support of the princely power in Moravia. The disagreements with his brother Jaromír Gebhart, from 1068 the Prague bishop, forced Vratislav to leave the seat at Prague Castle and to transfer the princely residence to Vyšehrad on the other side of the Vltava river. He founded here the Vyšehrad Chapter, subordinated directly to the Pope. He obtained the title of the Czech king in 1085 (only for his person, not hereditary) for the support of Emperor Henry IV. The ceremonial coronation was carried out at Prague Castle on 15 June 1086 in the Basilica of St Vitus, whose construction he completed three years later. Vratislav II supported the Slavonic lithurgy and at the Curia he tried to achieve its wider use. The effort to establish the Prague archbishopric was not successful.

Vladislav II (died 18 Jan 1174), a Czech prince and king from the Přemyslide dynasty, he ruled between 1140-72, as the king from 1158 (Vladislav I). His father Soběslav I (died in 1140) built the first stone princely palace at Prague Castle. In 1142 he stood up to the uprising of a part of the barons and most of the Přemyslides. In 1147 he participated in the second crusade into the Holy Land. In 1158 he obtained the royal title for his person (not hereditary) from Emperor Friedrich I Barbarossa for the promise to help him at his expedition against the rebellious north Italian towns. The Czech army excelled at the conquering of Milan. During his rule the first stone bridge across the Vltava was built, named after his wife Judita.

Přemysl I Otakar (around 1165 - 15 Dec 1230), a Czech prince and king from the Přemyslide dynasty. He ruled between 1192-93 and 1197-1230, as a king from 1198 (crowned in 1203). A son of King Vladislav I. During his youth he experienced the time of a political decline of the Czech state, when frequent changes of the members of the Přemyslide family on the throne provided the German rulers with the opportunity to intervene into the Czech affairs. His agreement with his brother Vladislav Jindřich (died in 1222), who made do with the title of the Moravian Margrave, ended years long strives between the Přemyslides and was a foundation of the consolidation of the Czech state. He took advantage of the weakening of the Roman Empire during the fights for the throne and strenthened the sovereignty of the Czech state and heightened its international prestige. His political skill was crowned by issuing the Golden Sicilian Bull, by which the German King Friedrich II confirmed the heredity of the royal title in the Přemyslide dynasty. The Czech king was confirmed as one of the seven electors of the emperor. His daughter Agnes was later adored as saint.

Wenceslas I (1205 - 23 Sep 1253), a Czech king from the Přemyslide dynasty. He ruled from 1230. The son of Přemysl I Otakar. In 1241 he organised the defence against the Tartar troops which went through Moravia from Poland to Hungary. Between 1247-49 he suppressed the uprising of Prince Přemysl II Otakar and a part of the nobility. His rule meant for the Czech state a period of a political, economical and cultural development. He supported the colonisation of the uninhabited areas, building castles, founding towns (in 1230 the founding charter of the Prague Old Town was issued). Tournaments of knights were held at his court. The beginning of the Czech Gothic culture falls into the period of his rule (the building of the Agnes Convent in Prague).

Přemysl II Otakar (1228 - 26 Aug 1278), a Czech king from the Přemyslide dynasty. He ruled from 1253. A son of Wenceslas I, called the „iron and golden King". Between 1247-49 he led an uprising against his father; defeated. Under his rule the Czech Kingdom reached the largest territorial extent (he gained among others Steiermark, Kärnten, Krain and the Aquileia patriarchy). In 1254-55 and 1267-68 he participated in the crusades into Prussia; he founded Königsberg (now Kaliningrad in Russia) on the Baltic coast, and tried to gain Lithuania. He lost most of the gained territories during his rule in the fights with Rudolf Hapsburg, with whom he competed for gaining the imperial crown. He did not succeed, paradoxically, because he was too powerful and the princes of the Empire wanted a weaker ruler whom they could manipulate. He was killed in the Battle of the Moravian Field on 26 August 1278. Přemysl II Otakar tried to consolidate the Czech state and cared for its economic development by founding new towns (in 1257 the founding charter of the Small Quarter was issued) and supporting colonisation.

Wenceslas II (27 Sept 1271 - 21 June 1305), a Czech king from the Přemyslide dynasty. He ruled from 1283. The son of Přemysl II Otakar. At the age of eight he was imprisoned by Ota of Brandenburg at Bezděz Castle, later he was transported from Bohemia and between 1279-83 he was kept in Brandenburg. In 1300 he was crowned the Polish King and in 1301 he accepted for his son Wenceslas III the Hungarian crown. Wenceslas II cared for universal development of the country. His rule was the climax of the economic and political rise of the Czech Kingdom in the 13th century. He supported the development of mining (especially the silver mines in Kutná Hora and Jihlava) and introduced a new silver coin - the Prague groschen. He tried to found a university in Bohemia and to issue a code of law for the kindgom; he did not succeed because of the opposition of the nobility. In Zbraslav he founded a Cistercian monastery, which served as a family tomb of the Přemyslides. His son Wenceslas III was assassinated in Olomouc in 1306; thus the Přemyslide dynasty died out on the spear side.

John of Luxembourg (10 Aug 1296 - 26 Aug 1346), a Czech king from the Luxembourg dynasty. He ruled from 1310. The son of the German - Roman King and Emperor Henry VII, father of Emperor Charles IV. He was brought up at the French court of Filip IV the Lovely. In 1310 in Speir he married Elizabeth Přemyslide, the daughter of Wenceslas II, which opened for him the way to the Czech throne. A brave warior and a skillful diplomat. He concentrated mainly on foreign policy (he annexed to the Czech crown the Cheb region, Upper Lusatia and a part of Silesia). Between 1330-33 he tried to establish a signoria under his leadership in Northern Italy. In 1334 he handed over, in fact, the rule of the Czech lands to his son Charles. He played an important role in the election of Charles as the German King in 1346. He was killed in the Battle of Crésy.

Charles IV (14 May 1316 - 29 Nov 1378), a Czech and Roman-German King from the Luxembourg dynasty. He ruled from 1346, the Roman-German King from 1355. Called „the Father of the Country". The oldest son of John of Luxembourg and Elizabeth Přemyslide, the most significant European ruler of the late Middle Ages. He was married four times. From 1323 he was educated at the French royal court, where he obtained a quality education (his tutor was among others Pierre de Rosieres, the later Pope Kliment VI). From 1334 he governed the Czech Kingdom (as the Margrave of Moravia) in place of his absent father. In 1344 he played an important role in the elevation of the Prague bishopric to the status or archbishopric. In the same year the building of the metropolitan Cathedral of St Vitus was started at Prague Castle. Prague became the residence of Charles, about which he took an extraordinary care. On 8 Mar 1348 he founded the New Prague Town, on 7 Apr 1348 a university in Prague, in 1357 he had a new stone bridge built across the Vltava (called after him). He rebuilt the Royal Palace at Prague Castle and at Vyšehrad and extended the Prague fortifications. He built Karlštejn Castle near Prague as a safe for the imperial coronation jewels. In 1355-56 he issued the *Golden Bull*, which had the force of a constitutional law. The Czech Kingdom as the main centre of the Roman-German Empire was generally promoted during his rule (in 1348 by annexing the Silesian principalities and Upper Lusatia he created a confederation of states of the Czech crown, which he extended by Lower Lusatia in 1368 and Brandenburg in 1378). The author of several books, for instance the autobiography *Vita Caroli* (The Life of Charles) or a legend about St Wenceslas.

Huss John (around 1371 - 6 July 1415), a Czech reformer. He studied and later taught at the faculty of arts of the Prague university (1409-10 its rector). In 1400 he was consecrated as a priest, from 1402 he preached in the Bethlehem Chapel in the Prague Old Town. The representative and leader of the Czech reformation movement, attempting at the remedy of the Christian Church and society by consistent application of the New Testament

ideas. He did not regard Church as an institution but as a community of the believers obeying God's law and predestined for salvation. He emphasised the role of the mother tongue instead of Latin. His ideal was the English thinker John Wickliff, and he shared his opinion that it is necessary to take from the Church the earthly property by the intervention of the secular power and to reestablish the apostolic mission of the Church. He gained the support of influential circles, including prominent personalities at the royal court of Wenceslas IV as well as a part of the Prague population. He played an important role in issuing the Decree of Kutná Hora (in 1409), which ensured superiority at voting for the Czech teachers at the Prague University. In October 1414 he went to a general council in Konstanz, where he was imprisoned in November 1414 and tried by the council court, which found some of his articles heretical. When Huss refused to retract his words, he was sentenced as a heretic and burnt to death. His death strenthened the reformatory movement, which culminated in the Hussite Revolution.

Wenceslas IV (26 Feb 1361 - 16 Aug 1419), a Czech king from the Luxembourg dynasty; the King from 1363 (he ruled independently from 1378), the German King from 1376 (he ruled between 1378-1400). A son of Charles IV. After his father's death he did not manage to solve the problems which accumulated during his rule. He caused a conflict with the Prague archbishop Jan of Jenštejn by his neutral attitude to the papal schism. The archbishop supported the Pope in Rome and aimed at greater political influence of the church in the Czech lands. The leaders of the Czech nobility united into the so called union of the lord and wanted to gain a decisive share in the governing of the Czech state (in 1394 and 1402 Wenceslas was even captured by the union and imprisoned). In 1400 he was deprived of the dignity of the Roman King, though he still used the title. From the end of the 14th century he and his court and counsellors supported the reformatory movement demanding the remedy of the Church and Christianity on a international scale. He did not intervene into the Hussite movement and by his passive attitude he let the events run their course, which culminated in the Hussite Revolution after his death.

Zikmund of Luxembourg (14 Feb 1368 - 9 Dec 1437), a Czech king from the Luxembourg dynasty, the King from 1420 (he ruled till 1436), the Hungarian King from 1387, the Roman-German King from 1410, the Roman-German Emperor from 1433. A son of Charles IV, the brother of Wenceslas IV. An educated ruler. He supported the Czech nobility against Wenceslas IV. He struggled for the reformation of the Roman Church and the solution of the papal schism. Therefore he supported the convocation of the Konstanz Council in 1414-18, where the only Pope Martin V was elected (during the council the church reformer John Huss was sentenced for his heretical opinions and burnt to death). After Wenceslas IV's death he was crowned as Czech King in 1420, however, the Hussites did not recognize him. The crusades against the Hussites led by Zikmund in 1420 and 1421-22 were unsuccessful. In 1431 he supported the convening of the Basel Council, whose aim was to continue in the church reform and to end the disagreement with the Hussites. In 1436 after large concessions he was accepted as the Czech King even by the Hussites.

George of Poděbrady (23 Apr 1420 - 22 Mar 1471), a Czech king; he ruled from 1458. He came from a Czech noble family. From 1448 the administrator of the land. After the sudden death of King Ladislav the Posthumous (from the Hapsburg family) he was elected king on 2 March 1458 by the decision of both the Hussite and the Catholic Estates (he was called the Hussite King). Between 1463-64 he stood up to the danger of international isolation by a scheme, which attempted to create an alliance of the European rulers, who would solve possible disagreements in a peaceful way. In 1465 a part of the Catholic nobility rebelled against the King, in 1466 the Pope Paul II declared George of Poděbrady dethroned and called a crusade against the Hussites. The King died during the war against the Hungarian King Mathias Korvin, who led the crusade and who had been elected Czech King by a part of the nobility.

Vladislav II Jagellon (1 March 1456 - 13 March 1516), a Czech king from the Jagellon family. He ruled from 1471, the Hungarian King from 1490. The son of the Polish King Kazimír IV. He was elected Czech King against the candidacy of the Hungarian King Mathias Korvin. Though a Catholic, he was recognized only by the Hussite oriented part of Bohemia, whereas in the other countries of the Czech crown it was Mathias Korvin who ruled till his death in 1490. He did not manage to stand up to the estate order of the state which made headway; he was under a strong influence of the nobility. In 1506 and 1507 he concluded succession agreements with the Hapsburgs. In his period there were conditions for the development of the late Gothic art (called the Vladislav Gothic). Its fine specimen is the Vladislav Hall in the Royal Palace of Prague Castle. His son Louis Jagellon died in 1526 after the lost battle of Mohacs with the Turks; in him the Jagelon rule in the Czech lands ended.

Ferdinand I Hapsburg (10 March 1503 - 5 July 1564), a Czech and Hungarian king from the Hapsburg family. He ruled from 1526, as the Roman-German King from 1531, the Roman-German Emperor from 1556. The son of Filip I the Lovely and Jane the Mad. The founder of the Austrian branch of the Hapsburg family. Educated in Spain. A skillful politician; he attempted at the firm connection and central administration of the countries which he ruled. He acted against the Estates and the non-Catholic religion. He pushed through the heredity of the throne and absolutistic tendencies. In 1547 he punished the uprising of the Czech Estates by confiscations and mainly by limiting the rights of the towns. He fought off the attacks of the Turks, who after the Battle of Mohacs in 1526 threatened his lands. In 1555 he contributed to concluding the Augsburg religious peace. From 1556 after the previous hostility to non-Catholics he endeavoured for religious peace with the Protestants and for a reform of the Catholic Church, he initiated the convoking of the Trident Council. In 1561 he managed to fill the Prague archbishopric after more than one hundred years. He endeavoured to perform recatholisation by peaceful means, mainly by the activity of Jesuits, which he called into the country. He founded colleges in Vienna, Prague (Klementinum) and Innsbruck and charged the Jesuits with the supervision over the educational system. At Prague Castle and in its neighbourhood after the fire in 1541 he started extensive Renaissance modifications (among others he founded the Royal Garden with the Royal Summerhouse).

Ferdinand of Tyrol, (14 June 1529 - 24 Jan 1595), an Austrian Archduke from the Hapsburg family; from 1568 the Count of Tyrol. A son of Ferdinand I, the governor in the Czech lands between 1557-67, from 1567 the governor in Tyrol. He was deprived of the succession after his marriage to Filipine Welser, a daughter of an Augsburg banker. He supported arts and culture, he led a bohemian life. During his stay in Prague he supported building activities in the Renaissance spirit (building modifications to Prague Castle, the Hvězda Summerhouse in the Game Preserve Bílá Hora).

Rudolf II Hapsburg (18 July 1552 - 20 Jan 1612), a Czech king from the Hapsburg family. He ruled between 1575-1611, the Hungarian King between 1572-1608), the Roman-German Emperor from 1576. He was brought up at the

Spanish court. He pushed through the anti-Reformation. Between 1593-1606 he waged war on the Osman Empire with varying success. The disagreements between Rudolf and his brother Mathias culminated in Mathias' rebellion. Mentally ill Rudolf was gradually deprived of the rule over individual countries in favour of Mathias, who was supported by the Hungarian, Austrian and Moravian Estates. He held power only in Bohemia and Silesia, in 1611 he was forced to abdicate even here. During his rule Prague became again the Emperor's residence. Thanks to Rudolf's liking for sciences and arts, it became not only the political, but also the cultural centre of Central Europe. Rudolf II as a sponsor attracted into Prague prominent contemporary scientists (Johannes Kepler, Tycho Brahe) and artists (Hans von Aachen, Giuseppe Arcimboldo, Bartolomeus Spranger). A result of the grand building activity was the prestigous Spanish Hall and a number of other buildings at Prague Castle. The rich collections of art and curiosities are kept partly in Vienna, part of them was transported to Sweden at the end of the Thirty Years War as a war loot.

of Rožmberk Petr Vok (1 Oct 1539 - 6 Nov 1611), a Czech nobleman from the significant Czech Rožmberk family. From 1592 the last member of the family and the ruler of the Rožmberk demesne. The brother of Vilém of Rožmberk (died in 1592), a prominent person of the Czech history in the second half of the 16th century. Petr Vok became famous for his philandering and drinking. However, he was interested in contemporaneous music and literature (he built an extensive library) and supported modern technological development (especially in mining). At the time of religious controversies he did not hold a clear-cut stance on these issues; through he came from a traditional Catholic family, he converted to Lutheranism, and in the end he enter the persecuted Moravian Brethren Church. As a member of a prominent Czech noble family, he had the possibility to get the highest offices of the country, however, he prefered the administration of his own demesne, though he influenced the public life of the country. From 1595 he stood up for Rudolf II's opponents. He exchanged with Rudolf II the Rožmberk Palace in Prague Castle for a palace in Hradčany Square.

Friedrich V of Falc (26 Aug 1596 - 29 Nov 1632), a Czech king (called the Winter King). He ruled between 1619-20, the Elector of Falc between 1610-23. The son-in-law of the English King James I (from 1613 the husband of his daughter Elizabeth). The leader of the Protestant Union. After dethroning Ferdinand II from the Czech throne he was elected on 26 Aug 1916 Czech King by the Czech Estates (crowned on 4 Nov 1619). The hopes of the leaders of the Czech Estates Uprising were connected with his person, they expected a rich foreign support. However, he did not have enough sense of political issues and preferred only Calvinism out of the other non-Catholic confessions. He did not manage to gain allies, after the Battle of the White Mountain he fled to Vratislav and then to the Hague. He lost both Bohemia and Falc and in January 1621 an imprerial anathema was pronounced against him. During his rule the St Vitus Cathedral at Prague Castle suffered large plundering.

of Valdštějn (Wallenstein) Albrecht Václav Eusebius (24 Sep 1583 - 25 Feb 1634), a Czech nobleman and general. A member of the Moravian Brethren Church, after 1606 he converted to Catholicism, from 1617 in the service of Ferdinand II, on whose side he stood also during the time of the Uprising of the Czech Estates between 1618-20. His career was intentionally connected with war, his cuirassiers participated in the Battle of the White Mountain in 1620. He enriched himself by the post-White Mountain confiscations, from this property he created a large principality around Frýdlant in northeastern Bohemia. He built a large palace in the Small Quarter in Prague. From 1625 the generalissimo of the imperial army. He had large success in waging war (in April 1626 he defeated the Danish near Dessau). He prepared a project of building the Baltic and Ocean navy of the Austrian Hapsburgs, in 1627 he got the Meklenburg area as a pledge. Valdštejn's offensive threatened the sovereignty of the imperial princes, and that is why the command was taken from him by the Emperor after urging the Catholic League. Then he took the side of the anti-Hapsburg coalition, from 1631 he led secret talks with the Czech exile and with the Swedish King Gustav Adolf and considered taking over the power in Bohemia. In 1631 after the Saxon invasion into Bohemia he was again charged with the command of the imperial army, in 1632 he drove the Saxon away, in September he fought off a Sweedish attack near Fürth (the first Swedish unsuccess during the Thirty Years War), in November he led a drawn battle with the Swedish, where the Swedish King Gustav Adolf was killed. In the summer 1633 he did not take advantage of his superiority in Silesia, which strengthened the distrust of the court and led to the anti-Valdštejn plot of the generals. He gradually lost controll over the army, on 18 Feb 1634 he was pronounced a traitor of the Empire by imperial decrees and on 25 Feb 1634 he and a few other officers were killed in Cheb. A number of artists were interested in his fate (F. von Schiller).

Komenský Jan Amos, in Latin Comenius (28 Mar 1592 - 15 Nov 1670), a Czech teacher, theologian, philosopher, social and religious thinker. A priest and the last bishop of the Moravian Brethren (from 1648). After the defeat of the Uprising of the Czech Estates in 1620 he was forced to leave his homeland and as a recognized scholar he became the political speaker of the Czech Protestant emigration. He died in Naarden in the Netherlands. Komenský connects the Czech Reformation tradition with the European religious and philosophical thinking. His extensive work is a profound humanist answer to the problems of the contemporary society (suffering from the Thirty Years War), to the national tragedy and to his personal (often cruel) experience from the life in exile. He tried to unite all human knowledge on the basis of science, which is accessible to everybody, and on the basis of faith.

Maria Theresa (13 May 1717 - 29 Nov 1780), a Czech and Hungarian queen from the Hapsburg family. She ruled from 1740 (crowned as the Hungarian Queen in 1741, the Czech Queen from 1743). The wife of the Roman-German Emperor Francis I of Lotringen. Her right of succession was denied by the foreign pretenders to the rule over the countries of the Hapsburg monarchy (the Prussian King Friedrich II, the Bavarian Elector Charles Albrecht supported by the French Bourbons) and caused a war for the Austrian heritage. A result of it was the loss of Silesia (1741-42 and 1744 Prague was occupied). During the Seven Years War between 1756-63 Prague was damaged by the artillery bombardment of the besieging Prussian troops. Maria Theresa's Enlightment reforms were revolutionary (the centralisation of the administration of the monarchy, introducing compulsory school attendance, the unification of measures and weighs, the building of the roads, the improvement of the postal connection, the restriction of the guild rights etc.). From 1765 her oldest son Josef II became her co-ruler, however, she did not agree with his radical opinions of an Englightenment rule, and till her death she kept a slower pace of the reforms. The building activity during the rule of Maria Theresa gave Prague Castle the present stately form. Two of her 16 children were significant from the historical viewpoint: her daughter Maria Antoinette, the wife of the French King Louis XVI, and her son Josef II, the Roman-German Emperor.

Josef II (13 Mar 1741 - 20 Feb 1790), a Roman-German emperor from the Hapsburg-Lotringen family; the co-ruler of her mother Maria Theresa from 1765, he ruled independently from 1780. In fact a Czech king; he was not crowned. His rule was a continuation of the Enlightenment absolutism and the Austrian centralism, however, he was more consistent in pushing through his own rationalist ideas. He subordinated the Church to a state supervision and took censorship from it, he tranferred the education of priests into general seminars under the state inspection, he abolished a number of monasteries and convents, from whose property he created a fund for supporting school and social policy, he abolished a number of regulations discriminating the Jews, he restricted censorship. In 1781 he issued the Toleration Letters Patent, by which religious freedom and the rights of the Protestants and the Orthodoxs were extended and the Letter Paten abolishing serfdom. In the framework of the centralisation of administration he united the four Prague towns (the Old Town, the New Town, the Small Quarter and Hradčany) into one town. He provided Prague Castle to the use of the army (many objects damaged).

Franz Josef I (18 Aug 1830 - 21 Nov 1616), an Austrian emperor and Hungarian king from the Hapsburg-Lotringen family, he ruled from 1848. In fact, a Czech king; he was not crowned. One of the most significant monarchs of the 19th century; he ruled for 68 years. He got even with the revolutionary movement of 1848-49 and at first he introduced a neoabsolutist regime, which he gradually loosened under the pressure of the liberal ideas and the national tension (in 1867 a federation of Austria-Hungary was made of Austria). He lost for good his influence in Italy and Germany, with which he led a common foreign policy. After the assassination of the successor to the throne, his grandnephew Franz Ferdinad d'Este in Sarajevo on 28 June 1914 the government made Franz Josef to sign an ultimatum to Serbia, which led to the First World War. Under Franz Josef I great political, economic and social changes set in in the Hapsburg monarchy (the end of feudalism and the completing of the industrial revolution). Persuaded about his divine choosing and about the commission of the monarchy, he accepted the restrictions on his absolute power and all modern tendecies against his will. He was a hardworking, precise official, with a sense of duty, skillful in politics, and simultaneously he held on introduced patterns. The outer appearance of his majesty was not affected even by the tragical events in his personal life (in 1889 the suicide of his only son Rudolf, in 1898 the assassination of his wife Elizabeth).

Masaryk Tomáš Garrigue (7 March 1850 - 14 Sep 1937), a Czech philosopher and statesman. 1918-35 the president of the republic. Between 1878-82 a reader of the Viennese University. From 1882 a professor of philosophy at the Czech University in Prague. He refused the Czech nationalism. He put emphasis on the development of the humanist ideas of the Czech Reformation and of the leaders of the Czech national revival. In December 1914 he left into exile (for Italy, Switzerland, France, England). From February 1916 the chairman of the Czechoslovak National Council in Paris. He struggled for the recognition of the new Czechoslovak state by the western powers. After the formation of the first Czechoslovak Republic (28 Dec 1918) he was elected president. After 1918 he was not a member of any political party; he kept significant influence on the public life in the Czechoslovak Republic mainly by his natural moral authority. Under President Masaryk Prague has again become the residential city; Prague Castle was chosen as the presidential seat. The necessary modifications to the interiors, courtyards and gardens were carried out in an original way by the Slovenian architect Josip Plečnik. Also the neo-Gothic completion of the St Vitus Cathedral was performed.

Havel Václav (5 Oct 1936), a Czech playwright and politician. Between 1989-92 the president of Czechoslovakia, from 1993 the president of the Czech Republic. From the 1960s he devoted to drama. After 1968 he was forced to leave the theatre; for some time he worked as a labourer and at the same time he was engaged in writing plays and in civil rights activities. A co-founder and one of the the first signatories of the Charter 77. In the 1970s and 1980s he was imprisoned several times, last time in 1989. In November 1989 he became the leader of the independent opposition which negotiated with the representatives of the Communist regime; a co-founder of the Civil Forum. In December 1989 after the abdication of G. Husák he was elected president of Czechoslovakia. He resigned from the presidency in July 1992 in connection with the disintegration of the Czecho-Slovak state. In February 1993 he was elected president of the Czech Republic. He has large authority both between the citizens and in the international sphere.

SIGNIFICANT ARTISTS IN BOHEMIA

alphabetical
list
of the artists
mentioned
in the book

Aachen Hans von (1551 or 1552 - 4 Mar 1615), a German painter, a representative of the Central European Mannerism. From 1598 active in Prague as a court painter of Emperors Rudolf II and Mathias. An author of religious and mythological paintings, allegories and portraits. His painting excelled in a refined composition and a cold wealth of colours. He bought works of art for Rudolf II, among others *Iliones* by Praxitel (today in the sculptural collection in Munich). He was elevated to the rank of nobility by Rudolf II.

Adrian de Vries (between 1546 and 1560 - 13 Dec 1626), a Dutch sculptor; a significant representative of the mannerism. Between 1601-12 he was in Prague as a court sculptor of Emperors Rudolf II and Mathias. From 1620 he was again in Prague. An author of free sculptures on mythological themes, reliefs (among others *Rudolf II supporting the art in Bohemia*), portraits busts of Rudolf II, statues of horses and fountains. The author of the bronze garden sculptures in the Valdštejn Garden in Prague (the originals were transported in 1648 into Sweden as a war loot).

Alliprandi Giovanni Battista (around 1665 - 13 March 1720), an Italian architect active in Bohemia; a representative of the radical dynamic Baroque. From 1706 the high Prague fortification builder. He designed palace buildings, castles and churches.

Arcimboldo Giuseppe (around 1527 - 11 July 1593), an Italian painter, engineer and musician; a significant representative of the fantastic art of the mannerism. Till 1592 active in Prague at the court of Emperors Maxmilian II and Rudolf II. In the spirit of the mannerism he created allegories and portraits composed of flowers, vegetables, fruit and animals. He was elevated to the rank of nobility by the Emperor.

Balko František Xaver, also Palko (3 Dec 1724 - 18 July 1767) - a Silesian painter; a representative of the high Baroque. In the 1750s he worked in Bohemia (author of altar paintings), later in Saxony and Munich.

Bílek František (16 Nov 1872 - 13 Oct 1914), a Czech painter and graphic artist; a significant representative of the Czech symbolism and spiritually conceived Art Nouveau. He created mainly ecstatically tense wooden sculptures expressing common symbols of human existence, mystical devotion and the desire for redemption. A museum has been established in Bílek's villa in Hradčany. The author of the wooden altar with Crucified Christ in the St Vitus Cathedral.

Brandl Petr (christened on 24 Oct 1668 - 24 Sep 1735), a Czech painter, one of the most significant representatives of the Czech high Baroque. An author of altar paintings and portraits, in which he expressed his extraordinary sense of the psychological characterisation. Excellent heads of saints, called beautiful old men.

Braun Matyáš Bernard (1684 - 15 Feb 1738), a Czech sculptor and carver of the Tyrol origin; one of the most significant representatives of the Czech high Baroque. Before 1710 he founded a sculptural workshop in Prague. He cooperated mainly with the architect F. M. Kaňka. The author of several statues on the Prague Charles Bridge.

Brokof Ferdinand Maxmilián (12 Sep 1688 - 8 Mar 1731), a Czech sculptor and carver of the German origin; one of the most significant representatives of the Czech high Baroque. He founded a significant sculptural workshop. The author of several statues on the Prague Charles Bridge. His father Jan Brokof carved out a statue of St John of Nepomuk, the prototype of similar statues of this saint all over Bohemia and abroad.

Caratti Francesco (around 1615-20 - Jan 1677), an Italian architect; one of the most significant creators of the early Baroque in Bohemia, a representative of the monumental architectural style, which was not followed in Bohemia. He worked for the nobility and the Church. Among others the author of the monumentally designed Černín Palace in Prague in Hradčany (after 1668), continuing in the tradition of the Roman architecture of the 16th century.

Colin Alexander (around 1526 - 17 Aug 1612), a Vlame architect and sculptor; a significant representative of the Renaissance north of the Alps. The author of the sculptural decoration at Heidelberg Castle, of the tombstone of Emperor Maxmilian I in Insbruck and of the sculptural decoration of the Royal Mausoleum in the St Vitus Cathedral at Prague Castle.

Dietzenhofer Kilián Ignác (1 Sep 1689 - 18 Dec 1751), a Czech architect; together with G. Santini the most significant representative of the high Baroque in Bohemia, a representative of its dynamic, radical branch.

The son of Kryštof Dientzenhofer, with whom whe colla- borated. A pupil of Johann Lucas Hildebrandt. His top work is the completion of the St Nicolas Church in the Small Quarter. He built the Convent and Church of St John of Nepomuk in Hradčany for the Ursuline nuns. He completed the Prague Loretto.

Dientzenhofer Kryštof (7 July 1655 - 10 June 1722) a builder and architect of the Bavarian origin; a signifi- cant representative of the high Czech Baroque. The fa- ther of Kilián Ignác Dientzenhofer. He brought into Bo- hemia and Germany the architectural motives of Guarino Guarini; probably the author of the group of the first buildings in the radical Baroque with a dyna- mic conception of mass and space. A builder of main- ly church buildings. He worked on the building of the Prague Loretto, the author of the front of the St Nicolas Church in the Small Quarter.

Filippi Giovanni Maria (after 1560 - after 1616), and Italian architect; a representative of the mannerism with early Baroque elements, one of the most signifi- cant architects of the first two decades of the 17th century in Central Europe. From 1602 the court build- er of Emperor Rudolf II; he brought into Prague the knowledge of the high Roman mannerism. The author of several buildings at Prague Castle, mainly of the new stables of Rudolf II, the New Hall (at present cal- led the Spanish) and the Mathias Gate, considered the first building aiming at the early Baroque in Prague (1613-14).

Fischer from Erlach Johan Bernhard (18 July 1656 - 5 Apr 1723), an Austrian architect; a significant repre- sentative of the European high Baroque. The father of Johann Emanuel Fischer from Erlach. He united the traditions of the Roman Baroque (Gian Lorenzo Berni- ni, Francesco Borromini) with the French Classicism. An author of palaces and churches mainly in Vienna and Salzburg. Also active in Prague, where he built the Clam-Gallas Palace in the Old Town and designed the tombstone of Vratislav of Mitrovice in the St Ja- mes Church in the Old Town. Probably the author of the design of the Diamond Monstrance in the Hradča- ny Loretto.

Fischer from Erlach Joseph Emanuel (12 Sep 1693 - 29 June 1742), an Austrian architect; a representative of the high Baroque and the Classicism. The son of Jo- hann Bernhard Fischer from Erlach. He continued the

work of his father in strenghtened classicist feeling. He designed the tombstone of St John of Nepomuk in the St Vitus Cathedral in Prague and probably also the tombstone of Leopold Šlik.

Grund Norbert (christened on 4 Dec 1717 - around 17 June 1767), a Czech painter; a representative of the Rococo. An author of a number of small, especially genre and gallant paintings.

Hilbert Kamil (12 Feb 1869 - 25 June 1933), a Czech architect and restorer of the medieval architecture; a representative of the late period of the neo-Gothic. The successor of Josef Mocker in the completion of the St Vitus Cathedral (1899-1933). As an author of the modifications to monuments, he abandoned the pu- ristic conception of his predecessor, his work was influ- enced by critical scientific research, he respected more the value of the monuments.

Janák Pavel (12 Mar 1882 - 1 Aug 1956), a Czech architect, designer and theorist; a significant repre- sentative of the modern architecture. He introduced modern conceptions into the Czech architecture; he went over from the Art Nouveau inspired by Otta Wag- ner and the cubism to the national decorative style and later to the functionalism. Besides his own work he was engaged in the reconstruction of monuments. From 1936 the architect of Prague Castle. He partici- pated in the renovation of the Černín Palace in Hrad- čany, the Ball-game House at Prague Castle, the Hvězda Summerhouse and the castle in Nové Město nad Metují.

Kaňka František Maxmilián (christened on 19 Aug 1674 - 14 July 1766), a Czech architect; a representa- tive of the high Baroque. A collaborator of Giovanni Santini and perhaps of G. Alliprandi. A very fruitful and successful author; his work anticipates the Rococo. He completed the Černín Palace in Hradčany in Prague.

Kosárek Adolf (6 Jan 1830 - 30 Oct 1859), a Czech painter; a representative of the Romanticism. An au- thor of especially romantic landscapes.

Kupecký Jan (1667 - 16 July 1740), a Czech painter; a significant representative of the high Baroque Euro- pean portrait art. Influenced by French representative portraits he came to an original style with a diversity of colours and a decorative pomp, but with a distinct interest in the psychological characterisation of portrayed persons. Also an author of genres and historical compositions. Although he did not live in Bohemia, his artistic opinion is very close to the Czech art.

Liška Jan Kryštof (around 1650 - 23 Aug 1712), a Silesian painter; a representative of the Baroque. After 1689 active in Prague. An author of frescos and hanging (mainly altar) pictures with an impressive composition and a deep colourfulness.

Mánes Josef (12 May 1820 - 9 Dec 1871), a Czech painter; the founder and a classic of the Czech modern art. He created in the spirit of the Romanticism the classic ideal of a Slavonic hero and of the national past, at the same time he anticipated the development of the modern realism. The author of the medallion pictures of the Old Time astronomical clock.

Mathey Giovanni Baptista (around 1630 - 1696), a French architect; a representative of the early Baroque. Between 1675-95 he worked in Bohemia. He brought into Bohemia the castle type with tree wings and the main central hall and a pavilion overtopping of the centre (the Trója Castle in Prague) and a church layout on the ground plan of the Greek cross with the main space vaulted by an oval cupola (the Church of St Francis of Seraphim in the Prague Old Town). He designed the Riding School of Prague Castle, and was active in the modifications to the Strahov Monastery.

Matyáš of Arras (around 1290 - 1352), a French architect; a representative of the post-classic Gothic architecture. Active in Avignone and from 1344 after an impetus by Charles IV in Prague, where he was to create for his contractor an ideal type of a French cathedral. He led the construction till his death, he built the eastern part of the choir with the gallery and pentagonal chapels. The members of his building foundry then continued in the construction, in 1356 they came over into Parléř's foundry, some of them went to another constructions (the Church of the Virgin Mary the Snowful in Prague). In the St Vitus Cathedral is preserved the Matyáš tombstone with a carved figural decoration and in the triforium is the Parléř portrait bust.

Maulbertsch Franz Anton (7 June 1724 - 8 Aug 1796), an Austrian painter and fresco painter; a prominent figure of the Central European painting in the late Baroque. A court painter of Empress Maria Theresa. At first

dramatically tense work gradually changed into an extreme formal loosening, where the light dominates over the colour. In Prague he decorated the Philosophical Hall of the Strahov Monastery.

Master of the Litoměřice Altar (the turn of the 15th and 16th centuries), a Czech painter; a leading figure of the Czech painting of the Vladislav late Gothic. Influenced by the Donau School. The peak of his paintings for the royal court is the St Wenceslas Cycle in the Chapel of St Wenceslas of the St Vitus Cathedral. The double portrait of King Vladislav Jagellon and his wife Anna is incorporated into the cycle.

Master of the Rajhradský Altar (active between 1415-1430), a Czech painter; a representative of the transition period from the classic to the late Gothic. He was active in Moravia. His paintings are characterised by dramatically given actions with considerably gesticulating figures and excited faces.

Master Theodoric, Dětřich (active between 1359-1368), a Czech painter; a representative of the high Gothic. He decorated for Emperor Charles IV the Chapel of the Holy Cross at Karlštejn Castle by wall paintings and 130 panel paintings of the saints who make up the Army of Christ, Heavenly Jerusalem.

Master of the Třeboň Altar (active between 1380-1390), a Czech painter; a prominent representative of the Czech painting from the beginning of the fine style, a figure of the European stature. His paintings excel in complicated expressing mystical and cosmological symbolism, complicated compositional structure and outstanding colourfulness.

Master of the Vyšebrodský Altar (active between 1340-1360), a Czech painter; a representative of the classic Gothic, a figure of the European stature. His work is characterised by the architectural dividing of space, linearity, a harmonious colourfulness and a lyrical conception. He worked probably in Prague for the Rožmberks and for the royal court of Charles IV.

Mocker Josef (22 Nov 1835 - 15 Nov 1899), a Czech architect and restorer; a representative of the monument conception of the purism and the architectural creation in the spirit of the romantic neo-Gothic. He participated in the completion of the St Stephen Cathedral in Vienna (the repair of a tower), in 1873 he was charged with the completion of the St Vitus Cathedral in Prague. Inspired by the Parléř Gothic he completed the western front with two towers.

Myslbek Josef Václav (20 June 1848 - 2 June 1922), a Czech sculptor; a founding person of the modern Czech sculpture. In his work we can see the influence of the Classicism, the neo-Renaissance and the Art Nouveau. His realism and lyrical sensitiveness manifested fully in his peak works, which include also the statue of kneeling Cardinal Schwarzenberg in the St Vitus Cathedral. The author of the St Wenceslas monument in Václavské Square in Prague.

Nosecký Siardus (12 Apr 1693 - 28 Jan 1753), a Czech painter and fresco painter; a representative of the high Baroque. From 1713 a member of the Premonstrantensian Order at the Strahov Monastery; active as a librarian. In the monastery he decorated the Thelogical Hall of the library, the abbot's dining room, the capitular hall, the Summer Refectory.

Pacassi Nicolo (5 March 1716 - 11 Nov 1790), an Austrian architect of the Italian origin; a representative of the late Baropue. A pupil of Joseph Emanuel Fischer from Erlach. From 1748 a court architect in Vienna. An author of the stately court late Baroque architecture of the Maria Theresa period in a sober monumental spirit with plastic accents. He participated in the completion of the imperial castle in Schönbrunn, he designed the general renovation and rebuilding of Prague Castle. Rococo elements can be seen in his interiors.

Parléř Petr (1332 or 1333 - 13 July 1399), a Czech architect, sculptor and carver of the Swabian origin; the most significant representative of the high Gothic in Bohemia, a brilliant designer, who introduced new construction principles (net vaulting) and elements (protruding corbel). In 1353 he was called from Köln on the Rhine by Emperor Charles IV into Prague to take over here (in 1356) the leading of the building of the St Vitus Cathedral after the deceased Matyáš of Arras. He modified the design and built the choir chapels on the rectangular ground plan, he built the sacristy with a protruding corbel, the southern vestibule and tower, the Chapel of St Wenceslas, he vaulted the choir by net vaulting. He carved out the tombstones of Přemysl I Otakar and Přemysl II Otakar, the author of 21 busts in the triforium (among others the bust of Emperor Charles IV and his four wives, the portrait of Matyáš of Arras,

the selfportrait). He built the Church of All Saints at Prague Castle. He was the director of the building of the Charles Bridge in Prague and the architect of the Old Town bridge tower.

Platzer Ignác František (6 July 1717 - 27 Sep 1787), a Czech sculptor; a representative of an original synthesis of the Viennese Classicism and the Czech tradition of the high Baroque. An author of large collections of carvings for church and monastery decorations, of garden sculptures (Dobříš), free and architectural sculptures. He carried out the sculptural decoration of the buildings at the Pacassi rebuilding of Prague Castle. The author of the sculptural decoration of the entrance gate to the *first courtyard* of the Castle (statues of the fighting giants).

Plečnik Josip (23 Jan 1872 - 7 Jan 1957), a Slovenian architect, furniture designer and town-planner; one of the most prominent representatives of the expressive trends of the Viennese modern style. In 1910 he arrived in Prague, where he taught at the School of Applied Arts. Between 1919-34 he was the architect of Prague Castle (on the basis of a personal invitation of President T. G. Masaryk). The author of the modifications to the three Castle courtyards, the flat of the president, the *Garden of Eden*, the Gardens *Na Valech* and *Na Baště*. He participated also in the adaptation of the Castle in Lány, the summer seat of the president. At the modifications to the Castle into the form of a respectable presidential residence he was inspired not only by the Czech architecture of the past periods, but also by the Mediterranean architecture (Greece, Crete, Egypt); he put his original stamp on the seemingly foreign elements and incorporated them into architectural, visual and ideal relations of the environment. He built the monumental Church of the Holiest Heart of the Lord in Prague Vinohrady.

Preisler Jan (18 Feb 1872 - 27 Apr 1918), a Czech painter and graphic artist; one of the most significant figures of the generation of the Czech modern art founders. He connected harmoniously the topical tendencies of the Czech painting at the end of the 19th century (naturalism, symbolism, decorativism), he emphasised the expressive meaning of colours.

Reiner Václav Vavřinec (8 Aug 1689 - 9 Oct 1743), a Czech painter; one of the most significant figures of the Czech high Baroque. He often completed the architecture of the churches of Kilián Ignác Dientzenhofer by ceiling frescoes (the Church of St John of Nepomuk near the Ursuline Convent in Hradčany). Also an author of ideal landscapes, battles and portraits.

Ried Benedict (around 1454 - 30 Sep 1534), a German architect active in Bohemia; the most significant representative of the Czech late Gothic. He connected the Czech late Gothic tradition with new Renaissance elements (the windows of the Vladislav Hall etc.) into a harmonious whole, expressing both the needs of representation and the new artistic feeling. A collaborator of Hans Spiess, with whom he designed the Royal Oratory in the St Vitus Cathedral. He built the new fortification of Prague Castle (till 1496) with large artillery bastions (the Powder Tower, the White Tower, the Daliborka Tower). He rebuilt residential rooms of the Castle. A master of the late Gothic vaulting: in the Old Royal Palace he built mainly the Vladislav Hall (the largest vaulted secular space in Central Europe) and the Riders Staircase. The author of the nave vaulting of the Cathedral of St Barbora in Kutná Hora. Elevated to the rank of nobility.

Rothmayer Otto (28 Feb 1892 - 24 Sep 1966), a Czech architect. A pupil of Josip Plečnik; later his long time friend and collaborator. In 1921 he was called by Plečnik to Prague Castle, where he participated in Plečnik's modifications and run the building work till his leave. Between 1935-56 he developed independently Plečnik's conception at the modifications to the Castle.

Santini Giovanni, his own name was Jan Blažej Santini-Eichel (4 Feb 1677 - 7 Dec 1723), a Czech architect of the Italian origin; one of the most significant and original architects of the Central European high Baroque, a representative of its dynamic trend and the creator of the so called Baroque Gothic. Influenced by J. B. Mathey, he was inspired by the work of J. B. Fischer from Erlach, Francesco Borrommini and Guarino Guarini. He emphasises light contrasts, he often used a central disposition with contrasting alternations of materials. He coped with the Czech medieval tradition in an original way by creating the so called Baroque Gothic (the renovation of the Church of the Virgin Mary in Sedlec near Kutná Hora). In Prague he designed among others the Mladota House at Prague Castle, the front of the Church of the Virgin Mary the Helpful near the Kajetán Mo-

nastery in the Small Quarter and probably he was one of the designers of the Šternberk Palace in *Hradčany Square*. His pilgrimage Church of St John of Nepomuk in Zelená Hora near Žďár nad Sázavou is marked down in the map of the world cultural heritage of the UNESCO.

Slavíček Antonín (16 May 1870 - 1 Feb 1910), a Czech painter, a leading figure of the 1890s generation and a prominent representative of the Czech impressionism in ladscape painting. Besides the Czech landscape he also painted Prague streets and embankments, where he expressed the loneliness of town people. Besides ancient spots he also painted wide panoramas capturing the atmosphere of the town.

Spiess Johannes (around 1440-50 - before 13 Nov 1511), a German architect, sculptor and carver; a representative of the late Gothic. He reached an exceptional mastery in net vaultings and other sculptural stone details (rich naturalistic decoration). From 1485 in the service of King Vladislav Jagellon at Prague Castle and in Central Bohemia. The designer of the Royal Oratory in the St Vitus Cathedral (together with his pupil Benedict Ried), also worked at Karlštejn.

Spranger Bartolomeus (21 Mar 1546 - 27 Sep 1611), a Dutch painter; a significant representative of the Central European mannerism. From 1581 he was active in Prague as a court painter of Rudolf II. He created an original style with marked plasticity and work with light. An author of mythological, allegorical and altar paintings and frescoes in the Emperor's palace. Elevated to the rank of nobility.

Stella Paollo della (around 1500-10 - Oct 1552), an Italian sculptor, architect and builder; a representative of the north Italian Renaissance and Mannerism. In 1537 he entered the service of King Ferdinand I Hapsburg. He applied here the knowledge of the Italian Mannerism, however, he adapted his work to the tradition north of the Alps (expressive manifestation). He designed the Royal Summerhouse and together with his assistants he decorated it with one hundred stone reliefs from the Antique mythology and history. He cooperated at the modifications to Prague Castle after the fire in 1541, he tried to rebuild and to complement the damaged parts into the original state.

Škréta Karel (1610 - before 1 Aug 1674), a Czech painter; one of the most significant representatives of the Czech high Baroque. Influenced by the Venetian colourism. He painted altar and hanging pictures, portraits, exceptionally mythological themes. He connected the Baroque sensualism and dramatic character with the sense of monumentality and genre details. He led a workshop with a number of pupils and collaborators.

Švabinský Max (17 Sep 1873 - 10 Feb 1962), a Czech painter and graphic artist; a representative of the modern Czech painting. At first influenced by the symbolism and the Art Nouveau, later he returned to the classic heritage of the Czech art of the 19th century and to its historical tendencies. He was an excellent author of a large number of painted and graphic portraits (portraits of figures of the Czech political and cultural life). The peak of his monumental work is the design of the stained glass windows and the mosaics in the St Vitus Cathedral.

Wolmut Bonifác (died before 28 Apr 1579), a German architect, builder and stonemason; a representative of the Renaissance, the most significant architect of the third quarter of the 16th century in Bohemia. From 1522 he worked in Vienna, where he worked at the completion of the St Stephen Cathedral. Between 1556-70 he worked as the royal architect in Prague. His work synthetizes the medieval Gothic tradition (the vaultings of the Old Diet at Prague Castle and the vaulting of the church in Prague Karlov) with the Renaissance, which he enriched by motives of the mannerism. He completed the upper storey of the Royal Summerhouse at Prague Castle and the Hvězda Summerhouse, he was building the Ball-game House of Prague Castle and the Ball-game House by the Hvězda Summerhouse. He roofed the tower of the St Vitus Cathedral by a Renaissance helmet, in the west he enclosed the nave of the St Vitus Cathedral by a Renaissance organ loft (at the modern completion of the Cathedral it was transferred into the north wing of the transept).